DARKNESS

MOVES

D A R K

UNIVERSITY OF CALIFORNIA PRESS   BERKELEY   LOS ANGELES   LONDON

N E S S

M O V E S

An

Henri

Michaux

Anthology,

1927-1984

Selected,

translated,

and presented

by David Ball

The publisher gratefully acknowledges the

contribution provided by the Literature in

Translation Endowment Fund, which is supported by

a generous gift from Joan Palevsky

University of California Press

Berkeley and Los Angeles, California

University of California Press

London, England

First paperback printing 1997

Library of Congress Cataloging-in-Publication Data

Michaux, Henri, 1899–1984

  [Selections, English 1994]

  Darkness moves an Henri Michaux anthology

  1927–1984 / translated by David Ball

    p cm

  Includes bibliographical references

  ISBN 978-0-520-21229-9 (pbk alk. paper)

  1 Michaux, Henri, 1899–1984—Translations into

English I Title

PQ2625 12A222 1994

082—dc20   92-12925

                      CIP

Printed in the United States of America

13 12 11

11 10 9 8 7 6 5

CONTENTS

ACKNOWLEDGMENTS

Ron Padgett's enthusiasm for Michaux and his fine poetic ear were invaluable to me from beginning to end of this project.

I want to thank Bill Oram, Elizabeth Harries, and Jefferson Hunter, colleagues at Smith College who were kind enough to read parts of the manuscript in various stages and comment on them incisively.

My ALTA-colleague Lynn Hoggard graciously took the time to criticize one section of the translation in detail; I gained much from it. For some of the texts in this volume, I also gained from reading two earlier translators of Michaux: Michael Fineberg and Richard Ellmann. Two of their lines in particular seemed just right to me; I took them.

An anonymous reader for the University of California Press carefully went over most of the manuscript twice. This reader's knowledge of French (and Michaux), sharp eye for detail, and critical, informed support have won my admiring gratitude.

Jeremy Larner ripped apart the first draft of my Introduction with gleeful ferocity, and I'm glad he did. His kinder comments about parts of the translation were helpful in a different way.

Above all, I was lucky enough to have the help of a translator, my wife Nicole Ball, in revising these texts—lucky, first because of what she could do (her familiarity with two cultures and her literary intelligence are extraordinary), and then, because of what she *would* do—it's hard to imagine anyone being so generous with her time. I'm grateful beyond words.

Acknowledgment is made to Editions Gallimard for permission to translate all the texts in this anthology; to New Directions Books to retranslate thirty-three pages from Henri Michaux: *Selected Writings*, Copyright © 1968 by New Directions Publishing Corporation, and reprinted by permission of New Directions Publishing Corporation; and to the Solomon R. Guggenheim Museum of New York and the Musée National d'Art Moderne of Paris for permitting and facilitating the selection and reproduction of Michaux's art in their collections. Jim Long and, again, Nicole Ball were most helpful in this part of the project, too.

D. B.

INTRODUCTION

Henri Michaux died in 1984 at the age of eighty-five. He was the author of more than thirty books of poems, prose poems, narratives, essays, journals, and drawings; his writings were translated into more than half a dozen languages, his paintings amply displayed in the major art centers of Europe and the United States. His place in world literature and art was secure, but difficult to define. Michaux stood alone.

When people who know his work try to relate Michaux to some movement or tradition, they don't come up with schools of poets, but with a range of great individual figures in literature and art: Kafka, Hieronymus Bosch, Goya, Swift, Paul Klee, Rabelais.... His strangeness has occasionally led him to be classified with the Surrealists (some critics feel they have to put him *somewhere*), but he never used their techniques: no *cadavre exquis,* no free association, no abstractly formulated attempt to destroy tradition and logic. A sentence like André Breton's "The color of fabulous salvations darkens even the slightest death-rattle: a calm of relative sighs" could never have been written by Michaux,[1] who tries to render his dangerous, magical world as clearly and concretely as possible. Whether in poetry, prose, India ink, or paint, his weird visions are not the result of some theory about the nature of art: they are messages from his inner space. In a sense he inhabits the realm the Surrealists merely longed for.[2]

No group, no label for him. John Ashbery defined him as "hardly a painter, hardly even a writer, but a conscience—the most sensitive substance yet discovered for registering the fluctuating anguish of day-to-day, minute-to-minute living." Wild and druggy enough to be venerated in the sixties by a poet like Allen Ginsberg (he called Michaux "master" and "genius"), and by the French rap star M.C. Solaar in the nineties, an inventor of fictions brilliant enough to be admired by Jorge Luis Borges ("his work is without equal in the literature of our time"), who was Henri Michaux?

His own "Some Information about Fifty-Nine Years of Existence" is a good place to start looking for an answer, although there are aspects of the man one could not possibly guess from that text. For example, although he was a very private person (he had a real horror of being photographed), he did have a circle of friends—particularly literary and artistic friends—and was an extremely courteous man.[3] Some of the dates in the "Information . . ." are wrong; the picture given is not only fragmentary and mythically literary (the poet as Outsider), but shifting and evasive; thus in 1935, we find this utterly maladjusted rebel (as Michaux has depicted himself) editing a literary review; something is wrong with this picture.

"Some Information about Fifty-Nine Years of Existence" is a highly personal, expressive account of his life to 1958, based on how Michaux saw himself and what he knew; in actual fact, it answers the question "Who am I?" the way autobiographical fictions do.[4] Perhaps the best way of getting an account of his work will be through a reader's fiction—a narrative, not of events in a life, but of the fundamental project in a work, based on what I know about Michaux and how I see him.

Let's say that from early childhood on, a man feels—more than most people do—how fragile he is, how hollow and weak ("I was born full of holes . . . I admit it, I'm an enclosed hollow . . . I built myself on an absent column"), encumbered by the world around him ("It began when I was a child. There was a big adult in the way");[5] he feels, too, how mobile and changing he is (who am I? this one? that one?), but he doesn't try to get rid of the feeling; on the contrary, he asserts its value:

> we are not made for just one self. We are wrong to cling to it. The preju-
> dice for unity. (Here as elsewhere, the will: impoverishing and sacrificing.)
> (. . .) There is not one self. There are not ten selves. There is no self.
> ME is nothing but a position in equilibrium.
>
> (Afterword to *Plume*, 1938)

He refuses to freeze himself into one adult identity, one way of being in the world ("Adult—finished—dead: nuances of the same state"); refuses to *act,* for stability or profit ("He who rejects the world builds no house in it"). He travels, both spatially (*Ecuador,* 1929; *A Barbarian in Asia,* 1933) and mentally (*Elsewhere,* 1948; etc.), but he travels precisely to get away from what "they" want. As he himself said, he traveled in order to "drive his country out of him, his attachments of all kinds and whatever elements of Greek or Roman culture or Belgian habits have become attached to him, despite himself. He travels *against*" ("Some Information . . ."). He rejects traditional Western education, philosophy,[6] art, and music:

> Books are boring to read. You can't move around in them as you wish. You
> are asked to follow. The trail is traced, one way.
>
> ("Reading," 1950, in *Passages*)

Heard Spanish music yesterday. Tells me nothing. Music for . entertainment. What I want . . . is music to question, to auscultate, to
approach the problem of being.

("First Impressions," 1949, in *Passages*)[7]

He also feels intense anxiety, "the obsessive beacon of fear," rage, and above all, "fatigue, fatigue" . . . What will become of him?

One obvious possibility is that he will be defined as hopelessly neurotic, or insane, and paralyzed—by himself or by others (they might lock him up). But this man has unusual verbal and visual gifts, and a still more unusual gift for hanging on to what he is, going with it, exploring it. It seems to him that the danger lies in *not* doing so: "he who hides his madman dies voiceless;" or conversely, "whoever rejects his demons badgers us to death with angels." With this in mind, he begins to write and to paint.

Without the slightest concern for realism, or sur-realism,[8] or for any literary fashion, he produces strange little fables,[9] "apparitions" in poetry or prose or paint,[10] pictures of fantastic predicaments and fantastic inventions and desires, coldly objective descriptions of strange voyages (both real and imagined), and above all "Exorcisms,"[11] maledictions, and other "poetry for power" (Michaux's title)—poems in strongly rhythmic, "hammering" free verse. It is here that we can see most clearly what he is about:

> Exorcism, a reaction in force, with a battering ram, is the true poem of
> the prisoner.
>   In the very space of suffering and obsession, you introduce such ex-
> altation, such magnificent violence, welded to the hammering of words,
> that the evil is progressively dissolved, replaced by an airy demonic
> sphere—a marvelous state!

(Preface to *Ordeals, Exorcisms*, 1945)

These are truly magical works for Michaux (and for many readers): like the art of "primitive" peoples, they are primarily produced to accomplish something, "to ward off the surrounding powers of the hostile world."

Of course the "magic" of these poems depends on the way the poet uses words, as he himself explicitly recognizes for at least one of their forms: "As for the magic of male-diction, it is, above all, hammering, hammering, hammering." But in a sense, all Michaux's work does not seem to aim at being fine art. He has a fundamental distrust of beautiful language, indeed of any language. His writing is not aesthetic (in his view) but performative. His art aims at showing what he sees, at channeling evil energy and dealing with it. He deals with it through the work. "I write so that what was true should no longer be true. Prison displayed is prison no longer." Perhaps this can help others as it helps him:

> I wrote *My Properties* out of hygiene . . . for my health . . . this book, this experiment which seems to have been born entirely from egotism—I would venture to say it is social . . . an operation within everyone's reach . . .
>
> To all those suffering, involuntarily, from their imaginations—I would like to have been useful to them in this way, at least.
>
> (Afterword to *My Properties*, 1934)

And in fact his work is recognized, admired, first by a few, then by many.

As he becomes more famous, he is asked to reflect, publicly, on his work and the world, and he does so in essays and poetic aphorisms. Above all he continues to delve into the repressed side of Western consciousness and art—the eerie mobility and fragmentation of the self—using words, paint and ink and pencil, and, for a period of about ten years, hallucinogenic drugs.

He also explores what is unacceptable in other ways: tentative, private, unfinished. Take this little passage from an essay on music:

> There is an instrument that can hardly be heard; it is played in Africa for oneself alone, inside the hut, or outside without bothering or attracting anyone. Rudimentary, archaic, apparently put together haphazardly, freely, by the village blacksmith, the *sanzas* (that is its name): no two the same, no good even for a slightly elaborated melody, it is independent of any scale.
>
> Anarchical. A music of murmurs, the opposite of music for competitions, compositions. Instrument to relieve us dreamily from all the noisemakers of this world.
>
> ("In the Changing Waters of Resonance," *Facing the Vanishing World*, 1975)

This description, and valorization, of an object may be read as a delicate metaphor for a system of values far removed from the norm. Who but Michaux would want an instrument that can't even play a melody? Toward the end of his life, working from the model of Chinese ideograms, he even dreams of a language of pure lines that would communicate intimately or "murmur," without forming any ideas too definitely: down with our swaggering languages, with their rigid, enslaving syntax and grammar! Let's have no alphabet—no words.[12]

In one sphere of activity, he can function in this mode fairly easily and does so all his adult life; he paints.

> Born, raised, educated in a purely verbal environment and culture (and be-
> fore the era of the invasion of images) I paint *to decondition myself*
>
> *(Emergences-Résurgences, 1972)*

Obviously, for a poet, such "deconditioning" cannot always be nonverbal. But it can be nonrational and non-Western, not limited by the categories that we traditionally impose on consciousness. Increasingly, he explores mystical experience, Eastern religions; until his death he strives, in poetry and prose, painting and music, to "coincide with [him]self," to "occupy [him]self," to achieve some kind of mobile, resolutely nonrational integration of his experience and consciousness, to integrate *The Space Within* and the space without.[13]

MICHAUX AND "THE PROBLEM OF BEING": FACING THE WORST

In a famous aphorism, Pascal wrote that "all the unhappiness of men comes from one thing: which is not to be able to remain at rest in a room"—hence, for Pascal, our frantic activity (*divertissement*) in the world. Michaux stays in the room and faces the unhappiness.

> Under the low ceiling of my little bed-room is my night, a deep abyss.
>   Constantly hurled down to a depth of thousands of feet, with a gulf sev-
> eral times that big below me, I hang on by the rough-spots with the greatest
> difficulty, dead tired, mechanically . . .
>
> ("The Night Moves")

It is terrifying to confront the mobile, isolated self, and especially terrifying to face its fragility. Here is a Meidosem, one of the many fantastic beings the poet invented:

> pierced by a thousand little transversal flows from extravasated blood burst-
> ing the arterioles, but it's not blood, it's the blood of memories, of the
> pierced soul . . . it's the reddened water of useless memory flowing out

. . . through small passages leaking all over—minuscule, multiple punctures.
A Meidosem bursts. A thousand small veins of his faith in himself burst.

That which is physically closest to one's self, most expressive of it, is also fragile: Michaux is obsessed by the vulnerability of the human face. (Surely his horror of being photographed has something to do with this; so do the many faceless portraits he produced.) In a typical show in "The Land of the Hacs," "the noble features—noble as even the most ignoble are—the features of that face were trampled on like some unimportant sugar-beet." And "In the Land of Magic,"

offenders caught in the act have their faces ripped off on the spot, [leaving] a huge, round, scabby clot; (. . .)
Anybody who has seen one will remember it forever. He has his nightmares to remember it with.

So the self can be stripped of its "face," its individual being, or it can hemorrhage out catastrophically. It can also be engulfed, as in the last sentence of "Space of the Shadows," or invaded: in "A Few Days of My Life among the Insects" the narrator has a hard time fending off a "huge female ichneumon-fly" who insists on sinking her egg-bearing rod into his kidneys "so as to pour out her abundant eggs, which I would then have had to nourish for months at a time, fetid victorious larvae." The horror is intensified by the monstrously unnatural sexual image: the male narrator is in danger of being raped and impregnated by a female insect.

Sexuality is not only monstrous "Among the Insects" (where the narrator also has intercourse with giant caterpillars). In a more ordinary world, five hideous women, one of them "A Mother of Nine," rape Michaux's character, Plume, until the blood flows. If they're in a bad mood, the giant female courtesans in "The Land of Magic" can "rip your head off in a flash, like a young herring's." The terrifying mobility of the self is matched by its weakness; its imminent destruction (*self*-destruction, in fact) is both horrifying and erotically attractive.

As the poet himself realizes, such a self creates monsters: "It soon became clear (from my adolescence on) that I had been born to live among monsters." In fact "with inner vision," he explores the actual lobe in his brain where they are produced: "The Monster Lobe." Indeed his texts swarm with monsters: not only "real" ones specifically called "monsters," which he meets everywhere (in his room, or on the stairs), but monstrous beings of all kinds. They may be monstrous in shape, like the "Pourpianes with green, quivering anuses"—here as elsewhere, the grotesque erotic detail recalls Hieronymus Bosch—or monstrous in size, like the giants mentioned above or the midget oak (see below); "Dwarves are born continually," says another narrator.

The creation of monsters is the clearest manifestation of what Freud, in his essay of that name, called the *Unheimliche,* the "uncanny,"[14] a complex of emotions that other psychoanalysts have called "the Not-me," the surging up of all the negative energies excluded from the ordinary self or the ego. It is the eerie, frightening feeling the universe may sometimes inspire in anyone, the flip side of religious awe. The word *uncanny* has, of course, etymological connotations of the un-known in English; in German, Unheimliche suggests what is un-homelike or un-familiar. Freud makes much of this, for it comes from the repression of what is all too familiar—of what one cannot live with. And in fact the universe is an unlivable place for Michaux. How can he survive in it?

The first condition is: knowledge. Poetry and painting are paths to that knowledge. So are drugs. In 1954,[15] after hesitating for a while, Michaux accepted the invitation of some friends (among them a neurologist) to experiment with mescaline, the active substance in the cactus used by certain Native American peoples to induce religious visions. Here Gilbert Lascault shrewdly points out that for Michaux—who, far from being a druggie, was rather "the water-drinking type" (as he himself says)—everything is a drug: fatigue, coffee, abstinence, even the effort at lucidity. All mescaline does is to show the poet what he is and has always desired. What he finds in mescaline, no doubt because it fascinates him, is not an escape from his anguish but a kind of "artificial hell"[16] in which anguish and loss of self dominate. He certainly doesn't use it for kicks: "Should one speak of pleasure? It was unpleasant," he writes in 1956 at the beginning of *Miserable Miracle,* his first book on mescaline. And in the epigraph to his third mescaline book, 1961:

> Drugs bore us with their paradises. Let them give us a little knowledge instead. This is not a century for paradise.
>
> *(Knowledge through the Abyss)*

With irrefutable, painful clarity, mescaline reveals to the poet that terrifying mobility, weakness, passivity, and tendency to dissolve which he had previously explored in fantasy. Passages like this one are typical in *Miserable Miracle:*

> I myself was a torrent, I was drowned, I was navigation. My great constitution hall, my ambassador's hall, my hall for gifts and exchanges into which I

usher foreigners for a first examination—I had lost all my halls with my servants. I was alone, shaken around violently like a dirty thread in an energetic wash.

In "Space of the Shadows," a somber narrative written a few years *before* the experiments with hallucinogens, the nature of space itself (a "horrible inside-outside") presents constant dangers to the female speaker. In *Turbulent Infinity* (1957), Michaux's second book describing his mescaline experiences, he himself is "Fluid, inside fluids. Dwelling lost. Have become outside oneself."

In one of the experiments related in *Miserable Miracle,* Michaux accidentally took an overdose and actually experienced the total destruction of his self (fortunately temporary). One of the ways he describes this ineffable experience ("so absolutely horrible . . . I can't find any way of saying it and I feel like a counterfeiter when I try") is by this image:

> incredibly fast, hundreds of lines of force were combing my being, which
> never managed to pull itself back together fast enough, which at the mo-
> ment of coming back together was raked by a new row of tines, and then
> again, and then again

The feeling of speed and now infinite mobility are heightened elements of Michaux's ordinary sense of being. This leads him to recall

> that very remarkable look of those wild-haired madwomen, not only the
> wind makes them look that way or their wandering hands, or their helpless-
> ness, but the imperative inner necessity of translating (at least in that way)
> the rapid, infernal combing-uncombing of their being—martyrized, pene-
> trated, drawn out like wires, indefinitely.

So mescaline puts the poet in contact with the feelings of those for whom the universe is *totally* unlivable: the insane. Later, when he has abandoned drugs and their dangers (overdose and especially addiction), he will take a less dramatic path to such knowledge; when he writes about drawings of hospitalized mental patients in "Ravaged People" (1976), it feels as if he is picturing madness from within.

There is another precondition for survival in Michaux's "room." Bad feelings must not be repressed, but intensified and pushed to their logical conclusions. The "logic" is not that of physical laws, but of mental reality; Freud would call it the primary process at work. Revolt is essential:

> In my night, I besiege my King, I get up little by little and I wring his
> neck.
> He regains his strength, I come back at him and wring his neck again.
>
> ("My King")

So is destructive rage. Michaux recognizes clearly enough that the "holes" that make up his very being, the "absent column" on which he has "built [him]self," are filled with "a wind, an emptiness" of "hate"; in fact, he says, "this is my health" ("I Was Born Full of Holes," in *Ecuador, 1929*). Thus, in daily life and in his "room":

> I can rarely see someone without beating him. Others prefer interior mono-
> logue. Not me. I prefer beating.
>
> ("My Occupations")

> You can say what you like, my darlings, but I do know how to have a good
> time. Only yesterday, I ripped an arm off a policeman. (. . .)
> My sheets are just about never white. It's a good thing blood dries fast.
> How could I sleep if it didn't?
>
> ("The Night Moves")

On the other hand, utter inattention to the worst catastrophes can be a great help:

> Stretching his hands out from the bed, Plume was surprised not to encoun-
> ter the wall. "Hmm!" he thought, "The ants must have eaten it . . ." and
> he went back to sleep.
>
> ("Plume")

In the last analysis, Plume's creator resembles his Meidosems: "clamped to their weakness, strong in a sense because of it, invincible even . . ." And as these last excerpts suggest, reading Michaux is not only a scary trip through the Unheimliche and the world of madness: it is a comic adventure.

HUMOR AND TERROR

Michaux survives, we smile. It's not surprising. The essence of what the Surrealists called *humour noir*, its ''sublimity,'' as they said, lies in ''the triumph of narcissism, in the invulnerability of the ego. . . . The ego refuses to let itself be injured . . . refuses to admit that traumas from the outside world can touch it.''[17] The greater the trauma, the greater the triumph.

Surely that's what happens when we read ''The Heroic Age,'' for example:

> The Giant Barabbo, in play, ripped an ear off his brother Poomappi.
> Poomappi said nothing, but as if absentmindedly he squeezed Barabbo's nose and the nose came off.
> In answer Barabbo bent down, broke off Poomappi's toes, and after first pretending he wanted to juggle them, quickly made them vanish behind his back.
> Poomappi was surprised.

—and so on, with more and more atrocious injuries being inflicted for a page and a half, until at last:

> The fight was over, at least for the day.

Sometimes the violent energy seems to mangle the language itself:

> He grabowerates him and grabacks him to the ground;
> He rads him and rabarts him to his drat.[18]

> ("The Big Fight")

Michaux's dark humor does not only work in mythical, unreal settings. In the texts about Plume—prose narratives three to four pages long—the catastrophes that occur to the character come from a widening crack in everyday experience. Thus an embarrassment in a chic restaurant ("the headwaiter came over, looked at him severely and said to him in a low, mysterious voice: 'What you have on your plate is *not* on the menu'") leads step by step, inexorably, to the police station, where a thuggish cop is promising to work Plume over until he "confesses"—and the text ends there, as a bad dream might. The dreamer survives. Unlike a bad dream, however, it's funny. Besieged by difficulties—"In a silly moment of distraction, Plume walked with his feet on the ceiling, instead of keeping them on the ground"—Plume blunders through life like a less clever Charlie Chaplin in a more fantastic universe.[19]

If narratives or poems of the self's survival against aggressively hostile forces can be amusing, so can the poet's own superaggressive forays into the world, sinister though they sometimes may be. Take this fairly typical piece from the *Plume* collection (1938):

THE OAK

I met an oaktree: as tall as my finger, and it was suffering. Of its four leaves, two were completely yellow. The others were drooping and had no sheen.

I could discover no enemy in the neighborhood, nor any excessive competition.

Some skillful parasite must have slipped into it. An oak, so what? what's that to a parasite?

So, I ripped it out, root and dead leaves, and up you go!

It's supposed to be tenacious, but to start living again when it was that far gone, no! it hadn't learned enough for *that*

There is nothing nice about the speaker, or about his world; this could be a terrible little tale of suffering, sickness, death, and destruction. But in fact I *enjoy* Michaux's reversal here, as he transforms mighty oak into sickly midget. Giants and dwarves everywhere: but the same monstrous metamorphoses and perversions of nature that populate Michaux's Bosch-like hells can be used in an entirely different mode. The whole text—especially the narrator's excessive, seemingly pointless rage and triumph—serves as an exorcism through humor; "exorcism through ruse" is the poet's own phrase for many of his works. The demon of rage is cast out through comic exaggeration, and the spell seems to work on the reader, too.

Just as the mutability of a hollow self swept by raging currents can be eerie and horribly painful—or amusing and pleasant—the transformation of nature and the suspension of its laws has both negative and positive values. We can see this quite clearly in the course of Michaux's explorations "In the Land of Magic" (1941), for example: the master-magicians accomplish both beautiful and terrible things. In a shorter, earlier, text, we find "magic" calming the very anguish that led to its creation:

> I used to be quite nervous. Now I'm on a new track: I put an apple on my
> table. Then I put myself inside the apple. What peace!

This is a recipe for identification with nature which recalls certain techniques of Zen Buddhism, says Michel Butor:[20] How can we enter into what we see in front of us? How to understand another person from the inside, and not only another person, but an animal—or a fruit? Like Cézanne, who spent years painting apples, Michaux wants to understand that "abyss of tranquillity" from within—no easy task. The poet was distracted from his efforts by the sight of passing women, among other things. It took years:

> I had to grope around, experiment—there's quite a story behind all this.
> Setting out isn't easy and neither is explaining it.
>   But I can tell it to you in a word. *Suffering* is the word.
>   When I arrived in the apple, I was ice-cold.

Suffering and ascesis in order to unite oneself with the universe, to reach final peace, "the peace that passeth human understanding"—these are the methods and goals of mystics in many religious traditions, particularly those of Asia.

"Magic," from which we have been quoting, dates from 1938; throughout his career, but increasingly in the last two decades, Michaux's work incorporates what Hinduism, tantric art, and Buddhism (not only Zen Buddhism) have taught him about consciousness, about *being*. The last two poems in the little anthology that Michaux himself selected for Gallimard in 1976 both bear this mark: "Toward Complete Being" ("Vers la complétude," 1967) and "Yantra" (1973). So do many of the texts in his four major collections from

1973 to 1985.[21] If some of their concepts and vocabulary come from the religions of Asia—the cosmogram, the "tantric hand," Purusha-Prakriti, the mandala—they serve to nourish the perennial personal concerns of Henri Michaux. Take the end of this "Outcome of Contemplation":

> Silence. The day of silence. Come back to it. Get back inside it. Impermanence has been left behind. As we free ourselves from impermanence, little by little, we find (some more, some less) in our calmed being, progressively, repeatedly deepened, Permanence, its radiance, the other life, the counterlife.

> (In *Facing the Vanishing World,* 1975)

This is not the only place in which Michaux tries to invoke (or create), rhythmically, a state of calm and permanence for the poet's raging, discontinuous self: it is suggested in "Magic" and we find it memorably performed in "To Act, I Come" (1949), the last section of "Poetry for Power," and elsewhere. So, too, for "the counterlife": the notion is crucial for Michaux from start to finish. Here it is connected to silence; but "the other life" is rooted not only in the religious silence of meditation, but in Michaux's old hostility to all that is fixed, defined—to his hostile distrust of language itself. He himself footnotes "the counterlife" thus: "Alone, without words. Words locate you. You have to reside in the non-located."

The year before he died, Michaux published *The Exalted Garden,* which is, in my view, the climax of mystic experience in his work. It is a little less than ten pages long and describes, tersely at the start and then in strongly rhythmed, poetic prose, the ecstatic feeling of oneness with the universe that the poet experiences in what is at first an ordinary country garden. It is the transformation and reversal of a *Western* myth: with an "Eve" as guide rather than temptress, this little space becomes a Garden of Eden, and one ordinary tree becomes something like a new and beautiful Tree of Knowledge. But the text begins, prosaically, "A bit of the prepared product remained." This ecstasy in the Garden is, like *By Surprise,* which Michaux published in the same year, one of his last texts "about" hallucinogenic drugs.

Again, the drug has acted as a revealer. If it once showed him horrors (horrors he always knew were there), it also taught him that the mind is far vaster than we usually think. For one thing, the mind has in it the capacity to experience *infinity*—infinity of space and time here and now (see *Knowledge through the Abyss,* below). Some people have always known this without the benefit of drugs; in European literature, Dante is one example. Just before "Toward Complete Being" and "Yantra" at the end of that little 1976 volume of selected poems, Michaux placed an amazing passage from his second "mescaline book," *Turbulent Infinity*: "I SAW THE THOUSANDS OF GODS." Which gods? "*The* thousands... " Apparently this is a vision of all the gods in the vast compass of the world's religions—a grandiose claim. Yet it is hard to read the text without thinking that he really saw them, that he "was given that marvelous gift." Religiously inclined or not (and the present writer is not), the reader feels the force of it, with a shock.

It is commonplace—because it is true—to say that great writers can extend our experience. Michaux does it more than most.

David Ball

NOTES

1. It was actually written by Breton and Philippe Soupault (my translation), the first sentence of "Eclipses" in *Les Champs magnétiques* (1919), a founding Surrealist text.

2 Malcolm Bowie makes this point in *Henri Michaux. A Study of His Literary Works* (Oxford: Clarendon Press, 1973), 24 Other useful books on Michaux in English.
—Virginia A. La Charité, *Henri Michaux*, Twayne's World Authors Series (Boston G. K. Hall, 1977)
—Laurie Edson, *Henri Michaux and the Poetics of Movement* (Saratoga, Calif.: Anma Libri, 1985).
—A special issue of *L'Esprit créateur*, edited by Laurie Edson (v. 26, no. 3, 1986) is devoted to Michaux.
There are fine writings about his art (and thus indirectly his poetic vision) in *Henri Michaux* (New York: The Solomon R Guggenheim Museum, 1978) and in John Ashbery, *Reported Sightings* (New York: Alfred A. Knopf, 1989).

3. In the *Cahiers de l'Herne* (1966), Patrick Gregory tells of how Michaux crossed all of Paris to return a pair of gloves to him; Allen Ginsberg relates the polite reception he gave to a couple of young American poets, even when one of them (Gregory Corso) hailed him on the streets of Paris with a "Hey, Henry!" you could hear on the docks of New York. And when I sent Michaux my first fumbling attempts at translating one of his poems years ago, he replied with a graciousness that moves me still.

4 His first book of poetic fictions was called, precisely, *Qui je fus* (Who I Was [Paris: N.R.F., 1927]). But only in the obliquest sense does it live up to its title.

5. As the reader will discover, most of the quotations from Michaux in this Introduction can be found in the present anthology

6. Michaux rejected *Western* philosophy: the Christian mystics were an exception from the start Later, and more lastingly, he will learn from Eastern mysticism and religion.

7. The dates in this Introduction are those of first publication—in this case, in *Mercure de France* Quite often, Michaux will publish a little text separately as a *plaquette*, an elegantly printed little book (usually with Fata

Morgana since the early 1970s), before putting these works together into an accessible collection (almost invariably with Gallimard)

8   I don't mean Surrealism doesn't interest Michaux; it does, and he writes about the movement, critically, in 1925, three years after his first published texts. But what he writes and paints himself is usually quite different.

9   *Fables des origines* is one of Michaux's first published works (1923). He will write fables—or myths—all his life, as many of the works in this anthology attest

10. The title of a small collection of poems and drawings published in 1946. Some are included in *La Vie dans les plis,* (*Life in the Folds* 1949); see below.

11. 1943; reprinted in *Epreuves, Exorcismes* (Ordeals, Exorcisms, 1945). But Michaux's "exorcisms" are by no means limited to one collection

12   In *Par des traits* (Through Lines, Fata Morgana, 1984), one of Michaux's last published texts: a hundred or so pages of inked lines (ideograms? little human figures? just lines, squiggles, and blots?), followed by a ten-page essay against "finished languages." As early as 1951, in *Mouvements,* Michaux had experimented with the possibilities of vaguely suggestive inkbrush strokes "in motion" and words in the accompanying poem. Now, in *Through Lines,* he ends with a call for

> The sign: finally delivering us from litanies of words, of phrases depending only on phrases, continuing in phrases, it would free the brain from its local over-occupation
>> Return to a primitive operation whose attraction has been indistinct but is now re- ceiving a new charge
>> Signs that would enable us to be open to the world differently, creating and develop- ing a *different function* in man, DISALIENATING HIM.

13. *L'Espace du dedans* (The Space Within) is Michaux's title for his 1944 anthology (Gallimard). Richard Ellmann's English translation was first published by New Directions, New York, in 1952.

14. Gilbert Lascault makes this observation in his extremely interesting essay in the *Cahier de l'Herne* devoted to Michaux (1966, reprint, Livre de Poche, n.d.)

15. And not in 1956, as he claims in "Some Information about Fifty-Nine Years of Existence."

16. For the French reader, this is an obvious contrast to Baudelaire's famous *Les Paradis artificiels* So is the epigraph to *Knowledge Through the Abyss,* below.

17   I'm quoting André Breton in his Preface to the *Anthologie de l'humour noir* (1939); he's quoting Freud. (Reprint, Paris· Jean-Jacques Pauvert, 1966; Livre de Poche, 15; my translation.)

18   *Il l'emparouille et l'endosque contre terre,*
     Il le rague et le roupète jusqu'à son drâle

19. "Our Brother Charlie" was Michaux's contribution on Chaplin to the special issue of the Belgian review *Le Disque Vert* in 1924, at the beginning of his literary career. "Difficulties" is the title of one group of texts (1930) in the 1938 collection titled *Plume*

20. *Improvisations sur Henri Michaux* (Fata Morgana, 1985), 68–69.

21. *Moments, traversées du temps* (Moments, Crossings of Time, 1973, including work from 1957–1970), *Face à ce qui se dérobe* (Facing the Vanishing World, 1975); *Chemins cherchés chemins perdus transgressions* (Paths Looked-For, Paths Lost, Transgressions, 1981); and the posthumous *Déplacements dégagements* (Displacements, Disengagements, 1985).

SOME INFORMATION ABOUT FIFTY-NINE YEARS OF EXISTENCE[1]

May 24, 1899.   Namur [Belgium].

Born into a middle-class family.

Father from the Ardennes.

Mother Walloon.[2]

One of his grandparents, whom he never knew, of German origin.

A brother, three years older.

Distant Spanish ancestry.

1900–1906.   Brussels.

Indifference.

Inappetence.

Resistance.

Uninterested.

He avoids life, games, amusements and variation.

Food disgusts him.

Odors, contacts.

His marrow does not make blood.

His blood isn't wild about oxygen.

Anemia.

Dreams, without images without words, motionless.

He dreams of permanence, of perpetuity without change.

His way of existing in the margins, always on strike, is frightening or exasperating.

He's sent to the country.

1906–1910. Putte-Grasheide.

Little village in la Campine.[3]

Five years in boarding school.

Poor, tough, cold school.

Classes are in Flemish.

His classmates, sons and daughters of poor peasants.

Secretive.

Withdrawn.

Ashamed of what surrounds him, of everything that surrounds him, of everything that has surrounded him since he came into the world, ashamed of himself, of being only what he is, scorn for himself and for everything he has known up to now.

He is still disgusted by foods, wraps them in paper and stuffs them in his pocket. Once he's outside, he buries them.

1911–1914. Brussels.

Returns to Brussels. Saved! So he does prefer one reality to another. Preferences begin. Watch out! sooner or later, belonging to the world will come in. He is twelve.

Ant battles in the garden.

Discovery of the dictionary, of words that do not yet belong to phrases, to phrasemakers, masses of words, words he can use himself in his own way. Goes to a Jesuit school.

With his father's help, he becomes interested in Latin, a beautiful language, which sets him apart from others, transplants him: his first departure. Also the first sustained effort he enjoys.

Music, just a bit.

1914–1918. Brussels.

Five years of German Occupation.

First French composition in school. A shock for him. The things he finds in his imagination! A shock even for the teacher, who pushes him toward literature. But he rejects the temptation to write; it could turn him away from the main point. What main point? The secret that, from his earliest childhood, he has suspected might exist somewhere. People around him are visibly unaware of it.

All kinds of reading. Research to discover his family, scattered through the world, his real parents, though not quite his parents either, to discover those who may "know" (Ernest Hello, Ruysbroek, Tolstoy, Dostoevsky).[4] Reads Lives of saints, the most surprising, the furthest removed from the average man. Also readings in bizarre writers, eccentrics or "Jeune Belgique"[5] who write in a strange style he would like to see still stranger. After his *baccalauréat*,[6] with the university closed because of the Occupation, two years of readings, of intellectual pottering about.

1919.　First year of medical school.
　　　 Doesn't show up at the final exams. Gives up studying medicine.

1920.　Boulogne-sur-Mer
　　　 Ships out as a sailor on a five-masted schooner.

　　　 Rotterdam.
　　　 Ships out a second time. On *Le Victorieux,* a ten thousand ton fine-looking vessel the Germans have just delivered to France. There are fourteen of us in a little crew's cabin, in the bow. Amazing comradeship, unexpected, invigorating. Bremen, Savannah, Norfolk, Newport News, Rio de Janeiro, Buenos Aires.
　　　 On the way back from Rio, the crew complains about the food,

refuses to go on and unanimously reports in sick. Out of solidarity, he leaves this lovely vessel... thus missing the shipwreck that will take place twenty days later, south of New York.

1921.   Marseilles.
All over the world, ships (formerly used to transport troops and food) are being laid up. Impossible to find a job. The big window closes once again. He is obliged to turn away from the sea.
Back to the city and people he detests.
Disgust.
Despair.
Various professions and jobs, all poor and poorly performed.
Top of his chart as a failure.

1922.   Brussels.
Reads [Lautréamont's] *Maldoror*.[7] Shock... which soon brings on the long-forgotten need to write.
First pages. Franz Hellens then Paulhan[8] see something in them, others see nothing at all.
Still reticent. He wouldn't like to ''have to'' write.
It prevents dreaming. It makes him come out.
He prefers to remain coiled up.
Leaves Belgium for good.

1924   Paris.
He writes, but still ambivalent.
Can't manage to find a pen name that would encompass him—him, his tendencies and his potentialities.
He continues to sign with his ordinary name; he detests it, he is ashamed of it, like a label marked ''inferior quality.'' Perhaps he hangs onto it out of faithfulness to his discontent and dissatisfaction.

So he will never produce anything proudly, but always dragging that ball and chain at the end of each work, thus keeping him from even a slight feeling of triumph and achievement.

1925. Klee, then Max Ernst, Chirico... Extreme surprise. Up to now, he had hated painting and the fact itself of painting, ''As if there still weren't enough of reality, of that awful reality,'' he used to think. ''But to want to repeat it, to come back to it!''
Various jobs. In a publishing house for a while, production department.

1927. Quito.
Year's trip to Ecuador, with Gangotena, an Ecuadoran poet possessed by genius and ill luck. He dies young and after him his poems, most of them unpublished, burnt up in a plane crash, disappear forever.

1928. Paris.

1929. His father dies. Ten days later, his mother dies. Voyages to Turkey, Italy, North Africa...
He travels *against*.
To drive his country out of him, his attachments of all kinds and whatever elements of Greek or Roman culture or Belgian habits have become attached to him, despite himself.
Voyages of expatriation.
Still, his rejection begins to yield just a bit to the desire for assimilation.
He will have a lot to learn, to learn to open up. It will take a long time.

1930–1931	in Asia.
	At last *his* voyage.
	India, the first people who, massively, seem to correspond to what is essential, who seek satisfaction in what is essential, at last a people that deserves to be distinguished from the others.
	Indonesia, China, countries about which he writes too quickly, out of his excitement and amazement at having been so deeply touched, countries about which he will then have to think and ruminate for years.
1932.	Lisbon-Paris.
1935.	Montevideo, Buenos Aires.
1937.	Begins to draw more than from time to time. First show. (Galerie Pierre in Paris.)
1938–1939.	Meudon.
	Edits the review *Hermès.*
1939.	Brazil (Minas Geraes and the State of Rio.)
January 1940.	Back to Paris. In July, the exodus [of refugees from the Germans]. Saint-Antonin. Then Le Lavandou.[9]
1941–1942.	Le Lavandou with the woman who will soon be his wife.
1943.	Back to Paris. German Occupation (the second one.)
1944.	His brother dies.

1945.   Weakened by food shortages, his wife catches tuberculosis. Together in Cambo. Improvement.

1947.   Almost cured. Voyages of convalescence and forgetting about troubles, in Egypt.

February 1948.   Death of his wife as a result of atrocious burns.

1951—1952—1953.   He writes less and less, he paints more.

1955.   Naturalized French.

1956.   First experiment with mescaline.

1957.   Art shows in the United States, Rome, London. Breaks right elbow. Osteoporosis. Hand unusable. Discovery of ''left man.''[10] Cured. And now?
Despite so many efforts in so many directions all through his life to change himself, his bones, without paying any attention to him, blindly follow their familial, racial, Nordic evolution...

H. M.

NOTES

1. Written by Henri Michaux for Robert Bréchon, *Michaux* (Paris. Gallimard, 1959).
2. French-speaking people from southern Belgium
3 Belgian countryside bordering on Holland

4. Ernest Hello was a mystical French Catholic writer of the late nineteenth century; he wrote against the "scientism" of his times Ruysbroek is the great Dutch mystic of the fourteenth century

5. Belgian review founded in the late nineteenth century which violently attacked the official literature of the time.

6. The examination that gives both a high-school diploma and entrance into the University in French-speaking countries

7 The Surrealists would claim Lautréamont as their spiritual ancestor because of his *Chants de Maldoror,* published 1868–1869.

8 Franz Hellens was a Belgian writer with Surrealist sympathies, Jean Paulhan, writer and editor of *La Nouvelle Revue Française,* was one of the most influential men in French letters in the first half of this century. He was to remain a close literary friend of Michaux's, his "man at Gallimard "

9. Small town on the Mediterranean.

10. *L'homme gauche* in French, with a pun on *gauche,* clumsy, as well as the opposition to the usual right-handed—or "right"—man

TRANSLATOR'S NOTE

The order of the texts in this anthology is roughly chronological—roughly, because Michaux would usually first publish a group of poems or just one longish text in a small book, often with his own illustrations, and then collect thematically linked pieces from a number of little books along with other work in a larger volume a few years later. (Titles of the larger collections are given in large bold capital letters at the start of each section of this anthology; titles of the little books in the larger collections are printed in smaller capitals. For example, "A Certain Plume," p. 61, was a small collection Michaux incorporated into *Plume*, title on p. 43.) He would sometimes put earlier and later work into the larger volume: clearly what counted for him was the connection between the texts, not the date of publication. Thus *The Night Moves*, an important collection published in 1935, includes *My Properties* (from 1929); *Plume* (1938) contains work from 1930 to 1938. Rather than dismantle the larger volumes, I have respected Michaux's intentions by grouping the selections from his major collections regardless of their internal chronology (although I have often indicated dates). An exception is *My Properties*, presented separately with one of his favorite pieces from *Who I Was* (1927) to represent his first two important years of publication; another exception is *Trying to Wake Up* (1945), printed separately for reasons explained in my introduction to that work; still another is *Passages (1937–1963)*, placed at the very end of this volume to give a special place to Michaux's reflections on literature and art.

The choice of texts has largely been determined by personal preference (mine and, whenever possible, Michaux's), and by the desire to give a representative selection of the variety of his work. I have not included his two remarkable travel journals—*Ecuador* (1929) and *A Barbarian in Asia* (1933)—because they are already available in English.

Many of Michaux's collections were published several times in editions revised by the poet. Texts translated for this anthology were taken from the most recent French editions, including the revised, expanded edition of *L'Espace du dedans (The Space Within: Selected Writings 1927–1959)*, published in 1966 with much material not in the 1951 New Directions anthology of that name, and his own 1976 *Choix de poèmes (Selected Poems)*.

Cuts in some of the works are indicated by . . . , or, for longer cuts, (. . .); Michaux himself often uses suspension points... and occasionally lines of dots, which I have faithfully reproduced.

Translator's footnotes are numbered and are found at the end of each section; Michaux's own notes are lettered, at the bottom of the page.

MICHAUX'S FRENCH

Henri Michaux upsets many of our preconceptions. One of them concerns the nature of poetic language. For poets, we are told, it is the signifier that counts, not the signified: the word is more important than the message (or, in one variant of this doctrine, is indistinguishable from it); words, their texture, their sound, their interplay, are what the poet calls our attention to; language is opaque. Whatever one may think of this theory—which some critics would extend to all literature and not only poetry—it certainly corresponds to a French reader's experience of Baudelaire, say, or Mallarmé, or even Rimbaud.

But Michaux is different. He distrusts language too much to valorize it by foregrounding it as the object of his texts. Language as object, as texture, doesn't seem to matter to him. His nonsense texts are an obvious exception to this; so are some of his "exorcisms." But most often, he uses language just the way poets are not supposed to, as if it were transparent, as an instrument, to get at the reality beyond it—extraordinary, strange, and mobile as that reality may be. In that sense, he translates relatively easily, whereas Baudelaire and Mallarmé simply do not exist as poets in English (in this reader's opinion).

On the other hand, he doesn't write ordinary French. Adverbs often are not exactly where they should be, and other changes are made in usual word order; articles and other words eliminated for conciseness; words are occasionally invented by the poet. Many words come from the sciences; Michaux has an unusually broad technical vocabulary for a poet, a result, perhaps, of his year in medical school. A few examples, or rather the precise English equivalents that the reader will find in this translation include occultation (astronomy); lyse (biochemistry); sinusoidal (mathematics); occiput, sinciput (anatomy); laminaria, ichneumon, balaenoptera, ambulacral (zoology); and from medicine, hemianopsia, hemiplegia, extravasated, and arteriole.[1] Above all he makes sudden little shifts in the level of language: he will quite naturally slip slangy expressions into his normally distinguished, formal, literary French. I have rendered these shifts and eccentricities in English whenever I could;

my goals were, on the one hand, not to flatten Michaux into ordinary English, but on the other, not to put him into an English that simply sounds *wrong*.

Above all—and parodoxically, for a writer who constantly complains of fatigue—his style fairly buzzes with energy; there are surprises in every line. So one must pay close attention to this poet's language, after all.

Three principles guided this translation.

1. The poem must be able to stand on its own as a poem in English.

2. The poem must be as close as possible to the meaning (in the simplest sense) of the original.

3. The poem should come as close as possible to the sound-pattern of the original. For prose, this last principle will be less important than the others—but in this volume, I would classify only Michaux's Prefaces and Afterwords as prose, since the other texts should be read with the same intensity one gives to poetry. In any case, we're dealing with an *equivalent* sound-pattern: no sound in French is exactly the same as a sound in English.

The notion of equivalency is essential. The overarching goal of this translation is to produce an English text that creates an effect equivalent to that created by the original. If a Michaux poem is an incantation, it should have an incantatory effect in English; if it has a savage, ironic feel to it, that's the way it should feel in our language.

Of course these principles often come into conflict with each other. That's where the translator has some hard choices to make, and where he realizes, again and again, that translation is not a science.

D. B.

1. But I translate *otite,* a common French term, as "earache" rather than "otitis."

WHO I WAS

MY PROPERTIES

The title of his first book of poems notwithstanding, Henri Michaux *is* fully Henri Michaux in these two little collections. The longish prose piece that gives the second book its name, for example, is typical in subject and poetic persona. Like Charlie Chaplin trying to paint a house by dipping his brush in a bucket with no bottom to it, the narrator keeps trying to put something—anything!—into his estates or "properties" (the ambiguity of the latter term is intentional), but whatever he puts there keeps disappearing... and we realize that we're actually seeing the imagination at work, desperately trying to build a little reality for the wavering, vanishing self. Michaux's subject is and will remain the "field of consciousness." And his speaker will keep the same characteristics, contradictory as they may be: like Chaplin, the poor narrator is quite sly in his own way, and (in other texts) capable of giving the odd kick in the pants to someone who annoys him, but liable to burst into tears at a setback. Insuperable difficulties are found elsewhere in this collection, too, as are the magical "Interventions" we find throughout his work, and the precise observation of fantastic creatures.

The form of these texts is also typical: indifferently poetry or prose, in "transparent" style (see "Michaux's French," above)—except, of course, for the nonsense poems, which do call attention to the language, by dismantling it.

(*Qui je fus*, N R F / Gallimard, 1927, *Mes propriétés*, Fourcade, 1929)

1

I

W A S

THE BIG FIGHT

He grabowerates him and grabacks him to the ground;
He rads him and rabarts him to his drat;
He braddles him and lippucks him and prooks his bawdles;
He tackreds him and marmeens him
Mandles him rasp by rip and risp by rap.
And he deskinnibilizes him at the end.

The other hesitates; he is bittucked, unapsed, torsed and ruined.
He'll be done for soon.
He mendles and marginates himself... but in vain,
The far-rolling hoop falls down.
Abrah! Abrah! Abrah!
The foot has failed!
The arm has broke!
The blood has flowed!
Gouge, gouge, gouge,
In the big pot of his belly there's a great secret
You hags all around us crying into your handkerchiefs,
We're amazed, amazed, amazed
We're watching you
We're looking for the Great Secret, too.   *3*

PROPERTIES

MY PROPERTIES

In my properties everything is flat, nothing moves; there is a shape here and there, but where can that light come from? No shadows.

Occasionally when I have the time, I look around, holding my breath, on the alert; and if I see something emerge, I shoot out in a flash and jump on the spot, but the head—for usually it's a head—sinks back into the swamp; quickly I start digging, it's mud, just ordinary mud or sand, sand…

All this doesn't open on to a fine sky, either. Even though there is nothing over it, seemingly, you have to walk with a stoop as in a low tunnel.

These properties are my only properties, and I've lived in them since childhood, and really very few people own poorer ones.

Often I wanted to lay out fine avenues in them, I'd put in big landscaped grounds…

It's not that I like grounds, but… still.

At other times (it's a mania of mine, it comes back again and again after all my failures), in life outside or in an illustrated book I see an animal I like, a white egret for example, and I say to myself: now *that* would be nice in my properties, and then maybe it could multiply—and I take lots of notes and try to learn about everything in the animal's life. My documentation gets fuller and fuller. But when I try to transport it into my property, it always has a few essential organs missing. I struggle. I already have a feeling nothing will come of it this time, either; and as for multiplying, on my properties there is no multiplying—as I know all too well. I busy myself with the new arrival's food, with its air, I plant trees for it, I sow grass, but such are my detestable properties that if I turn my eyes away, or if I'm called out for a moment, when I come back there's nothing left, or only a layer of ash that might, at most, reveal a last wisp of scorched moss... at most.

And if I stick to it, it's not that I'm stupid.

It's because I am condemned to live in my properties and I've really got to make something out of them.

I'm going to be thirty soon, and I still don't have a thing; naturally I get upset.

I do manage to form an object, or a living thing, or a fragment. For example a branch or a tooth, or a thousand branches and a thousand teeth. But where can I put them? Some people effortlessly succeed in making clumps of plants, crowds... whole arrangements.

Not me. A thousand teeth, yes, a hundred thousand teeth, yes, and some days in my property I have a hundred thousand pencils in front of me, but what can I do in a field with a hundred thousand pencils? It's not appropriate—or else let's throw in a hundred thousand draughtsmen.

Fine, but as I work to form a draughtsman (and when I've got one, I've got a hundred thousand), there go my hundred thousand pencils up in smoke.

And if I'm preparing a jaw for the tooth, or a digestive and excretory system, as soon as the envelope is ready, when I'm putting in the pancreas and the liver there go the teeth—gone!—and soon the jaw, too, and then the liver, and when I'm up to the anus, only the anus is left; I'm really disgusted, because if I have to go back to the colon, the small intestine and the gallbladder again, and everything again and again, in that case, no! No.

In front and in back, right away it disappears—it just can't wait a second.

That's why my properties are always absolutely bare of everything, except for some living thing, or a series of living things, which only reinforces the general poverty and is like a monstrous, unbearable advertisement for the general desolation.

So I rub everything out, and only the swamps are left, without anything else, swamps that are my property and will drive me to despair.

And if I persist, I really don't know why.

But sometimes it all becomes animated, life swarms all over. It's visible, there's no doubt about it. I'd always had a feeling there was something in it, I feel full of zest. But now here comes a woman from the outside, she's riddling me with innumerable pleasures, but so close together that it's all only one instant, and carrying me away in the same instant many, many times around the world... (As for me, I haven't dared to invite her on a visit to my properties in the state they're in, of poverty, of quasi-inexistence.) Fine! on the other hand, worn out as I am from so many trips I can't understand at all, which were just so much perfume, soon I run away from her, cursing women once again. And now, utterly lost on this planet, I go wailing after my properties which are nothing, but which are familiar ground all the same, and don't give me that impression of *absurdity* I find everywhere else.

I spend weeks looking for my land, humiliated, lonely; you can insult me as much as you like at times like this.

I sustain myself with the conviction that it's impossible for me not to find my land, and, in fact, one day, a little sooner, a little later, there it is!

What happiness to be on home ground again! It has that *look,* no place else has it. It's true there are a few changes, it seems to me it slopes a bit more, or it's a bit moister, but the texture of the earth—it's the same texture.

Perhaps there are no abundant crops there. But that texture, you see—it really means something to me. If, however, I go up to it, it blurs into the mass—a mass of small halos.

No matter, it's clearly *my land.* I can't explain it, but confusing it with other lands would be like confusing myself with someone else: it's impossible.

There's my land and me; then there are foreign places.

Some people have magnificent properties, and I envy them. They see something elsewhere that they like. Good, they say, this will be for my property. No sooner said than done, there it is in their property. How is the transfer carried out? I don't know. Trained in acquiring, in accumulating, from early childhood, they can't see an object without immediately planting it in their property—it happens automatically.

You can't even call it greed; call it reflex.

Some of them are not even quite aware of it. They have magnificent properties that they keep up by the constant exercise of their intelligence and their extraordinary capacities, and they're not even aware of it. But if you should need a plant, however uncommon it may be, or an old carriage of the kind used by Juan V of Portugal, they leave for a moment and immediately bring back what you asked for.

Those who are good at psychology—I mean, not book psychology—may have noticed that I told a lie. I said my properties were land. Now, that has not always been the case. On the contrary, it is quite recent, although it seems so old to me, spanning a few lifetimes, even.

I am trying to remember exactly what they used to be in days gone by.

They were like whirlwinds; like huge pockets, slightly luminous pouches, and they were made of an impalpable though highly dense substance.

Sometimes I go out with a woman I used to be quite close to. The tone of our conversation quickly becomes distressing. Then I brusquely take off for my property. It has the form of a bishop's staff. It is vast, luminous. Light pierces this luminosity and steel crazily trembling like water. And I feel good there; it lasts a few moments, then, out of politeness, I return to the young woman, and I smile. But this smile is such that... (no doubt because it excludes her), she walks out and slams the door.

That's how it goes with my friend and me. It's always like that.

We'd be better off separating for good. If I had big, rich properties, of course I would leave her. But as things are, I'd better hang on for a while.

To come back to the "land." I was talking about despair. No, on the contrary, a piece of land gives you reasons to have all kinds of hope. You can build on a piece of land, and I'll do it. Now I am sure of it. I am saved. I have a base.

Formerly, since everything was in space, with no ceiling, no ground, naturally if I put in a living thing I would never see it again. It would disappear. *It disappeared by falling,* that's what I hadn't understood—and I thought it was because I hadn't built well! I would come back a few hours after putting it in, and every time I was astonished by its disappearance. Now that won't happen to me again. It's true my land is still swampy. But I'll dry it out little by little and when it's good and hard, I'll set up a family of workers on it.

It will be nice to walk around on my land. You'll see what I can do with it. I have a huge family. You'll see all kinds of types in it, I haven't showed it yet. But you'll see it. And its development will amaze the world. For it will develop with the avidity and passion of people who have lived a purely spatial life longer than they wished, and who wake up beside themselves with joy, to put on shoes.

Also, in space, any living thing used to be too vulnerable. It wasn't decorative, it stood out like a sore thumb. And all the passersby would smack at it like a target.

Whereas land, once again...

Oh, it's going to revolutionize my life.

Mother always predicted I'd be wretchedly poor and utterly worthless. Fine. Up to this land she has been right; after the land, we'll see.

I've been the shame of my parents, but we'll see about that, and besides, I'm going to be happy. There will always be lots of company around. You know, I used to be very lonely, sometimes.

A DOG'S LIFE

I always go to bed very early, dead tired, and yet you couldn't find any tiring work in the course of my day.

Maybe you couldn't find any.

But what suprises *me* is that I can hang on till evening, and that I'm not forced to get into bed by four o'clock in the afternoon.

What tires me out like that are my continual interventions.

I've already said that in the street I fight with everybody; I slap some man, grab women's breasts, and using my foot as a tentacle I sow panic in the cars of the Metro.

As for books, they harass me more than anything else. I just can't leave a word with its original meaning or even its form.

I catch it and after a few tries I uproot it and lead it definitively away from the author's flock.

There may easily be thousands of sentences in a chapter and I've got to sabotage every one of them. It is absolutely essential to me.

Occasionally, certain words remain like towers. I have to go about it a few times and then, when my demolition has already gone pretty far, all of a sudden, while passing by an idea, I can see that tower again. So, I hadn't knocked it down enough, I have to go back and find the poison for it, and I spend an endless amount of time in this way.

And once the whole book has been read, I lament, for I haven't understood a thing... naturally. Couldn't enhance myself with anything. I stay thin, and all dried up.

I used to think that when I had destroyed everything, I would be well adjusted, right? Maybe. But it's long in coming, it's really long.

SCREAMING

A whitlow causes atrocious suffering. But what made me suffer most was that I couldn't scream. For I was in a hotel. Night had just fallen and my room was in between two others where people were sleeping.

So, I started taking some big bass drums from my skull, and brass, and an instrument with more resonance than an organ. Now, using the prodigious strength that the fever was giving me, I made a deafening orchestra out of them. Everything was shaking with its vibrations.

Then, sure at last that my voice would not be heard over this tumult, I began to howl, to howl for hours, and little by little, I managed to get some relief.

A SAINT

While circulating through my accursed body, I came to a region where the parts of myself were few and far between; to live there, you had to be a saint. In times gone by, I had truly aspired to sainthood, but now that illness was forcing me into it, I struggled against it and I still struggle, and it's obvious that I'm not going to survive like this.

If I had been given the opportunity, fine! but to be forced into it—no, I just can't stand it.

INTERVENTION

In the past, I had too much respect for nature. I would stand before things and landscapes and let them do what they wanted.

That's over and done with: now I will *intervene*.

So, I was in Honfleur and I was getting bored. Then I resolutely put a bit of camel into it. That did not seem particularly appropriate. No matter, it was my idea. Besides, I acted on it with the greatest caution. First I brought them in on the most crowded days, Saturdays on the Market Place. The traffic jam that followed was indescribable, and the tourists said: "Oh, what a stink! The people here are so filthy!" The smell gained the port and began to overpower the odor of shrimp. People were coming out of the crowd covered with dust and hairs of the lord knows what.

And at night, you should have heard the pounding of the camels' hooves as they tried to cross the canal locks, bong! bong! on the metal and the beams!

The invasion of the camels was carried out with order and safety.

The inhabitants of Honfleur could now be seen squinting all the time with that suspicious look peculiar to camel drivers when they inspect their caravan to make sure nothing is missing and they can continue their journey; but I had to leave Honfleur on the fourth day.

I had also launched a passenger train. It sped out of the Grande Place and rolled resolutely forward with no regard for the weight of the material; it shot forward, saved by faith.

It's a shame I had to leave, but I doubt very much if calm will soon return to that little town of shrimp and mussel fishermen.

A SICK MAN'S DISTRACTIONS

Sometimes, when I'm feeling really low and I'm always alone too and I'm in bed, I have my left hand do obeisance to me. It raises itself on my forearm, turns toward me, and salutes me. My left hand is extremely weak, and quite distant toward me. Lazy, too. For it to move, I have to force it a bit. But as soon as it has begun it keeps on going, with a genuine desire to please me. It goes into such genuflections and is so courteous to me that even a third party would be moved.

INSECTS

As I went farther west, I saw nine-segmented insects with huge eyes like graters and latticework corselets like miners' lamps, others with murmuring antennae; some with twenty-odd pairs of legs that looked more like staples; others of black lacquer and mother-of-pearl that crunched underfoot like shells; still others high legged like daddy longlegs with little pin-eyes as red as the eyes of albino mice, veritable glowing coals on stems with an expression of ineffable panic; still others with an ivory head—surprisingly bald, so that suddenly one had the most fraternal feelings for them—so close, their legs kicking forward like piston rods zigzagging in the air.

Finally, there were transparent ones, bottles with hairy spots, perhaps: they came forward by the thousands—glassware, a display of light and sun so bright that afterward everything seemed ash and product of dark night.

THE EMANGLOM

It's a shapeless animal, one of the hardiest, three-quarters muscle, and all muscle on the outside, which is almost one foot thick all over. It can climb any rock, even smooth ones.

That skin, normally so amorphous, turns into crampons.

No animal attacks it; too high off the ground for a rhinoceros to crush, it might knock the rhino over instead, as it lacks only speed.

Tigers would break their claws without putting a dent in it, even a flea or a horsefly—or a cobra—can't find a sensitive spot.

And although it is marvelously aware of everything that happens around it (except apparently at the height of summer), absolutely no senses have been found in it.

To eat, it goes into the water: there is a lot of bubbling and above all movement in the water, and fish—perfectly intact—come floating to the surface belly up.

Deprived of water, it dies; the rest is mystery.

On the banks of the rivers where the Emanglom spends a good deal of time, it is not unusual to find crocodiles all smashed to bits.

THE URDES RACE

In this country, they do not use women. When they want pleasure, they go into the water, and then toward them comes a creature rather like an otter, but bigger, even more supple (and have you ever seen an otter go into the water? it slips in like a hand), toward him come these animals and fight over him, wrap themselves around him and knock each other about so much that if he hadn't put on light wooden floaters, the man would sink straight to the bottom, however strong a swimmer he might be—and he would be serviced on the bed of the river, if I may use the word. This animal winds itself around him like a sticky ribbon and does not readily let him go.

What makes these animals particularly attractive is that they are both supple and strong. At last man meets his superior.

Rich people breed them for themselves and their guests.

They also take care to provide empty waters where children may swim.

As for nubile young people, they must be watched carefully the first times they go to the river, for pleasure and sudden astonishment make them lose their strength too quickly and get dragged down to the bottom.

Everyone knows how treacherous water is in this way. As they are almost in a faint, they have to be pulled out of the water by means of long poles.

The nature of their pleasure is like ours, but for women, nothing. However, men make mothers of them and put them on their right-hand sides in bed—just as they do everywhere else.

DEATH OF A PAGE

Unbornished, vunished and already more raggled than rigged.

…A little thing and dying.

Alogol! Alopertius! Alogol! Help, I beg of you…

There is a druin, fuin, sen sen lom.

There is a luin, suin, sen sen lom.

…A little thing and dying.

But he's as upright, nyah! swaggerom,

As all chivalry or Cardinal of France.

ARTICULATIONS

And aller, aller et allero
And bitch!
Sarcospell on Sarico,
Andoran for talico,
Or'll ándora your ádogo,
Adogi.
Crass, crass like Chícago,
And ass-kicks to poverty.

(. . .)

None of the willed imagination of the professionals. No themes, developments, construction, or method. On the contrary, only the imagination that comes from the inability to conform.

These pieces, without preconceived connections, were written lazily from day to day, following my needs, the way it came, without pushing, following the wave, always attending to what was most pressing, in a slight wavering of truth—never to construct, simply to preserve.

(. . .)

Anybody can write *My Properties.*

Even the invented words, even the invented animals in this book were invented "from my nerves," and not constructed according to what I think about language and animals.

H. M.
(1934)

THE

NIGHT

MOVES

The room, the poet... and *The Night Moves:* in visions, and in narratives that dramatize currents of consciousness and sometimes take on the status of myths. Which is, perhaps, why Michaux put *My Properties* into this book. Like the title text of the 1929 collection, the later ''My King,'' for example, can be read as a myth of the imagination; it is a representation of the Son in perpetual, unavailing revolt against the Word of the Father. Hopeless, but funny, it feels like Beckett as much as Kafka.

In his ''Drawings with Commentary,'' the artist-poet introduces a project he will have all his life: not to *describe* the world of the drawing—any more than his verbal work describes the visual world—but to enter into it and embrace its strangeness.

(*La Nuit Remue*, Gallimard, 1935, revised edition, 1967)

2.

Under the low ceiling of my little bedroom is my night, a deep abyss.

Constantly hurled down to a depth of thousands of feet, with a gulf several times that big below me, I hang on by the rough spots with the greatest difficulty, dead tired, mechanically, helplessly, wavering between disgust and perseverance; the ant-climb continues with interminable slowness. The rough spots grow tinier and tinier, I can hardly make them out on the perpendicular wall. Abyss, night, terror, all fuse together, increasingly indissoluble.

3.

Already on the way up the stairs she'd begun to be not very big. When she finally reached the fourth floor, by the time she was crossing the threshold of my room, she was hardly any taller than a partridge. No, no, in that case I'd really rather not. A woman, fine! but not a partridge. She knew perfectly well why I had called her. It wasn't to... well!

So why keep at it against all reason and savagely hold me back by the leg of my pants? The last kick I gave her made her fall all the way down to the concierge's rooms. I certainly did not want that. She made me do it, honestly. I honestly think so.

And now, at the bottom of the stairs, her little moans, moans, moans, like all evil beings.

4.

...They appeared, slowly exfoliating from the beams in the ceiling... A drop appeared, swollen as an egg of oil, and heavily fell, a drop fell, an enormous belly, on the floor.

A new drop formed, a dark but gleaming womb, and fell. It was a woman.

She made extravagant and no doubt horribly painful efforts, and failed completely.

A third drop formed, swelled up, fell. The woman formed in it was instantaneously flattened, but nevertheless made such an effort... that she turned over.

In one flip. Then all movement stopped.

Long were her legs, long. She could have been a dancer.

Once again a drop formed and swelled—the terrible tumor of a life formed too quickly—and fell.

The bodies kept piling up, living pancakes, but quite human except for the flattening.

Then the drops stopped flowing. I lay down near a heap of tiny women, with stupor in my spirits, heartbroken, thinking neither of them nor of myself, but about the bitterness of daily life.

5.

There are always three of us in this galley. Two to keep the conversation going and me to row.

How hard is our daily bread, hard to earn, hard to get paid!

These two chatterboxes are my only distraction, but it's still awfully hard to see them eating my bread.

They talk all the time. If they didn't talk all the time, the immensity of the ocean and the noise of the storms would surely get the better of my courage and my strength, they say.

It isn't easy to push a boat forward all by yourself with a pair of oars. Even if the water offers little resistance... It does offer some, believe me. It does resist, and there are some days, especially...

Oh, how gladly would I lay down my oars!

But they have their eyes on me, since they have nothing else to do but that—and chatter away and eat my bread, my little ration, cut into a dozen times over.

6.

You can say what you like, my darlings, but I do know how to have a good time. Only yesterday, I ripped an arm off a policeman. It may have been the striped arm of a sergeant. I'm not sure. I ripped it off energetically, and threw it out in the same way.

My sheets are just about never white. It's a good thing blood dries fast. How could I sleep if it didn't?

My arms go wandering about all over, into bellies, into chests, into the organs called secret (secret to some people!).

My arms always bring something back, my fine drunken arms. I don't always know what it is, a piece of liver, chunks of lungs, it's all the same to me, as long as it's warm, wet, and full of blood.

Actually what I would like is to find some dew, very soft, truly soothing.

A white arm, fresh, carefully covered with satiny skin, isn't a bad take. But my nails, my teeth, my insatiable curiosity, the trouble I have getting used to superficial things... Well, that's the way it is. He who went for a kiss brought back a head.

Pray for him, he rages for you.

MY KING

In my night, I besiege my King, I get up little by little and I wring his neck.

He regains his strength, I come back at him and wring his neck again.

I shake him again and again like an old plum tree, and his crown wobbles on his head.

And yet, he is my King, I know it and he knows it, and of course I'm at his service.

Still, in the night, the passion of my hands strangles him relentlessly. No cowardice though, I come in with my bare hands and I squeeze his Kingly neck.

And he's my King, the one I've been vainly strangling for so long in the privacy of my little room; his face, bluish at first, becomes normal after a little while, and his head pops up again, every night, every night.

In the privacy of my little room, I fart in my King's face. Then, I burst out laughing. He tries to present a calm countenance, clean of all insult. But I fart in his face without stopping, except to turn around to him and burst out laughing in his noble face, which tries to maintain its majesty.

This is the way I act with him, endlessly beginning my shadowy life.

And now I throw him down on the ground and I sit on his face—his august face disappears—my rough oil-spotted pants, and my behind (because after all that's what it's called) remain, without embarrassment, on that face made to rule.

And I don't hesitate, not me! to turn left and right, whenever I feel like it and even more often than that, without worrying about his eyes or his nose being in the way. I only leave when I'm tired of sitting.

And if I turn around, his imperturbable face reigns, still.

I slap him, I slap him, then I wipe his nose mockingly like a child's.

However, it is quite obvious that he is the King, and I his subject, his only subject.

I boot him out of the room with kicks in the ass. I cover him with kitchen scraps and garbage. I break dishes on his legs. I cram low, well-aimed insults into his ears, hitting him deeply and shamefully with calumnies you might hear on the streets of Naples, particularly dirty and detailed, so that just to hear them is a stain you can't get rid of, a revolting suit made to measure: the very dung of existence.

Well, I have to begin all over again the next day.

He has come back; he is there. He is always there. He can't clear off for good. He absolutely has to impose his accursed royal presence on me, in my room—which is small enough already.

All too often I become involved in lawsuits. I run up debts, I get into knife fights, I abuse children, I can't help it, I just can't really manage to get the spirit of the Laws into my head.

When the Other Side has made its complaint to the tribunal, my King hardly listens to my reasons and takes up the Other Side's case, which becomes an indictment in his august mouth, a terrible preliminary that's really going to do me in.

Only at the end does he bring in a few trifling restrictions.

The Other Side, feeling that it's a small matter indeed, prefers to withdraw those few subsidiary complaints, and the bench strikes them. It's enough for the Other Side just to be sure of the rest.

At this point, my King takes up the argument from the start, always as if it were his own, but cutting it down slightly a bit more. Once this has been done, and an agreement reached on these details, he takes up the argument again from the beginning, and, weakening it little by little in this way, from step to step, from fresh start to fresh start, he reduces it to such nonsense, that the shamefaced bench and all the magistrates wonder who dared to convoke them for trifles of this sort, and a negative verdict is delivered amid the hilarity and jeers of the public.

Then, my King, paying no more attention to me than if I were not involved at all, rises and goes away, impenetrable.

One may wonder if this is really a job for a King; yet here's where he shows what he is—that tyrant, who can let nothing, nothing, happen without showing off his powers of enchantment, crushing, with no appeal possible.

What an idiot I was to try to throw him out! Why didn't I leave him in that room, calmly, calmly, without paying any attention to him.

But no. Idiot that I was—and as for him, seeing how easy it is to reign, he'll soon tyrannize over a whole country.

Wherever he goes, he makes himself at home.

And no one is surprised, it's as if he has belonged there forever.

They wait, they don't say a word, they wait for Him to decide.

In my little room animals come and go. Not at the same time. Not intact. But they go by—a petty, ludicrous procession of the forms of nature. The lion comes in with his lowered head bruised and dented like an old ball of rags. His poor paws flapping. It's hard to see how he can move forward—wretchedly, in any case.

The elephant comes in all deflated and less solid than a fawn.

And so it goes for the rest of the animals.

No appliances. No machines. The automobile comes in thoroughly laminated and might make a parquet floor at a pinch.

Such is my little room where my inflexible King wants nothing, nothing that he has not knocked around, mangled, reduced to nothing, a room where I, on the other hand, have asked so many to be my companions.

Even the rhinoceros, that brute who can't stand man, who charges at everything (and so solid, carved in rock), the rhinoceros himself one day came in as an almost impalpable fog, evasive and without resistance... and floated.

The little curtain over the skylight was a hundred times stronger than he was, a hundred times stronger than he—the strong, impetuous rhinoceros who stops at nothing.

But my King does not want rhinoceroses to enter in any fashion other than weak and trickling.

Another time, maybe he'll let him get around on crutches... and, to hold him in, a semblance of skin, a thin child's skin that could be torn by a grain of sand.

This is how my King authorizes the animals to parade before us. Only like this.

He reigns; he has got me; he does not care for distractions.

This tiny little rigid hand in my pocket, that's all that's left of my fiancée.

A tiny hand, dry and mummified (could it really have been hers?). That's all he left me of Her.

He took her away from me. He lost her for me. He reduced her to nothing for me!

In my little room, the palace ceremonies are as wretched as can be.

Even snakes are not low enough, don't grovel enough for him, even a motionless pine would offend him.

Also, what appears at his Court (in our poor little room!) is so incredibly disappointing that the lowest worker would not envy him.

Besides, who but my King—and I, because I'm used to it—could find some respectful being in those advances and retreats of dark matter, those little flurries of dead leaves, those few drops that fall, grave and desolate, in the silence.

A vain homage, moreover!

Imperceptible are the movements of His face, imperceptible.

THE MAIN POINT

Man—his essential being—is only a point. It is this point alone that is swallowed up by Death. That's why he must be careful not to be encircled.

One day, in a dream, I was surrounded by four dogs and a nasty little boy commanding them.

The trouble, the unbelievable difficulty I had in hitting him, I shall never, never forget. What an effort! No doubt I hit some sort of being, but whom? In any case, my opponents were defeated enough to disappear. Don't think I was fooled by their appearance, though: they weren't anything but points either—five points, but very strong ones.

And another thing: that's how epilepsy begins. The points march on to you and eliminate you. They *blow,* and you're invaded. How long can you put off your first fit, I really wonder.

WEDDING NIGHT

When you come home on your wedding day, if you stick your wife in a well to soak all night she is flabbergasted. Even if she had always been vaguely worried about it...

"Well, well," she says to herself, "so that's what marriage is like. No wonder they kept it all so secret. I've been taken in by the whole business."

But since her feelings are hurt, she doesn't say a thing. That's why you can plunge her into it for a long time, over and over, without making any trouble in the neighborhood.

If she didn't understand the first time, it's not very likely that she'll catch on after that, and you have a good chance of being able to continue with no problems at all (except for bronchitis) if you really want to.

As for me, since I suffer even more in other people's bodies than in my own, I had to give it up right away.

EVERYBODY'S LITTLE PROBLEMS

An ant doesn't worry about an eagle. The furor, the ferocity of the tiger means nothing to him, the ferocious eye of the eagle does not fascinate him, not in the slightest.

In an anthill, there is never any question of eagles.

Little waves of light don't worry a dog at all. However, a microbe who sees the light coming in (parts of the rays just a bit smaller than it is, but numerous, numerous and hard) gets desperate when it feels the innumerable beats that are going to dismember it, shake it to death—even the cursed gonococcus that does so much to complicate relationships between men and women is seized with despair, and, against its will, gives up its difficult life.

ad finished some pencil drawings,

d when I found them in a drawer

ew months later, I was surprised,

by something I had never seen before,

rather never understood, which was

n revealed, and here it is:

I.

These are apparently three men; each man's body, his whole body, is encumbered with faces; these faces shoulder each other and sickly shoulders tend toward cerebral and sensitive life.

Even the knees are trying to see. This is not a joke. At the price of all stability, they have considered turning themselves into mouths, nose, ears and above all turning themselves into eyes; desperate sockets taken from the kneecap. (Like they say: the kneecap complex, the most complex of all.)

Such is my drawing, such it continues.

A face, thirsting to reach the surface, has left the depths of the abdomen, invaded the thoracic cavity, but in the process of invading it has already become many, it is multiple, and a mattress of heads certainly lies beneath it and would be revealed by auscultation, except that a drawing can't be auscultated.

This heap of heads more or less forms three characters terrified of losing their being; on the surface of the skin their staring eyes burn with the desire to know; they are consumed by the anxiety of losing the spectacle for which they have emerged into life, into life.

In this way, dozens and dozens of these heads appeared—the horror of these three bodies—a scandalously cerebral family, ready to do anything at all for knowledge; even the instep wants to get some idea of the world and not just the ground, of the world and the world's problems.

So nothing will agree to be a waist or an arm: everything has to be a head, or nothing.

All these pieces form three people, baffled, utterly lost, supporting each other.

2.

How he stares! (his neck has lengthened so much it is one-third of his person.) How afraid he is to stare! (his head has swung round to the far left.)

A few hairs act as antennae and vehicles for fear, and his terrified eyes also act as ears.

The wild-looking head has a hard time reigning over two or three straps (are they straps, bits of intestine, nerves in their sheath?)

Unknown soldier escaped from some war or other, ascetic body, reduced to a few barbed wires.

4.

As for this one, his three arms are not too many to protect him, three arms in a row, one right behind the other, with hands ready to push away any possible intruder.

For when you're lying down, your enemy will take advantage of it, in fact he's just itching to hit you.

Behind three raised arms, the hero of peace awaits the coming offensive.

5.

Here, the squid turned into a man, with his eyes too deep. Each one has annexed a little brain, separately, for itself alone (a pair of eyeglasses turned into a head!), but most assuredly they think too much. They think in big halos, in excavations, that's the danger: the spyglass is an aid to sight but not to thought and clears out the head (the man) as it works, by the shovelful.

6.

It would certainly be a flame, if it weren't already a horse, it would be a really good horse, if it weren't in flames. He leaps through space. How far from being a rump it is, that rump bursting with burning plumes, with impetuous flames! As for his legs, they have the tenuousness of insect antennae, but their hooves are sharply defined, perhaps a bit too "pastille-ish." That's why he's *my* horse, a horse no one will ever ride. And a light, doubtless sensitive banner around his head gives him an almost feminine delicacy, as if he were blowing his nose in a lace handkerchief.

Luckily, luckily I drew him. Otherwise I never would have seen one like that.

(. . .)

7.

That horse is saying something to that stag. He's telling him something. He's much bigger than he is. His head towers over him from above, quite a meaningful head: he must have suffered a great deal, for a long time, from humiliating situations (he has come out of them now.) His eyes are full of reproach. Have you ever seen wrinkles above and around the eyes of a horse, straight wrinkles going up to the top of its forehead? No. And yet no horse looks more like a horse than he does. Without those wrinkles, he would not express himself with such authority. Naturally this is not a horse you can ever see in harness... although there are worse tragedies.

And there, a bit further on, another animal comes running. It stops, whoa! on its legs, it looks around, tries to get the hang of the situation, you can tell it realizes what's going on.

Meanwhile, the first one, which has not stopped talking to the stag, tells him, through his expressive stillness: How could you? really, where do you get your nerve? The stag acts like a dumb animal. Besides, it's only a fallow deer, how could I possibly have made the mistake of saying it was a stag?

8.

In a garden of flowers, of fowls, of flycatchers, of hillocks and tented seeds parachuting through the air, the graceful hydrocephalic giant rolls forward on his skate-skooter. Skate-*wagon,* for one can sit in it, although not comfortably; it has a high, narrow back, tilted up like a plumed tail, but still higher than its highest point there appears—while a long steady hand guides the steering handle—appears and soars the majestic head with its good-natured brow, an intelligent egg, delightfully oval, designed for turns or to give ideas room to grow.

On an entirely different plane, although quite near him, a clown is running at top speed on his woolen legs.

9.

Not only hair is growing on this head, but a round of fair damsels. Or rather, they are gathering to form a round, and already three are at their places and going out to take the others by the hand. And all that on what? on the great dreaming head of the pretty black princess with tiny little breasts, oh, tiny little waist, oh, tiny little princess.

10.

Is it in order to see that these two have come on to this page? Or to be frightened, to be frozen with terror at the strange sight they see, that they are the only ones to see?

And nothing to digest their terror with. No support. No body. No, no one will ever have a body here.

But perhaps once their fright has passed, they will turn their backs on the paper, those silent lovers, leaning on each other in their delicate thinness, alone with each other, on the other side of the world, having come here like a chance detail, leaving again, unnoticed, for other barren plains.

UNDER THE OBSESSIVE BEACON OF FEAR

It's still only a small halo, nobody sees it, but *he* knows that out of it will come the fire, a tremendous fire will come, and him smack in the middle of it, he's going to have to adjust, to keep on living as before (How you doing? O.K., and yourself?), ravaged by the conscientious devouring fire.

.   .   .

(. . .)

.   .   .

...and fear makes no exceptions.

When a deep-sea fish goes mad and swims anxiously over to the fish in its family at a depth of two thousand feet—bumps into them, wakes them up, accosting them one after the other:

"Don't *you* hear the sound of running water?"

"You don't hear a thing down there?"

"Don't you hear something going 'cheh,' no, softer: 'chee, chee'?"

"Watch out, don't move, we'll hear it again."

Oh, Fear, you terrible Master!

The wolf is afraid of the violin. The elephant is afraid of mice, pigs, firecrackers. And the agouti shudders in its sleep.

THE VILLAGE OF MADMEN

Once so lively, now a deserted village. Huddled under an open shed, a man was waiting for the rain to end; now, it was freezing cold, there would be no chance of rain for a long time to come.

A farmer was looking for his horse among the eggs. It had just been stolen. It was a market day. Countless were the eggs in countless baskets. Surely the thief had thought of this to discourage pursuit.

In a room of the white house, a man was dragging his wife toward the bed.

"Do you mind!" she said. "What if I were your father!"

"You can't be my father," he said, "since you're a woman, and besides, no man has two fathers."

"See, you're worried, too."

He left, disheartened; a Gentleman in evening dress passed by him and said:

"There are no more queens nowadays. There's no point going on about it, there *are* no more." And he walked away, muttering threats.

EM AND THE OLD DOCTOR

Returning from the Indies with a swollen leg oozing pus all over, Em went out of his way to consult an old doctor who lived in the Black Forest, and showed him his leg and the pus.

"Oh," said the Doctor, "maybe a few worn-out, old microbes are still in there... A few worn-out old microbes... "

As the young man was worried about his leg bones that would be destroyed by the microbes:

"No, I don't think so," said the Doctor, "I rather think they're at their wit's end. Their best days are over, believe me." And with a peaceful smile, he sent him on his way.

The Giant Barabbo, in play, ripped his brother Poomappi's ear off.

Poomappi said nothing, but as if absentmindedly he squeezed Barabbo's nose and the nose came off.

In answer Barabbo bent down, broke off Poomappi's toes, and after first pretending he wanted to juggle them, quickly made them vanish behind his back.

Poomappi was surprised. But he was too good a player to show anything. On the contrary, he acted like someone for whom a few toes less is no problem at all.

However, in a spirit of repartee, he sliced off one of Barabbo's buttocks.

You may be sure that Barabbo was extremely attached to his buttocks—to both of them—but he hid his feelings and immediately took up the fight once again. With great cruelty and great strength, he ripped off Poomappi's lower jaw.

Poomappi was disagreeably surprised. But there was nothing he could say. It was a fair blow, it had been struck face to face, without any cheating whatsoever.

Poomappi even tried to smile: it was hard, oh, was it hard!

The outside didn't lend itself to smiling, and neither did the inside. So he wasted no more time in this effort, but continuing his train of thought, he took up the fight again, aimed for the navel, smashed open his abdomen, and tried to insert Barabbo's own foot into the hole; first he succeeded in twisting it up, then in anchoring it inside the wound like a post.

Barabbo was surprised.

His balance on one toe-less leg left a great deal to be desired. But he showed nothing, acted like someone who is at ease, who has supporters everywhere, and waited.

At this moment Poomappi, who had almost won, made a great mistake. He came up close.

Then, quick as an arrow, Barabbo dove down, he was upon him, dislocated one of his arms, hung on to the other, dislocated it too, and fell so cleverly on top of the unfortunate Poomappi that he broke both his legs.

Lying face to face, both equally exhausted, and overwhelmed with pain, Poomappi and Barabbo vainly tried to strangle each other.

Poomappi's thumb was right on the neck, but he lacked the strength to squeeze effectively.

Barabbo's hands still had some strength in them, but his hold was bad; he squeezed away uselessly at Poomappi's neck.

Faced with this extraordinary concourse of adverse circumstances, the hearts of the two brothers failed; they looked at each other for a few moments with growing indifference, then, turning around, each one to his own side, fainted.

The fight was over, at least for the day.

TOWARD SERENITY

He who does not accept the world builds no house in it. If he is cold, it's without being cold. He is hot without heat. If he chops down birches, it's as if he were chopping down nothing at all, but there are the birches, on the ground, and he takes his agreed-upon wages, or else he only takes a few punches. He takes the punches like a gift without any particular meaning, and he goes on his way, without being surprised.

   He drinks water without being thirsty, he sinks into the rock without harm.
   Under a truck, with a broken leg, he looks just the same as usual and thinks of peace, of peace, of peace so hard to reach, so hard to keep, peace.

   Although he has never gone out, the world is familiar to him. He knows the sea quite well. The sea is constantly beneath him, a sea without water, but not without waves, not without vastness. He knows the rivers. They run through him constantly, without water but not without languor, not without sudden rapids.
   Hurricanes without air rage inside him. The immobility of Earth is also his. Roads, cars, flocks go through him endlessly, and a great tree without cellulose but quite hard ripens inside him like a bitter fruit, bitter often, sweet rarely.

   Living thus at a distance, always alone at the rendezvous, without ever holding a hand in his hands, with a hook in his heart he thinks of peace, of that cursed throbbing peace, all his, and of the peace that is said to be above that peace.

(1934)

PLUME,

preceded by

Far-Off

Inside

Michaux continues to turn his fears and magical interventions into poetry, and sometimes into strongly-rhythmed prose poems like "Song of Death." It is the more prosaic texts in this collection, however, which are no doubt his most famous: those in the "Plume" sequence. In a sense, Plume continues the adventures of the narrators of "My Properties" and "My King" in a still more comic mode. Michaux himself saw all these texts as versions of his own being:

you can't write something like "My King" unless you have the idea of pushing things through to the end... I lose myself [in them], painfully. It is painful to write texts that are so confessional: *Plume, My Properties*

But "Plume" seems less a confession than a humorous strategy for survival. It is, as Michel Butor suggests, paraphrasing a line from a Michaux poem, "Weigh no more than a *plume* and everything will be all right."

In his Afterword to this volume, the poet reflects at some length on the nature of the self and its relationship to his writing. This text is given in full.

(*Plume, précédé de Lointain intérieur*, Gallimard, 1938, revised edition, 1963)

MAGIC

I

I used to be quite nervous. Now I'm on a new track:

I put an apple on my table. Then I put myself inside the apple. What peace!

It looks simple. And yet I'd been trying for twenty years; and I would never have succeeded if I had wanted to begin like that. Why not? Perhaps because I would have thought myself humiliated, given its small size and its slow, opaque life. This is possible. The thoughts of the level below are rarely edifying.

So I began in another way and united myself to the Scheldt River.

The Scheldt at Antwerp, where I found it, is big and wide, with high waves. When ocean liners appear, it takes them. It's a river, a real one.

I decided to make myself one with it. I stood on the dock at all hours of the day. But I scattered myself into many useless sights.

And then, despite myself, I would look at women from time to time, and a river really won't stand for that, and neither will an apple or anything in nature.

So, the Scheldt and thousands of sensations. What was I to do? Suddenly, when I had given up everything, I found myself... I won't say in its place, because to tell the truth I never quite managed that. The Scheldt is constantly flowing (that's a real difficulty) and slides toward Holland, where it will find the sea and elevation zero.

I'm coming to the apple. There, too, I had to grope around, experiment—there's quite a story behind all this. Setting out isn't easy and neither is explaining it.

But I can tell it to you in a word. *Suffering* is the word.

When I arrived in the apple, I was ice-cold.   *45*

IV

That cavity in my front tooth was pushing its needles all the way up into the root, almost under my nose. A nasty feeling!

What about magic? Certainly, but you have to move in massively under your nose. What imbalance! And I hesitated, my thoughts elsewhere—on a study of language.

Meanwhile an old earache, which had been dormant for three years, woke up and so did its tiny perforation in the depths of my ear.

So I had to make up my mind. If you're wet, you might as well jump into the water. If you're knocked off balance, you might as well get a new perch.

All right. I drop my studies and I start concentrating. In three or four minutes, I erase the pain from the earache (I knew the way). For the tooth, I needed twice as much time. It was in such a funny spot, right under my nose. Finally it disappeared.

The difficulty is to find the place where you're in pain. Once you've got yourself together, you go toward that spot, groping in your night, trying to circumscribe it—since nervous people can't concentrate, they feel pain everywhere—then, as you enter it, you aim at it more carefully, for it gets small, very small, ten times as small as the point of a pin; still you keep watching over it without letting go, with increasing attention, throwing your euphoria into it until you no longer have any point of suffering before you. That means you've actually found it.

Now you have to stay there without pain. Five minutes of effort should be followed by an hour and a half to two hours of calm and insensibility. This applies to people who are not particularly strong or gifted; at any rate, that's the time I need.

(Because of the inflammation of the tissues, there remains a sensation of pressure, of a small isolated block, like the feeling that remains after the injection of a liquid anesthetic.)

V

I am so weak (or rather, I used to be), that if my mind could coincide with anyone at all, I would immediately be subjugated and swallowed up by him and completely dependent on him; but now I keep my eye on it, I'm attentive—dogged, rather—at being always, very exclusively, me.

Thanks to this self-discipline, now I have more and more chance of never coinciding with any mind at all and being able to move around freely in this world.

Better still! Now that I've come to be so strong, I would gladly challenge the most powerful man alive. What would his will matter to me? I have become so sharp and circumstantial that if I were right in front of him he wouldn't be able to find me.

VISION

She was washing her hands in soapy water, when suddenly it changed into cutting crystals, into hard needles, and the blood (as it has the knack of doing) flowed out and away, leaving the woman to her own devices.

A little while later, as often happens in this century so obsessed with cleanliness, a man came in, and he, too, intended to wash up: he rolled his sleeves all the way up, covered his arm with foamy water (it was real foam now), deliberately, attentively—but dissatisfied, he broke it with a sharp blow on the edge of the sink, and began to wash another, longer arm that grew out of him immediately, as a replacement for the first one. It was an arm softened by a more abundant, silkier down, but once he had soaped it up thoroughly, almost lovingly, suddenly he gave it a mean look, suddenly dissatisfied, he broke it, "Hai!", and yet another one that grew out in its place, he broke that one in the same way, and then the next one and then another one, and then yet another one (he was never satisfied) and so on up to seventeen—for in my terror, I was counting! Then he disappeared with an eighteenth that he preferred not to wash but to use just as it was for the needs of the day.

THE LOCK-EATER

In the corridors of the hotel, I met him walking around with a little lock-eating animal.

He would put the little animal on his elbow, and then the animal was happy and would eat the lock.

Then he would walk further down the hall, and the animal was happy and another lock would be eaten. And so on for several, and so on for many. The man was walking around like someone whose home had expanded. As soon as he opened a door, a new life would begin for him.

But the little animal was so hungry for locks that its master soon had to go out again and look for other break-ins, so that he got very little rest.

I did not want to ally myself with this man. I told him that what *I* liked best in life was going out. He looked blank. We weren't on the same side, that's all, or else I would have allied myself with him; I liked him but he did not suit me.

GOING HOME

I was hesitant about going back home to my parents. When it rains, I said to myself, how do they manage? Then I remembered there was a ceiling in my room. "So what!"—and, distrustful, I refused to return.

Now they can call me in vain. They whistle, they whistle in the night. But in vain do they use the silence of the night to reach me. It is absolutely in vain.

THEY WANT TO STEAL MY NAME

As I was shaving this morning, spreading and pulling up my lips a bit to get a tighter surface that would resist the razor nicely, what do I see? 3 gold teeth! And I've never been to the dentist in my life!

Oh, oh!

And why?

Why? To make me doubt myself, and then to take my name of Barnaby away from me. Ah! they're pulling hard on the other side, hard, hard.

But I'm ready too, and I hold on to IT. "Barnaby," "Barnaby," I say softly but firmly, and then on their side all their efforts are reduced to nothing.

NATURE, FAITHFUL TO MAN

No, when you light a big wood fire, there is absolutely no instance of the dark not going away at once, of its merely leaving nonchalantly and as if reluctantly. It is on such points that the human spirit founds its security and not on the notion of good and evil.

Not only is water always ready to boil and just waiting to be heated up, but the ocean itself, at the height of its furor, has only the form of its bed that a sunken continent obliges it to occupy. The rest is scratches of the wind.

Because of this submissiveness, water is pleasing to the weak; ponds, lakes, are pleasing to them. They lose their feeling of inferiority. They can breathe at last. These great spaces of weakness go to their head as pride and sudden triumph.

Let them relish it, for in a split second a scornful girl and a skeptical father will boot them off that extraordinary platform where they thought they would reign forever.

SUNDAY IN THE COUNTRY

Macarities and Macarretons were strolling down the easygoing road.

Dervies and Stewemies were frolicking in the fields.

One parmegardienne, one tarcadame, an old paricaridelle (all shrinkonied and curetinous) were rushing to town.

Garinettes and Firewolflies were chatting gaily together.

Riling from group to group, a handsome Ballus from the Bormulacea family met up with Zanicotta. Zanicotta smiled, then the modest Zanicotta turned away.

Alas! in a glance, the paricaridelle had seen all.

"Zanicotta!" she cried. Zanicotta was frightened and ran away.

The old sun surrounded by clouds was slowly taking shelter on the horizon.

They could smell the fragrance of the end of a summer's day, faint, but profound, a future recollection indefinable in their memory.

The choughing and cheeving of the sea could be heard in the distance, deeper than a while ago. All the bees had already gone back to their hives. There remained a few mosquitoes in pin formation.

In their turn, the rowdiest youngsters in the village wended their way toward their cottages.

Standing on a height, the village formed a more sharply silhouetted height. Parkbeamed and agostrawed, with its little roofs all engreed and crute, it stood out against the sky like a little boat, excessively overcast, overdecked and brilliant, brilliant!

The excited paricaridelle and a few old whitechaplettes, dirty wrinks and real gossips, creeled against everything, spied on the stragglers. The future held a sob and tears. Zanicotta had to shed them.

BETWEEN CENTER AND ABSENCE

It was at the very beginning of a convalescence—mine, no doubt, but who knows? who knows? fog! a fog! we are so exposed, we're exposed as can be...

"You filthy quacks," I said to myself, "You are crushing inside me the man whose thirst I quench."

It was at the doorway of a long-lasting fear, autumn! autumn! fatigue! I was waiting on the "vomit" side, I was waiting, I could hear my caravan stretching out in the distance, laboring toward me, sliding, sinking in, sand! sand!

It was in the evening, the evening of fear, the evening was coming, implacably hauling away. "The cranes," I said to myself, "The cranes are glad to see the beacons in the distance... "

It was at the end of the war of the limbs.

"This time," I said to myself, "I'll get through, I was too proud before, but this time I'll get through, I'm getting through... " What extraordinary simplicity! Why didn't I figure you out?... Guilelessly, the chicken hatches, perfect, from an ordinary egg...

It was during the thickening of the Great Screen. I COULD SEE! "Can it be," I said to myself, "Is it really possible to fly over oneself?"

It was at our arrival, between center and absence, in Eureka, in the nest of bubbles...

(1938)

DRAGON[1]

A dragon came out of me. He pulled out a hundred tails of flames and nerves.

What an effort I made to force him to rise, whipping him over me! His lower part a steel prison: I was locked inside. But I kept at it and his furor I withstood and the bars of the implacable jail finally came apart little by little, forced by the impetuous whirling motion.

It was because everything was going so badly, it was in September (1938), it was on a Tuesday, that's why I had to take on this peculiar form in order to live. And so I fought for myself alone when Europe was still hesitating, and set forth as a dragon, against the evil forces, against the endless paralysis that arose from what was happening, over the voice of the ocean of mediocre men whose immense importance was once again suddenly, dizzyingly, revealed.

IN THE NIGHT

In the night
In the night
I have united with the night
With the endless night
With the night.
Mine, queen, queen of mine.
Night
Night of birth
Filling me with my cry
My flowering spikes.
You, invading me
with howl howl swells
all over ocean swells
smoking dense
and bellowing,
are the night.
Here lies the night, relentless night.
And its brass band, and its beach,
Its beach above, its beach all over,
Its beach drinking, with its weight king, sinking things beneath,
Beneath it, beneath thinner than a thread
Beneath the night
The Night.

(1930)

NIGHT OF INCONVENIENCES

There are few smiles in this universe.

He who moves through it has an infinite

number of encounters that wound him.

However, you don't die in it.

If you die everything starts all over again.

Plows of white sugar or blown glass or china are an obstacle to traffic. So are spills of curdled milk when they come up to your knees.

If by chance each of us should fall into a cask, even if its bottom is gone and your feet are free, walking and moving around become difficult.

If, instead of barrels, they are small pavilions (joyful to other people, no doubt, but...) walking is terribly tiring.

So is a world with old ladies' backs for sidewalks.

Bundles of glass sticks hurt you, it's unavoidable. Bundles of glass hurt, bundles of tibias are frightening instead.

Walls of rotten meat buckle and collapse, even if they are quite thick. I don't think you could live in them without keeping an eye on them all the time.

When you notice fine veins of steel in your hand, it dampens your spirits considerably, your palm stops being a hollow: now it's a small shirt taut with pus, an inconvenience; what you can do with your hands is kept to a strict minimum.

A crater in an adorable cheek opening under your kiss has very little charm. Its rotten lace is not seductive. You turn away.

Black lemons are frightful to see. A sweater of earthworms may provide warmth, but it provides it at the expense of many other feelings.

Men who fall, cut in half through the middle, human shards, those big shards of bones and flesh, hardly make good companions.

Heads that no longer communicate with the belly except through lianas, whether dry or moist—who would still dream of talking to them intimately, that is, without second thoughts, in a natural way? And with zinc lips, what affection is still possible? And what if the poor were given pies made of stewed ball-bearings? who would not boast of being rich?

When butter loses its balance on the knife and suddenly expands, falling like a tombstone—watch your lap!

And now there are octopus bodies on the pillow!

And what if your tie becomes flowing glue,

And your eye a blind sparsely-downed duckling, who will be killed by the first cold of winter,

And your bread turns into a bear demanding its share and ready to kill.

And what if the birds of prey who want to move from one part of the sky to the other, blinded by who knows what idea, from now on use your own miraculously enlarged body as a path, clearing their way through the fibers of the large tissues; with their crooked beaks, they create useless damage and the claws of those cursed birds get clumsily caught up in the essential organs.

And as you seek your safety in flight, what if your legs and your back split like stale bread, and every movement breaks them more and more, more and more... How are you going to manage now? How can you manage?

SONG OF DEATH

When wide-winged fortune, fortune had carried me off by mistake to its joyful country with the others, suddenly, but suddenly! as I was breathing easy at last, infinite little firecrackers in the atmosphere blasted me and then knives popping out from all over stabbed me again and again, so that I fell back on the hard ground of my country, forever mine from now on.

When straw-winged fortune, fortune had raised me for a moment above all the anguish and the groans, a host a thousand strong, veterans used to mortal combat, hidden in the dust of a high mountain while my mind was elsewhere, suddenly hit us like a missile, and I fell back on the hard ground of my past, past forever present from now on.

When fortune once again, cool-sheeted fortune had welcomed me gently, as I was smiling to everyone around me, giving away everything I owned, suddenly I was grabbed by who knows what from below and behind, suddenly, like an unhooked pulley, I toppled in a huge swoop and fell back on the hard ground of my fate, fate forever mine from now on.

When fortune once again, oil-tongued fortune had washed my wounds, fortune like a hair picked up and braided into your own had taken me and united me indissolubly to her, suddenly as I was already soaking in joy, suddenly Death came and said: "It is time. Come." Death, forever Death from now on.

(1930)

I. A PEACEFUL MAN

Stretching his hands out from the bed, Plume was surprised not to encounter the wall. "Hmm," he thought, "the ants must have eaten it... " and he went back to sleep.

A bit later his wife caught him by the arm and shook him: "Look," she said, "you good-for-nothing! While you were busy sleeping, they stole our house from us." And in fact, sky stretched out uninterrupted on every side. "Oh well, it's over and done with," he thought.

A bit later they heard a noise. It was a train hurtling right at them. "Judging by the rush it seems to be in, it will surely get there before us," and he went back to sleep.

Next the cold woke him up. He was all soaked in blood. A few pieces of his wife were lying next to him. "When there's blood," he thought, "there is always so much un-pleasantness; if only that train hadn't gone by, I would have been delighted. But since it has gone by already... " and he went back to sleep.

"Come now," the judge was saying, "how can you explain the fact that your wife was so badly wounded she was found cut into eight pieces, whereas you, who were lying next to her, could not make a move to stop it, and did not even realize it? That is the mystery. That is the whole question."

"I cannot help him in this line of inquiry," thought Plume, and he went back to sleep.

"The execution will take place tomorrow. Does the prisoner have a statement to make?"

"I'm sorry," he said, "I haven't been following the affair." And he went back to sleep.

II. PLUME AT THE RESTAURANT

Plume was having lunch at the restaurant when the headwaiter came over, looked at him severely and said to him in a low, mysterious voice: "What you have on your plate is *not* on the menu."

Plume apologized immediately.

"Well sir," he said, "since I was in a hurry, I didn't bother reading the menu. I ordered a chop, just like that, thinking that perhaps you had one, or if you didn't, that you could easily find one nearby, but I was ready to order something quite different if there were no chops around. The waiter didn't seem particularly surprised, he went away and brought it in a bit later and so...

Naturally I'll pay the price for it, whatever it may be. It's a nice cut of meat, I won't deny it. I'll pay the price without hesitation. If I had known, I would gladly have chosen another kind of meat or simply an egg—and anyway I'm not very hungry any more. I'll pay you right away."

But the headwaiter does not move. Plume is terribly embarrassed. After a while, when he looks up... Uh-oh! Now the manager is standing there in front of him.

Plume apologizes immediately.

"I did not realize," he says, "that chops weren't on the menu. I didn't look at it, because I have extremely bad eyesight, and I didn't have my pince-nez on me, and besides, reading always gives me a terrible pain. I asked for the first thing that came into my mind and more to elicit other suggestions than out of personal taste. The waiter, who no doubt had other things on his mind, didn't think twice about it, he brought me this, and as for me, I'm quite absentminded and I began to eat, so... I'll pay you personally as long as you're here."

But the manager doesn't move. Plume feels more and more embarrassed. As he is holding a bill out to him, he suddenly sees the sleeve of a uniform; it's a policeman standing in front of him.

Plume apologizes immediately.

Well sir, he had come in to rest a bit. Suddenly, they shouted at him point-blank, "And for Monsieur? You would like... ?" "Oh, a glass of beer." "And then what?... " the angry waiter had shouted; so, more to get rid of him than for any other reason, Plume had said: "O.K., a chop!"

He was no longer thinking about it by the time it was brought in on a plate; then, well, since there it was right in front of him...

"Listen, if you would try to settle this business, it would be very nice of you. Here's something for you."

And he holds out a hundred franc bill. As he hears receding footsteps, he thinks he's home free. But now it's the police commissioner standing there.

Plume apologizes immediately.

He had an appointment with a friend. He had looked for him in vain all morning. So, since he knew that his friend walked by this street on his way home from the office, he had come in here, had taken a table near the window and moreover, since there might be a long wait and he didn't want to look as if he were reluctant to spend money, he had ordered a chop—just to have something in front of him. Not for a moment did he think of eating it. But since he had it in front of him, mechanically, without having the slightest idea of what he was doing, he had begun to eat.

They should realize that he wouldn't go to a restaurant for anything on earth. He always has lunch at home. It's one of his principles. This was a case of pure absentmindedness, the kind of thing that can happen to anyone when he's upset—a moment of thoughtlessness, no more than that.

But the commissioner has phoned the head of the criminal division: "Come on," he says to Plume as he hands him the phone. "Explain yourself once and for all. It's your only chance." And a policeman, shoving him roughly, says to him: "From now on you've got to walk the straight and narrow, got it?" And as firemen are pouring into the restaurant, the manager says to him: "Look what a loss I'm going to take. A real disaster!" And he points to the dining room: all the customers have rushed out.

The men from the Secret Police are telling him: "It's going to get rough, we're warning you. You'd better confess everything, the whole truth. This isn't the first job we've handled, believe you me. When it starts going this way, it's really serious."

Meanwhile, a huge, tough cop over his shoulder is saying to him: "Listen, I can't do anything about it. I've got orders. If you don't talk into the phone, I start hitting. Get it? Confess! I'm warning you. If I don't hear you, I start hitting."

III. PLUME TRAVELS

Plume can't say he is treated with excessive consideration when he travels. Some people walk right over him without a word of warning, others matter-of-factly wipe their hands on his jacket. He has ended up getting used to it. He would rather travel inconspicuously. As long as he can, that's what he will do.

If they snarlingly serve him a root on his plate, a big fat root: "Come on, eat. What are you waiting for?"

"Oh, certainly! Fine!—right away." He doesn't want to get into trouble for no good reason.

And if, at night, they refuse him a bed: "Look! You didn't come so far just to sleep, did you? Come on, take your trunk and your things, it's the time of day when walking is easiest."

"All right, all right, sure... certainly. I was just kidding, of course. Oh yes, it was a... joke." And off he goes again into the dark night.

And if he's thrown off a train: "Aha! So, you think we've been heating up this locomotive for three hours and we've hitched up eight cars to transport a young man your age, in perfect health, who can be perfectly useful here, who has no need whatsoever to go there, and you think that's why we've dug tunnels, blown up tons of rocks and laid hundreds of miles of track in all kinds of weather, not to mention that we have to watch the line continually for fear of sabotage, and all that in order to... "

"All right, all right, I understand completely. I got on just to—oh, just to look around. That's all, really. Just curious, O.K.? And thanks a million." And he goes back on the road with his luggage.

And if, in Rome, he asks to see the Coliseum: "No way! Listen, it's in bad enough shape already. And then the gentleman will want to touch it, lean on it, sit down... that's why we only have ruins left all over the place. We've learned our lesson—a hard lesson—but in the future, no, it's all over now, understand?"

"All right, all right. It was... I only wanted to ask you for a postcard, a snapshot maybe... if by any chance... " And he leaves the city without having seen a thing.

And if, on the steamer, the Purser suddenly points at him and says: "What's this guy doing here? Well! there's certainly a problem with the discipline down below, it seems to me. Quick, throw him back down in the hold. The second watch has just rung." And he walks off whistling a tune, while Plume breaks his back slaving away all through the crossing.

But he doesn't say a thing, he doesn't complain. He thinks of the unfortunate people who can't travel at all, whereas *he* travels, he travels continually.

IV. IN THE APARTMENTS OF THE QUEEN

As Plume was coming into the palace with his credentials, the Queen said to him:

"Now then. The King is extremely busy at present. You will see him later. We shall visit him together, if you wish, about five o'clock. His Majesty is quite fond of Danes, His Majesty will be pleased to receive you, perhaps you could take a walk with me while you're waiting.

As the palace is very large, I'm always afraid of losing my way in it and suddenly finding myself in the kitchens; you can easily imagine that for a Queen, it would be *so* silly. We'll go through here. I know the way quite well. Here's my bedroom."

And they went into the bedroom.

"As we have over two hours before us, perhaps you could read to me a bit, but I don't have anything very interesting here. Perhaps you play cards. But I must confess that I always lose immediately.

At any rate don't stay on your feet, it's tiring; when one is seated one soon gets bored, so perhaps we could lie down on this divan."

And they lay down on the divan.

But she soon got up again.

"It is always unbearably hot in this room. If you would help me get undressed, I'd be most grateful. Afterwards we can have a proper chat. I would so like to have some information about Denmark. Besides, this frock is so easy to take off, I wonder how I stay dressed all day long. This frock just slides off without one's realizing it. You see, I raise my arms, and now a child could pull it into his hands. Naturally I wouldn't let him. I'm quite fond of them, but there is so much gossip in a palace, and anyway children lose everything they touch."

And Plume undressed her.

"Now then, don't you stay like that. Someone who's all dressed in a bedroom seems so very stiff, and then I can't stand seeing you like that, it makes me feel as if you're going to walk out and leave me all alone in this enormous palace."

And Plume got undressed. Then he lay down in his shirt.

"It's still only a quarter past three," she said. "Do you really know so much about Denmark that you can talk to me about it for an hour and three quarters? I won't be that demanding. I can understand how difficult it would be. I'll give you a bit of time to think about it. And look here, meanwhile, since you're here I'm going to show you something I find most intriguing. I'd be curious to know what a Dane will think of it.

See, under my right breast, right here, I have three small signs. Not three: two little ones and a big one. See the big one, it almost looks like... That *is* truly strange, isn't it, and look at the left breast, nothing! utterly white!

Listen, tell me something, but do examine it carefully first, take your time... "

And so Plume examined. He touched, groped about with unsure fingers, and the search for realities made him tremble, and his fingers moved over and over through their curved trajectory.

And Plume pondered.

"You are wondering, I see," said the Queen after a few moments, "(I can see now that you know your stuff.) You want to know if I don't have another one. No, I don't," she said, and she became all ashamed, she blushed violently.

"And now tell me all about Denmark, but press yourself up against me, so that I can listen to you more attentively."

Plume moved forward; he lay down next to her and now he could no longer disguise his condition.

And sure enough:

"See here," she said, "I thought you had more respect for the Queen, but after all since there you are, I would not wish *that* to prevent us from talking about Denmark afterward."

And the Queen drew him to her.

"And keep caressing my legs," she was saying, "or else I get distracted right away, and I won't remember why I lay down... "

It was then that the King walked in!

. . . .

Terrible adventures, whatever your plots and your beginnings, painful adventures, guided by an implacable enemy.

VII. PLUME'S FINGER WAS HURTING HIM

Plume's finger was hurting a bit.

"You'd better see a doctor," said his wife. "Often all it takes is a little ointment."
And Plume went.

"One finger to cut off," said the surgeon, "no problem at all. With anesthesia, it takes six minutes at the most. Since you're rich, you have no need for so many fingers. I'll be delighted to perform this little operation for you. After that, I'll show you several models of artificial fingers. Some of them are extremely graceful. A bit expensive no doubt. But naturally there's no question of cutting corners. We'll give you the best there is."

Plume sadly looked at his finger and apologized.

"Doctor, it's the index finger, you know, a most useful finger. In fact I was just going to write my mother again. I always use my index finger when I write. My mother would be worried if I put off writing her any longer; I'll come back in a few days. She's a very sensitive woman, she gets upset so easily."

"No problem," the surgeon said, "here's some paper, white paper, with no letterhead of course. A few heartfelt words from you will put her right.

Meanwhile I'll call the Hospital and tell them to set everything up, so all we'll have to do is get out the sterilized instruments. I'll be back in a minute... "

He was back in a flash.

"Everything's perfect, they're waiting for you."

"So sorry, Doctor," said Plume, "you see, my hand's shaking, there's nothing I can do about it... umm... "

"There, there," said the surgeon, "you're quite right, it would be better not to write. Women are terribly sharp, especially Mothers. When it's their son, they can spot a bit of hesitation anywhere, and then make a mountain out of a molehill. For them, we're just little children. Here's your hat and your cane. The car is waiting for us."

And they went into the operating room.

"Listen, Doctor. Really... "

"Oh!" said the surgeon, "don't worry, you're being over-scrupulous. We'll write that letter together. I'll think about it while I operate on you."

And bringing the mask to his face, he put Plume to sleep.

"At least you could have asked my opinion," said Plume's wife to her husband.

"Don't go thinking it's so easy to find a lost finger once again.

I don't much like the idea of a man with stumps. As soon as your hand gets a bit too bare, you can just forget about *me*.

Cripples are nasty, they become sadistic right away. But I haven't been brought up the way I was brought up just to live with a sadist. You probably thought I'd volunteer to help you with those things. Well, you were wrong, and you should have thought before you... "

"Look," said Plume, "don't worry about the future. I still have nine fingers, and besides, you may change."

VIII. PULLING OFF HEADS

All they wanted to do was to pull him by the hair. They had no desire to hurt him. All at once they ripped his head off. Surely it wasn't on tight. It never comes off just like that. Surely it was missing something.

When it's not on shoulders any more, it's in the way. You have to give it away. But you have to wash it, because it smears the hand of whoever gets it. They had to wash it. Because the one they gave it to, with his hands already covered with blood, is beginning to get suspicious, is beginning to look at them like someone who's waiting for an explanation.

Oh, we found it while we were working in the garden... We found it in the middle of some other heads... We picked this one because it seemed fresher. If he preferred another one... we could go take a look. Meanwhile, he can keep this one...

And they go off, followed by a look saying neither yes nor no, a fixed stare.

What about going over to the pond. You can find lots of things in a pond. Maybe a drowned man will fill the bill.

You think you'll find whatever you want in a pond. You come back from it quickly and you come back empty-handed.

Where can you find heads ready to give as a present? Where can you find them without making too much of a stir?

"On my side, I do have my cousin. But, we practically have the same head. Nobody will ever believe I found it just like that."

"Oh, as for me... There's my friend Pierre. But he's strong enough not to let it get pulled off just like that!"

"Well, we'll see. The other one came off so easily."

And so they go off, full of their idea, and they come to Pierre's house. They drop a handkerchief. Pierre bends down. As if to help him up, laughing, they pull him back by the hair. The head comes off, ripped out.

In comes Pierre's wife, furious: "That drunk, he's spilled the wine again! He can't even drink it any more, he has to spill it all over the floor. And now he can't even get up... "

And she goes off to get something to clean things up. So they hold her back by the hair. The body falls forward. The head remains in their hands. A furious head, swinging back and forth, with long hair.

A big dog bounds in, barking loudly. They give it a good kick and the head falls off.

Now they have three of them. Three is a good number. And besides, there's some choice here. They're really not the same heads. No: a man, a woman, a dog.

And they go back to the one who already has a head, and they find him waiting.

They lay the bouquet of heads on his lap. He sets the man's head to the left, near the first head, and the dog's head and the head of the woman with its long hair on the other side. Then he waits.

And he looks at them with a look saying neither yes nor no, a fixed stare.

"Oh, we found these at a friend's place. There they were, right in the middle of his house... Anyone at all could have taken them away. There weren't any others. We just took the ones that were there. Another time we'll have more luck. After all, it *was* a bit of luck! Luckily, there are plenty of heads around. Still, it's kind of late now. To find them in the darkness... By the time we clean them up, especially the ones in the mud... Well, we'll try. But with just the two of us, we can't bring back whole carts-full, O.K.?... Let's go. Maybe some more of them have fallen since a while ago. We'll see... "

And they go off, followed by a look saying neither yes nor no, a fixed stare.

"Oh, you know me, *I* don't care. No, really! Take my head, go back with it, he won't recognize it. He doesn't even look at them. Tell him... Hey, as I went out, I tripped over this. It *is* a head, I believe. I'm bringing it to you. And that will be all for today, all right?..."

"No, old pal, you're all I've got."

"Come on, come on, don't get mushy. Take it. Come on, pull, pull hard—harder, for God's sake!"

"No. See, it's not working. This will be our punishment. Now, try mine, pull, pull."

But the heads won't come off. Real murderer's heads.

They don't know what to do, they come back, they return, they come back, they leave again, they leave again, followed by that waiting look, a fixed stare.

Finally they get lost in the night, and that is a great relief for them; for them, for their conscience. Tomorrow, they'll take off in some random direction and they'll follow it as far as they can. They will try to start their lives over. It is quite hard. But one must try. One must try not to think of all that, to live as before, like everybody else...

IX. A MOTHER OF NINE!

Plume had just barely arrived in Berlin, he was going to enter the Terminal Building, when a woman accosted him and proposed to spend the night with him.

"Don't leave, I beg you. I am the mother of nine children."

And calling her girlfriends to the rescue, she roused the whole neighborhood, he was surrounded, there was a little crowd and a policeman walked up. After listening to them: "Don't be so hard-hearted," he said to Plume, " ...A mother of nine!" So they pushed him along to a squalid little hotel, eaten by bedbugs for years. When there's enough for one, there's enough for two. There were five of them. They immediately divested him of everything he had in his pockets and shared it among themselves.

"So!" said Plume, "this is what it means to be robbed, it's the first time it's ever happened to me. That's what happens when you listen to policemen."

He took back his jacket and started getting ready to leave. But they became violently indignant: "What! What do you think we are—thieves? We paid ourselves first as a precaution, but you're going to get something for your money, kiddo." And they got undressed. The mother of nine was covered with pimples and so were two of the others.

Plume thought: "Not exactly my type, these women. But how can I get that across without hurting their feelings?" And he pondered.

Then, the mother of nine: "Hey, girls, you won't believe it, but I'll bet this guy's another one of those little show-offs who's afraid of syphilis. Matter of luck, syphilis!"

And they took him by force, one after the other.

He tried to get up, but the mother of nine: "No, don't be in such a rush, kiddo. As long as there's no blood, there's no real satisfaction."

And they did it again.

He was nearly dead with fatigue, when they got dressed.

"Come on," they said, "hurry up, it's a quarter past midnight, and the room's only paid up to midnight."

"But after all," he said, thinking of the 300 marks they had confiscated, "perhaps with the money you have received, you could pay the supplement until morning?"

"Hey, this guy's really incredible! So it's supposed to be our treat, huh? You've got to be kidding!"

And, dragging him from his bed, they threw him down the stairs.

"Well!" thought Plume, "later on, this will make a terrific memory of my trip."

X. PLUME IN CASABLANCA

Once he got to Casablanca, Plume remembered that he had a lot of errands to run. That's why he left his suitcase on the bus; he would come back to get it once he had finished his most pressing business. And he went to the Hotel Atlantic.

But instead of asking for a room, reflecting that he still had a lot of errands to run, he thought it better to ask for the address of the Société Générale Bank.

He went to the Société Générale, had his card sent in to the assistant director, but once he was introduced, rather than showing his letter of credit, he thought it appropriate to inquire about the main attractions of the Arab quarter, Bousbir, and the Arab cafés, for you just can't leave "Casa" without having seen the belly dance, even though the women who dance it are Jewish and not Moslem. So he inquired about the place, was driven to the Arab café, and already had a dancer sitting at his table ordering a bottle of port when he realized that really this was all a lot of foolishness: on a trip, with its unaccustomed fatigue, the first thing you need is food and drink; so he left and went to the Roi de la Bière restaurant in the new city; he was going to sit down at a table when he reflected that when you travel it's not enough to eat and drink, one must be careful and make sure that everything is in order for the next day's trip, so that instead of playing the sultan at a table, it would be a good idea to find out right away where the ship he had to take the next day was anchored.

It would be time well spent. He was already busy doing this, when it occurred to him to go see what was happening at Customs. There are days when they won't let a box of ten matches get through, and whoever they find carrying a box like that, either on him or in his luggage, will really be in for it. But on the way, thinking how often the Medical Department is left to ignorant doctors who could easily stop someone in perfect health from getting on board, he had to admit he would be well advised to show himself in his shirtsleeves, rowing a boat, bursting with vigor despite the cool of the night, and this is what he was doing when the police, always suspicious, questioned him, heard his answer and from then on would not let him out of their grasp.

XII. PLUME ON THE CEILING

In a silly moment of distraction, Plume walked with his feet on the ceiling, instead of keeping them on the ground.

Alas, when he noticed, it was too late.

Already paralyzed by the blood that had immediately collected, piled up in his head like the iron in a hammer, he no longer knew what he was doing. He was lost. With terror, he saw the far-off floor, the armchair once so inviting, the whole room an astonishing abyss.

How he would have liked to be in a vat full of water, in a wolf trap, in a safe, in a copper water-heater, rather than here, all alone, on this ridiculously deserted ceiling that offered no resources; and coming back down from it would be tantamount to committing suicide.

Misfortune! Misfortune always following the same man... whereas so many other people all over the world continued to walk calmly on the ground, people who surely were no better than he was.

At least if he could have entered the ceiling and ended his unhappy life peacefully if rapidly inside it... But ceilings are hard, and can only "return" you—that's the right word.

No choice in misfortune, you're given whatever is left. As he persisted desperately, ceiling mole that he was, a delegation from the Bren Club which had gone to look for him found him by raising their heads.

By means of a raised ladder, they took him down without a word.

They were embarrassed. They apologized to him. Just to be on the safe side, they accused an absent organizer. They flattered Plume's pride: he had not lost heart, whereas so many others would have become demoralized, thrown themselves into space and broken their arms and legs and more, for the ceilings in this country are quite high and date almost without exception from the period of the Spanish conquest.

Plume awkwardly brushed off his sleeves without answering.

AFTERWORD

More than once, I have felt "passages" of my father in myself. Immediately, I would rebel. I have lived against my father (and against my mother and against my grandfather, my grandmother, my great-grandparents); since I didn't know them, I could not fight against more distant ancestors.

By doing this, what unknown ancestor have I allowed to live in me?

In general, I did not follow their bent. By not following their bent, of what unknown ancestor did I follow the bent? Of which group, of which average of ancestors? I used to vary constantly, to make them run—either them, or me. Some of them hardly had time to blink, and then disappeared. One would only appear in such and such a climate, in such and such a place, never in another, in such and such a position. Their great number, their struggle, the quickness of their appearance—another inconvenience—I didn't know to whom I could turn for support.

We are born of too many Mothers. — (Ancestors: mere chromosomes carrying moral tendencies, what's the difference?) And then, other people's ideas, the ideas of my contemporaries, everywhere phoned into space, and friends, attempts to imitate or to "be against."

Yet I really would have wanted to be a good director of a laboratory, with a reputation for having been a good manager of my "self."

In pieces, scattered, I would defend myself and still, there would be no director of tendencies or I would immediately dismiss him. He would get on my nerves right away. Was he the one who was abandoning me? Was I the one who was leaving him? Was I the one who was keeping *me?*

The young puma is born spotted. Afterward, he surmounts the spots. It's the puma's strength against the ancestor, but he can't surmount his carnivorous tastes, his pleasure in killing, his cruelty.

For too many thousands of years, he has been occupied by conquerors.

Self is made out of everything. A certain inflection in a sentence—is this another me trying to appear? If the YES is mine, is the NO a second me?

"Me" is never anything but provisional (changing in relation to this one or that one, an ad hominem "me" changing in another language, in another art) and pregnant with a new character who will be set free by an accident, an emotion, a blow on the head—excluding the preceding character, and to everyone's astonishment, formed instantly. So he was already fully formed.

Perhaps we are not made for just one self. We are wrong to cling to it. The prejudice in favor of unity. (Here as elsewhere, the will: impoverishing and sacrificing.)

In a double, triple, quintuple life, we would be more comfortable, less gnawed and paralyzed by a subconscious hostile to the conscious mind (hostility of the other, deprived "selves").

The greatest fatigue of the day and of a life may be caused by the effort, by the tension necessary to keep the same self through the continual temptations to change it.

We want too much to be someone.

There is not one self. *There are not ten selves. There is no self. ME is only a position in equilibrium.* (One among a thousand others, continually possible and always at the ready.) *An average of "me's," a movement in the crowd. In the name of many, I sign this book.*

But did I want this? Did we want it?

There was pressure (tightening screws).

And then? I placed it. I had a lot on my hands.

Each tendency in me had its own will, as each thought, as soon as it appears and is organized, has its own will. Was it mine? This man has his will in me, that one—a friend, a great man of the past, the Gautama Buddha, many others, lesser ones: Pascal, Ernest Hello?[2] Who knows?

The will of the greatest number? The will of the most coherent group?

I did not want to want. I wanted, it seems to me, *against myself,* because I had no desire to want and nonetheless I wanted.

...As a crowd, I found my way around my moving crowd. As every thing is crowd, every thought, every instant. Every past, every uninterruption, every transformation, every thing is something else. Nothing ever definitively circumscribed, capable of being circumscribed, everything: relations, mathematics, symbols, or music. Nothing fixed. Nothing is property.

My images? Relations.

My thoughts? But perhaps thoughts are precisely only annoyances of the self, losses of equilibrium (phase 2), or regaining equilibrium (phase 3) of the thinker's motion. The phase 1 (equilibrium) remains unknown, unconscious.

The true, deep, thinking flux no doubt happens *without conscious thought,* without images. The perceived equilibrium (phase 3) is the worst, the one that everybody finds odious after a while. The history of Philosophy is the history of the false positions of conscious equilibrium that have been adopted one after the other. And then... *is it through the "flame" part that fire can be understood?*

Let us avoid following an author's thought[a] (even if he were a new Aristotle); rather, let's look at what he has in the back of his mind, what he's getting at, the imprint that his desire to dominate and influence—although well hidden—tries to make on us.

Besides, WHAT DOES HE KNOW ABOUT HIS THOUGHT? He's pretty badly informed about it. (As the eye does not know what makes the green of a leaf, although it sees it admirably well.)

He does not know the components of his own thought; sometimes barely the first components—but the second ones? the third? the tenth? No, neither the distant components, nor what surrounds him, nor the determinants, nor the "Oh!" of his era (which the lowest high school substitute-teacher will know three hundred years from now).

His intentions, his passions, his *libido dominandi,* his compulsive lying, his nervousness, his desire to be right, to win, to seduce, to surprise, to believe and have others believe what he wishes, to fool people, to hide—his appetites and his disgusts, his complexes and his whole life harmonizing, unbeknownst to him, with the organs, the glands, the hidden life of his body, his physical deficiencies, everything is unknown to him.[b]

His "logical" thought? But it circulates in a casing of paralogical and analogical ideas, a straight road cutting through circular paths, seizing (you can only seize by cutting) bleeding sections of this so richly vascularized world. (All gardens are hard for trees.) False simplicity of first truths (in metaphysics) followed by extreme multiplicity—that's what he's trying to get accepted.

In one point, too, will and thought converge, inseparable, and become false thought-will.

In one point, too, the examination of false thought—thought like, in microphysics, the observation of light (the path of the photon)—falsifies it.

Any progress, every new observation, every thought, every creation, seems to create (at the same time as light) a zone of darkness.

---

[a]Thought is also less important than the perspective in which it appears
[b]Music-thought that makes him harmonize millions of circumstances, so that it is rather surprising that when reading one of them and thinking it over, one is not ipso facto enlightened about countless phenomena, an endless chain of lightning flashes, osmoses, reactions

In ten pages of the Tao-ti-ching of Lao-Tzu, if one reads them well, one should also find the Chinese wheelbarrow, gunpowder, as well as Asiatic cholera, Sun Yat Sen and if Japan will soon be beaten

All knowledge creates new ignorance.

All consciousness, a new unconscious.

Every new contribution creates new nothingness.

So, reader, *you're holding in your hands, as often happens, a book the author did not write,* although a world participated in it. And what does that matter?

Signs, symbols, impulses, falls, departures, relations, discords, everything is there to bounce up, to seek, for further on, for something else.

Between them, without settling down, the author grew his life.

Perhaps you could try, too?

      Henri Michaux

NOTES

1. Although this text comes from the same period as *Plume,* it was not actually published in that book, but in *Peintures* (G L.M , Paris, 1939); reprinted in the second edition of *L'Espace du dedans (The Space Within)* (Gallimard, Paris, 1966) and again in Michaux's own anthology. *Choix de poèmes* (Gallimard, Paris, 1976), our source for this translation.

2. See *Some Information*, n. 4, p. xxx.

ORDEALS,

EXORCISMS

The title of this little collection of poems and prose texts (121 pages in the original edition) could define much of Michaux's work. Its Preface is particularly important: in it, he explains the function of art-as-exorcism and its reason for being: "to ward off the surrounding powers of the hostile world." As in *Facing the Locks,* a collection he published almost ten years later, some of the texts in *Ordeals, Exorcisms* reflect, more clearly than usual, a reality outside the self—in this case, the Nazi Occupation of Europe. If Michaux's basic situation is one of exploring the sicknesses of the self inside a room, there are times when the outside world will come to resemble the prison of a sick man's room: from 1940 to 1944, all of France seemed to be transformed into a prison or a hospital.

   This work also reflects the poet's continuing preoccupation with inner space, the field of consciousness, the imagination and its monsters... Most of it could have been produced at any period of Michaux's career.

(*Epreuves, exorcismes 1940–1944,* Gallimard, 1945, new edition, 1967)

PREFACE

It would be truly extraordinary if perfect harmony emerged from the thousands of events that occur every year. There are always a few that stick in your throat; you keep them inside yourself; they hurt.

One of the things you can do: exorcism.

Every situation means dependency, hundreds of dependencies. It would be unheard-of if this state of affairs were perfectly satisfying or if a man—however active he might be—could really fight against all these dependencies effectively.

One of the things you can do: exorcism.

Exorcism, a reaction in force, with a battering ram, is the true poem of the prisoner.

In the very space of suffering and obsession, you introduce such exaltation, such magnificent violence, welded to the hammering of words, that the evil is progressively dissolved, replaced by an airy demonic sphere—a marvelous state!

Many contemporary poems, poems of deliverance, also have an effect of exorcism, but of exorcism through subterfuge. Through the subterfuge of our subconscious nature that defends itself with an appropriate imaginative elaboration: Dreams. Through planned or exploratory subterfuge, searching for its optimum point of application: waking Dreams.

Not only dreams but an infinity of thoughts exists in order to allow us "to get by," and even some philosophical systems were essentially exorcistic, although they thought they were something else entirely.

Their effect is similarly liberating, but their nature is quite different.

Nothing here of that rocketing surge, impetuous and seemingly super-human, of the exorcism. Nothing of that kind of gun turret that takes shape at those moments when the object to be driven away, rendered as it were electrically present, is beaten back by magic.

This vertical, explosive rush upward is one of the great moments of existence. The exercise cannot be recommended enough to those who despite themselves live in unhappy dependence. But it is hard to start the motor—only near-despair will do the trick.

The understanding reader will realize that the poems at the beginning of this book were not made out of hatred of one thing or another, but to shake off overpowering influences.

Most of the following texts are in a sense exorcisms through subterfuge. Their reason for being: to ward off the surrounding powers of the hostile world.

VOICES

I heard a voice in those unhappy days and I heard: "I shall reduce them, these men, I shall reduce them and already they are reduced although they don't realize it yet. I shall reduce them to so little that there will be no way of telling man from woman and already they are no longer what they once were, but since their organs can still interpenetrate they still think themselves different, one this, the other that. But so terribly shall I make them suffer that there will no longer be any organ that matters. I shall leave them only their skeletons, a mere line of their skeleton for them to hang their unhappiness on. They've run enough! What do they still need legs for? Their movements are small, small! And it will be much better that way. Just as a statue in a park makes only one gesture, whatever may happen, even so shall I petrify them—but smaller, smaller."

I heard that voice, I heard it and I shuddered, but not all that much, because I admired it, for its dark determination and its vast though apparently senseless plan. That voice was only one voice among hundreds, filling the top and bottom of the atmosphere and the East and the West, and all of them were aggressive, wicked, hateful, promising a sinister future for man.

But man, panicky in one place, calm in another, had reflexes and calculations in case of hard times, and he was ready, although he might generally have appeared hunted and ineffectual.

He who can be tripped up by a pebble had already been walking for two hundred thousand years when I heard the voices of hatred and threats which meant to frighten him.

THE LETTER

I am writing to you from a land that was once full of light. I am writing you from the land of the cloak and shadow. For years and years, we've been living on the Tower of the flag at half-mast. Summer! Poisoned summer! And since then it has always been the same day, day of the encrusted memory...

The hooked fish thinks of the water as long as he can. As long as he can, isn't that natural? You reach top of a mountain slope and you're hit by a pike-thrust. Afterward your whole life changes. One instant smashes in the door of the Temple.

We ask each other for advice. We don't know any more. One doesn't know any more than the other. This one is frantic, that one nonplussed. All of us at a loss. Calm exists no longer. Wisdom lasts no longer than an inspiration. Tell me: with three arrows shot into his cheek, who would walk around looking natural?

Death took some of us. Prison, exile, hunger, hardship took the others. Great sabers of shuddering slashed through us, then everything base and sneaky passed through us.

Who on our soil still feels the kiss of joy in the very bottom of his heart?

The union of wine and the self is a poem. The union of self and woman is a poem. The union of heaven and earth is a poem, but the poem we have heard has paralyzed our understanding.

Our song in unbearable grief could not be uttered. The art of carving in jade has stopped. Clouds go by, clouds shaped like rocks, clouds shaped like peaches, and as for us, we too go by like clouds, full of the vain powers of suffering.

We no longer like the day. It howls. We no longer like the night, haunted by worries. A thousand voices to sink into. No voice to lean on. Our skin is sick of our pale faces.

Vast events. The night, too, is vast, but what can it do? The thousand stars of night can't light a single bed. Those who knew no longer know. They jump with the train, they roll with the wheel.

"Stay within oneself?" Don't even think about it! On the island of parrots, no house is isolated. In the fall, villainy showed its face. The pure is not pure. It shows its stubbornness, its vindictiveness. Some can be seen yelping. Others can be seen ducking out of the way. But grandeur is nowhere to be seen.

The secret ardor, the farewell to truth, the silence of stone slabs, the scream of the knife victim, the world of frozen rest and burning feelings has been our world and the road of the puzzled dog our road.

We could not recognize ourselves in the silence, we could not recognize ourselves in the screams, nor in our caverns, nor in the gestures of foreigners. Around us, the countryside is indifferent and the sky has no purpose.

We have looked at ourselves in the mirror of death. We have looked at ourselves in the mirror of the sullied seal, of flowing blood, of decapitated surging, in the grimy mirror of humiliations.

We have gone back to the glaucous springs.

LABYRINTH

Life, a labyrinth, death, a labyrinth
Labyrinth without end, says the Master of Ho.

Everything hammers down, nothing liberates.
The suicide is born again to new suffering.

The prison opens on a prison
The corridor opens another corridor:

He who thinks he is unrolling the scroll of his life
Is unrolling nothing at all.

Nothing comes out anywhere
The centuries, too, live underground, says the Master of Ho.

AFTER MY DEATH

I was transported after my death, I was transported not into a closed space, but into the immense vacuum of the ether. Far from being depressed by this immense opening in all directions as far as the eye could see, in the starry sky, I pulled myself together and pulled together all that I had been and all I was just about to be, and finally all I had planned to become (in my secret inner calendar), and squeezing the whole thing together, my good qualities too, and even my vices, as a last rampart, I made myself a shell out of all this.

Around this nucleus, energized by anger, but by a clean anger no longer based on blood, cold and whole, I set about playing porcupine, in a supreme act of defense, in an ultimate refusal.

Then, the vacuum, the larvae of the vacuum that were already extending their soft pockets tentacularly toward me, threatening me with an abject endosmosis—the larvae, astonished after a few futile attempts on this prey that refused to give in, retreated in confusion and disappeared from view, leaving alive the man who deserved it so much.

Free, henceforth, on this front, I used my power of the moment, the exaltation of the unhoped-for victory, to weigh towards Earth, and repenetrated my motionless body, which the sheets and blanket had luckily prevented from growing cold.

With surprise, after this struggle of mine which outdid the efforts of giants, with surprise and joy mixed with disappointment I came back to the narrow closed horizons where human life, to be what it is, must be lived.

IN THE COMPANY OF MONSTERS

It soon became clear (from my adolescence on) that I had been born to live among monsters. For a long time they were terrible, then they ceased being terrible and after great virulence they weakened little by little. Finally they became inactive and I lived among them in serenity.

This was the time when others, still unsuspected, began to form and one day would come before me, active and terrible (for if they were to come and spring up only to be idle and kept on leash, do you think they would ever come?), but after filling the whole horizon with darkness they began to weaken and I lived among them in serenity, unperturbed, and this was a fine thing, especially since it had come close to being so hateful, almost fatal.

And they who at first had been so excessive, repulsive, disgusting, took on such delicate contours that despite their impossible forms, one would almost have classed them as a part of nature.

Age was doing this. Certainly. And what was the clear sign of this inoffensive stage? It's quite simple. They no longer had eyes. With the organs of detection washed away, their faces—although monstrous in form—their heads their bodies were no more disturbing than the form of the cones, spheres, cylinders or volumes that nature displays in its rocks, its pebbles and in many other domains.

THE MONSTER LOBE

After my third relapse, through inside vision I saw my brain all sticky and in folds, macroscopically I saw its lobes and centers, none of which were functioning any more, and instead, I expected to see pus or tumors forming inside there.

As I was searching for a lobe that might still be healthy, I saw one, unmasked by the shrinkage of the others. It was at the height of its activity and a very dangerous activity too, for it was a monster lobe. The more I saw it, the more certain I was.

It was the monster lobe, usually reduced to an inactive state, which, given the failure of the other lobes, suddenly, by a powerful act of substitution, was supplying me with life; but it—the life of monsters—was welded to mine. Now, all my life, I had always had the greatest difficulty in keeping them in their place.

Here, perhaps, was the ultimate attempt of my Being to survive. In what monstrosities I found support (and in what way!), I would not dare relate. Who would have thought that life was so precious to me?

From monster to monster, from caterpillars to giant larvae, I kept on clinging...

THE MONSTER ON THE STAIRS

I met a monster on the stairs. When you looked at him, the trouble he had in climbing them hurt terribly.

Yet his thighs were impressive. He was even, so to speak, all thigh. Two heavy thighs on plantigrade paws.

The top did not seem clear to me. Little mouths of darkness, darkness or..... ? This being had no true body, except just enough soft, vaguely moist zones to tempt the dreaming penis of some idle man. But perhaps that wasn't it at all, and this big monster, probably a hermaphrodite, crushed and bestial, was unhappily climbing a flight of stairs that would no doubt lead him nowhere. (Although I had the impression that he had not set out just to climb a few short steps.)

Seeing him was upsetting, and surely it was not a good sign to have met up with a monster like that.

You could see he was vile immediately. But in what way—that was not at all certain.

He seemed to carry lakes on his undefined mass, tiny lakes, or were they eyelids, enormous eyelids?

IN THE HOSPITAL

The pain is atrocious. They have given me a room in the hospital at some distance from the others.

I share it with a coughing woman.

No doubt they expected that with the screams my suffering would soon wrench out of me I would destroy the sleep of all the patients in the ward.

No! Every morning I examine my strength on the one hand, and the progress of my pain on the other, and I decide as firmly to hold on today as, irrevocably, the next, to let myself give in to the screams of my infernal suffering that I can now only hold back with extreme difficulty whose overflow is imminent, imminent, if it has not already been reached. Yet the next day again I resist the growing pressure that is well beyond what I thought I would be able to stand.

But why, oh why did they give me a coughing woman who lacerates my rare moments of peace and is shredding to pieces, disastrously, the little continuity I can still manage to keep, in this terrible harassment of pain?

TRYING

TO

WAKE

UP

Although Michaux included this piece in *Passages 1937–1950* and again in the expanded *Passages 1937–1963,* it was first published separately in 1950 and written in 1945. It is closer to "My Properties" or even "Space of the Shadows" (in *Facing the Locks*) than to the other texts in *Passages,* most of which are essays.

In this work, Michaux deals concretely with a problem that may be formulated abstractly as follows: if we have no sense of being solidly centered in our bodies, how can we construct a more or less stable self, a center of consciousness? how can we manage to get through the day? Here's how...

(*Arriver à se réveiller,* Bettencourt, 1950, Gallimard, 1954 and 1963)

TRYING TO WAKE UP

The night leaves me cadaverous.

The corpse has to be revived.

However, I don't have the impression of being a dead body in the morning.

If someone could see me at that time in accordance with my impressions, I would appear as a sea of clouds, a globulous sea of masses of flakes, a huge object that no doubt borders on the stratosphere.

Cloud though I may be, I am well aware that this state has its enemies, that I will soon have to become active again, definite, reduced in size… and that it would be wise to start moving in that direction (if it isn't too late for me to wake up, ever). I get busy immediately.

To manage that, to manage to reach the shape that, I sense, must be most favorable for me, I gropingly aim at becoming a shape with feet or legs or pseudopods.

With many legs, I hope to find the floor more rapidly; I seem to be dangerously far away from it.

But I can't begin that way. The gaseous planet (or the immensely gigantic chloroformed amoeba) that I have become won't allow it yet.

Courage! In this mass a will remains.

This headstrongness without a body is vaguely growing.

Without knowing exactly what being I am, in fact without thinking or worrying about it, but sure that there will be a better chance of raising myself up with pseudopods—even clumsy ones moving every which way—than without them, I try to extract myself with many feet from the layer of sleep. For it so happens that there is layering in this false cloud, not, it is true, through the weight of the center of my person which is probably denser (a center I cannot feel at all, nor can I feel heterogeneousness) but rather the way you sometimes lie in the bed of a constantly repeated melody without being able to get out of it, no matter how hard you try.

In this serious situation (serious, for at these moments I don't have the encouraging memory of how I have gotten out of it before—more than once, in fact thousands of times) I do not turn to pseudopods (strangely enough), but—and this shows the solid (or childish) confidence I have in mechanics—I turn to tried and true instruments of lifting: blocks and tackles, cranes, loading masts, all of them enormous, cranes of the kind one would need for a superskyscraper of two hundred stories, dizzying blocks and tackles, multiple belts, cardan gears and others whose names I don't know because I may have seen a drawing of them or their form just once, but now they're miraculously here again in a situation that is tragic for me, requiring the use of the best devices available.

It would seem that trying to hoist up my gaseous supermass by means of these instruments is so blatantly inappropriate that even a half-conscious idiot, a semicorpse would realize it.

Hmm... All I know is, this doesn't wake me up.

(. . .) Then come attempts at getting out through some sort of huge scrapers stuck under my mass (grandiose images, but weak as bits of wool, even though I put all the steel I can think of into them).

Then, in silence and exhaustion, I come back to my paralysis, the one indisputable reality.

Although the instruments I've used have never once succeeded in moving me, as far as I can recall, I always turn to them at the beginning of my awakening.

Luckily, I don't meet with the same lack of success in my attempts at lifting with pseudopods, otherwise I would never wake up.

When I begin to bud, to form even the crudest of legs, even sorts of stumps, I know I'm beginning to enter the path of deliverance.

And when real legs take shape, dividing my being up and down...

But I'm not up to that yet. I even still have to come back to my lifting instruments again, even though they have given me so little help up to this point.

Everybody has his mistakes, his invincible mistakes of behavior. At least one might expect some adjustments, a choice of tools more appropriate to the goal pursued.

Now, what appears is even more inappropriate, in still greater abundance.

This is when long, frail bones begin to appear, proportionate to the length of the body—that is, up to hundreds of yards long—almost threadlike in spots, in continual danger of splitting or breaking loose, for instead of fitting through apophysis and holding together through ligaments, they fit together (I really don't know why) either through piles of hundreds of turning plates or through whistling spools wobbling dangerously, threatening to fall out and break loose. It would make a turnip anxious!—a balance unable to give a tenth of the satisfaction needed by the awakened man, who doesn't know what to do, while the real paralysis of his body still prevents him from gaining any confidence at all.

Then everything stops in a dissolving fog. Please, let me "keep" something!—for it happens, unfortunately, that at the critical moment, exhausted by the effort, I fall asleep again, and everything will have to begin all over again later, God only knows how.

New, new tentative experiments, again an attention distributed feverishly (in a way, *placidly*, too) throughout a thousand points of this construction of bones that is only holding up by a few miracles, (. . .) again attention to the delicate foot-shaped supports, when at last...

at last, with no warning, no preparation, there comes into the cage of the enormous and enormously empty edifice of bone and fog, there comes into me with no further delay a vertical surge

...and as soon as there is a surge, I have noticed, everything changes. Another center appears, a real one this time, easy, strong, willful, not at all hardworking, with no need to work, a kind of *well in the air* that is my real life and my self, and then in a few seconds the fat swollen being of a while ago is gone. And, as a dozen drops or so may remain from a huge steam-cloud, there remain, from the huge, excessive, cloudy mass, a neck, some skin, hands, a chest, me between white sheets and... which soon moves. Oh! such a little bit! But this delightfully light, supple, hardly perceptible lifting immediately speaks volumes about my possibilities. Soon I'll be able to get up. I am now just a few minutes away, and with no obstacles on the road to the near future, I am now a man like any other.

It happens, but much more rarely, that I awake (from this half-sleep I've been talking about) on four legs. In that case I need more time to return to biped shape, because—I think—of a certain propensity I have for living in that state, which I don't have for my cloud shape. I'd certainly be prevented from doing so even if I wanted to, and I would be too afraid to stay that way. Although, after all... I've come out of it many times in the course of my life. But all it takes is once, when you forget how to deal with it and you stay that way forever, until you die.

Thus it is that I have been fascinated by quadrupeds and multipeds much more than most men who lose interest in them after the age of twelve, whereas I kept that interest to the age of thirty-five.

I will have lived most of my life as a galaxy.

P.S. I. People who dream have always seemed to me superficial sleepers. Probably afraid to "lose their man."

P.S. II. During the morning that follows, before eating or drinking, I am in drunken equilibrium.

—Indeterminate—

—Uncircumscribed—

Neither leaf, nor man, nor anything. I'm still waiting for what the day will hold for me—and I look at the things that present themselves to me as if they were presenting themselves to my own future, as if I were being asked to have a career as a pigeon, a leaf, a little girl, a hedge, a pebble, and I say neither yes nor no.

No precise desires. I reject neither pigeon, nor hedge, nor horse, nor pebble, nor little girl. No. I am still undecided.

In the afternoon, it will be different. I'll rub them out with no problem at all, those horses, hedges, the not-me's. No danger of them swallowing me up. The moment has passed.

This volume includes texts composed over a ten-year period, from the 1936 *Voyage to Great Garaband* to the 1946 *Report from Poddema*. "The author has often lived elsewhere," as he says in his Preface, and in fact will continue to do so: Michaux's "reports from abroad," often in the form of letters or explorer's descriptions, precede the publication of *Elsewhere*. We find them in his two "real" travel books, of course (*Ecuador,* 1929, and *A Barbarian in Asia,* 1933) but in other works, too; and he will keep on sending out these "reports" long after *Elsewhere* is published. Why not? "Soon [these strange lands and peoples] will be encountered everywhere," says Michaux, and he was right: "The Nonese and the Olibarians," for example, written in 1936, gives an excellent account of the French and their German masters during the Occupation (1940–1944)... or perhaps it is an allegory of the South African blacks and their white government in the 1980s.

There is also a connection between these "elsewheres" and strange currents in the mind, as we may suspect already and will see still more clearly when Michaux gives us his reports on voyages through mescaline country in the late fifties and sixties, and further explorations of madness later on.

(*Ailleurs,* Gallimard, 1948, revised edition, 1967)

PREFACE TO *ELSEWHERE*

The author has often lived elsewhere: two years in Garaband, about the same in the Land of Magic, a bit less in Poddema. Or a lot more. There are no precise dates.

He did not always particularly like these countries. Here and there, he nearly got used to them. Not really. When it comes to countries, the more one distrusts them the better.

He came back home after each trip. His resistance isn't infinite.

Some readers have found these countries a bit strange. That won't last. The impression is already fading.

He who sought to escape the World becomes its translator, too. Who can escape? The container is closed.

You'll see: these countries are perfectly natural after all. Soon they will be encountered everywhere... Natural as plants, insects, natural as hunger, habit, age, custom, customs, as the presence of the unknown bordering on the known. Behind that which is, which nearly was, which tended to be, threatened to be, and which among millions of "possibles" began to be, but was unable to settle in completely...

H. M.

IN THE LAND OF THE HACS

As I was coming into that village, I was drawn by a strange noise to a crowded square; in the middle of it, on a raised platform, were two half-naked men wearing heavy wooden clogs solidly attached to their feet, fighting each other to the death.

Although this was by no means the first savage spectacle I had witnessed, I did feel queasy a few times at the sound of the clogs thudding into the bodies, so dull, so subterranean.

The crowd was not talking, not shouting, but woowooing. Rattling with complex passions, these inhuman moans rose up like enormous draperies around this really "bastardly" fight, in which a man was going to die without grandeur.

And what always happens happened: a hard, dumb clog crashing into a head. The noble features—noble as even the most ignoble are—the features of that face were trampled on like some unimportant sugar beet. The word-making tongue falls in, while the brain inside can't cook up another thought, and in its turn, the feeble hammer of the heart takes its hits—and what hits!

There, he's really dead now! So the other one gets the purse and the satisfaction.

"Well," my neighbor asked, "what do you think of it?"

"How about you?" I said, for one must be prudent in these countries.

"Well," he answered, "it's a show, a show like any other. In our tradition, it's number 24."

And with these words, he cordially bid me good day.

.　　.　　.

I saw the fight between two brothers. For four years, they had avoided each other, building up their strength, getting into perfect condition. When they met, it seemed they didn't realize it. They began to feel each other dreamily, all the while spattering each other with mud, as if to make unrecognizable the family features they were about to humiliate—to humiliate, oh, unimaginably!

The old hatred stemming from childhood rose in them little by little, while they slapped that sticky, leprous earth all over each other and danger surged up in them—up to their noses, to their ears, to their eyes, a dark warning. And suddenly they were two demons. But there was only one hold. Swept away by their momentum, the elder fell into the mud with the other one. What frenzy down there! Tremendous seconds! Neither one got up again. The back of the elder appeared for an instant, but his head could not turn out of the swamp and sank back into it, irresistibly.

.　　.　　.

They also have "General Fire Companies." Big ones, smaller ones, always resting squarely on the shoulders of a boy.

If you look hard, you will see some of them slipping off with fire baskets in rich neighborhoods.

Believe me, you'd better make a deal with those youngsters, before the fire takes on proportions that attract a crowd thirsty for emotion, which won't lift a finger to save your house.

Certainly not. The crowd is crazy about fires.

THE EMANGLONS

Whenever you are close to the murmur of a stream and the glitter of light on the little waves and ripples of water, you may also expect to find a few Emanglons.

The Emanglons constantly feel scratched by the murmur of the little leaps of the water in a stream, scratched and healed up immediately afterward.

That is why you can see them at their best near running water. Like convalescents still a little sick but well on their way to recovery, they are quite open to others, and it is just possible that if the stream is very jumpy and cascading, and really annoying (though simple and kept in its little frame), it is just possible that they will pay attention to you and address you politely.

Then you can feel pleasure emanating from them. But since they are not used to expressing themselves, especially with foreigners, what comes forth is, along with a few words, an abundance of cluckings—full of excellent intentions, no doubt.

. . .

When the Emanglons travel during the daytime, they are wrapped up and sealed like packages. They hate the sun (except in the forest where it is broken into crumbs), and the idea of worshiping it would never occur to an Emanglon. Besides, in the cruel light of the sun they feel themselves watched. And they hate being watched.

They gladly go out at night, with bearers carrying multicolored lanterns that spread out through the woods, silent, but enjoying the sight more than one would think.

The most skillful climb on to branches to hang lights on them at different heights. Some of them sit in these branches, where they feel an intense pleasure, and it is sometimes necessary to bring them home inanimate and absent from themselves.

. . .

Sometimes, on his doorstep, you can see an Emanglon sneeze. Once, twice, three times, a hundred times, for a whole day. He has a right to do that. Of course. Of course...

He would have less of a right to remain inside his house—at least if he's someone who's going to sneeze away for whole hours and weeks, which sometimes happens (for they are prone to spasmodic sneezing). No, no one could stand that. It would be too much to ask of the Emanglons' nerves.

That's what a sneezer has got to understand. If he insists on remaining inside, he must know what he's risking by being so stubborn. In order to put an end to the ordeal the whole family is enduring through his fault, if anyone close to him—a sister, a friend of the household—should smash in his skull with a hammer, no court in the land would convict the person who sacrificed himself in this way. The act was unavoidable. The judge himself would have picked up the hammer just as he did. No one can be condemned for that.

The Emanglons also have no trouble getting rid of people who are hard of hearing, who force them to speak loudly—something intolerably irritating.

THE CORDOBESE

Not one of them is free from bile.

The quickest people in the world to take offense, the most eaten away by affronts (which they feel everywhere), hesitating not between anger and calm, but between several angers.

Their faces loaded with jealousy, constantly cooked and soaked over and over in it, in outrages to their honor, in resentments—especially in the evening—invaded by poisonous juices, seasoned, tensed, superimposed, spotted, paled, darkened by successive waves of bitterness.

A hundred different expressions of anger: with some, it turns into shivering so violent it makes them take to their beds; with others, into fever, hiccups, spasms, little verbal peaks, whirling arms; anger more dangerous in someone who rarely feels it, as its customary path is not already traced—more devastating, striking randomly, with no exit, as if it were going to rip his chest open.

Anger without cruelty, atrocities or murder, for rather than be free of it altogether, they prefer the pride of being its master, its center, its victim. (Anger: strength. Murder: onanism.) One must know how to hold oneself back.

The women have all the fine vivacity of the men, without their bilious demon; full of spirit, slim, with pure, rested faces. Now that disconcerts the men, those machos, never tired, but ridiculed by such grace—hence new attacks of anger, with the women always astonished by these fits of fury, like birds insulted by rats.

Men and women on the edge of the abyss of love, never meeting.

Love songs in Cordobia: beautiful with energy, wrenched out of the depths, going far, but somewhat showy.

A country more visited by sadness than truly sad. Houses built in inconvenient places: infuriating, but madly classy.

The air—freezing or burning—burns your mucous membranes. Thirst. They keep their thirst. Thirst is sharper than slaking.

They worship one God, revengeful, hard, absolute, inclined to see evil everywhere and just waiting for them all when they die. His reign will have no end.

(The Cordobese are related to the Ebelli, the Ecrelli, the Ficres and the Pajaris.)

THE GAURS

They are avidly religious. What have they not sacrificed to religion? Their ways are rude: they eat their food raw. For the gods alone there is cooked nourishment. They prepare it with tremendous care, and a master sauce-chef works constantly at cooking up a large variety of dishes—whole sheep, fowls.

The god sniffs it in, his nostrils all brown, greasy, scabby. But he never gets tired of seeing innocent animals thrown alive into steaming pots under burning sauces, and years and years must go by before his nose becomes obstructed by the progressive deposits of smoke particles and he publicly stops tasting the animal sacrifices and sniffing the most intense aromas.

Then, with a clear conscience, they stop feeding him until some misfortune occurs; then they throw themselves at his feet in contrition (others promptly unstuff his nostrils) and humbly offer him up the sacrifice of their cattle, which, out of spite and bad faith, they had hoped to keep from him.

I don't know all their gods, but I do know a few of them, as I've seen them being paraded around on holidays; they are also on permanent display in certain places, where a large number of them are to be found in groups, each with its band of worshippers and its master sauce-cook.

The god *Bannu* prefers chickens, pimentos, and antelope eyes. The god *Xhan*, grilled meat, with the victims burnt to the bone. The god *Sannu* feeds on entrails and live animals steamed in a double boiler. The god *Zirnizi* prefers small rodents, larks, and nightingales, but they have to be slowly burned into the finest, most delicate ash.

The god *Kambol*, who has tasted of man, alas, is fond of man or rather of girl, of flesh tending toward the fullness of woman, flesh still "climbing uphill." That's what he wants. Naturally, they try to fool him with pigs that are still young—between pig and piglet—and here and there, the better to confuse him, there is a hand, a finger, a delicate arm laid out on all this piggery.

They gain a few human lives, of course, but they can't frustrate him indefinitely, for he really knows men, he is the god who knows men best, and unlike many others, he appreciates them and has only the sweetest words for them.

As they are generous (although perhaps merely out of fear), the Gaurs cannot understand coldness and avarice in others: "Come on," they will say to some foreigner passing through, "you have four children, and you can't even give two to such a powerful god!" (The god Kambol.) Such irreligiousness they find stupefying. They are seized by wrath, divine wrath, and, to repair the outrage, they massacre all those impious people and offer them up to their greedy gods. (In this country, I cannot advise you strongly enough to travel alone, with just the slightest bit of luggage that you can hide in a ditch if necessary.)

Sometimes a pious Gaur, walking by the pots of the Great Kambol, sees him with a meager and almost insulting pittance, a puny baby with no more than skin on his bones and nothing to be gotten out of him really, or else deceitful meats—pigs and calves and young gazelles; then the pious Gaur, with an aching heart, ashamed of such poverty, but poor himself, quickly cuts off one of his fingers—a meager offering, no doubt, but with many excuses he presents it piping hot to the god, drenched in the blood impetuously gushing out, the human blood that the god likes so much.

．　　■　　．

The god *Mna* is the deafest and the greatest. They are sure that if *he* could only hear them, it would be the end of all their miseries—which are countless, for I have never seen a people so riddled with illnesses (I describe a few further on).

This is why, on his tiny little ear, they have hung another ear, huge, elephantine, with deep folds, spread out heavily behind his head like a train. And there are always big official loudmouths, priests and children of priests with shrill, penetrating voices, to cry out words of supplication to him, naturally only after they have alerted him by a preliminary procession of firecracker throwers and trumpet players chosen from the most powerful lungs among the Gaurs.

Oh! he is so hard of hearing, if only he could see! Well, no. Nothing to hope for on that score. Never has the shadow of an eye, never has the merest drop of a crystalline lens appeared in his face. They can't fool themselves with this kind of hope, they can really only count on this profoundly deaf god's vanishing sense of hearing—for in days gone by he apparently could still hear a little (although frequently all wrong)—and thus on his immediately distributing what was asked of him, because as soon as he understands what is happening, he has no greater wish than to satisfy men: he can refuse them nothing. Alas, now he really seems to be moving toward total deafness, and one wonders, with terror, what will happen when he reaches it.

.　　.　　.

The god of the waters is lying down. It is out of the question for him to get up. The prayers of men do not interest him in the slightest, nor their vows, nor their pledges. Little does he care for sacrifices. He is the god of water above all.

He has never really paid attention when the Gaurs' crops were rotted by the rain, when their herds were carried away by floods. He is the god of water above all. Yet they have well-educated priests. But they don't really know enough to tickle him. They study, search through their traditions, fast, meditate, and it is possible that in the long run they will succeed in reaching him and in making themselves heard over the voice of the waters, which is so very dear to him.

.　　.　　.

How impudent we are, we who live only for ourselves, our family, our country, as if all that were not equally vile!

One must take good care, when traveling through the land of the Gaurs, always to have a plentiful provision of statuettes on hand and visibly offer them sacrifices, and to order three or four supplementary dinners and have them burnt in the fire with a little air of mystery.

The atmosphere was infectious, and I had begun to perform regular devotions to a little lamp of red glass that I had in my baggage. One evening it was irresistible: I offered it up an ox and from that time on, I couldn't help bringing it offerings, spending whole nights lost in worship, surrounded by a crowd of supplicants, of the sick, and if a particularly devout person had not—luckily—stolen my lamp from me in the hope of obtaining great miracles in his favor, I would have given my pants for it. But this theft discouraged me and I left the country soon afterward.

.   .   .

At the end of a tree-lined road, in a loathsome little pond, is a god with shining, excited eyes.

What's the good of setting him apart, off at such a distance, since one must come to him anyway?

It is not without anguish that one begins walking down this lane.

For sacrifice is not enough. One must make martyrs, and make a martyr out of somebody one loves. This god, called "The Simple One," is satisfied neither by blood, nor by life, nor by sauces. He wants only intimacy.

Just let a father who tenderly loves his son appear at the end of the lane and immediately his eyes begin to shine in the distance; and one realizes, alas, that here the god has what he needs, and that he can appreciate it.

.   .   .

When a Gaur, overwhelmed with misfortunes, raises his arms to the sky (if he still has the strength), the priests call him violently to order: "Sacrifice, sacrifice!" they tell him. And taking advantage of his weakness and disarray, they take his goats away from him and everything he owns. For they are always traveling far and wide to places where there is some distress, cataclysm or flood, to make people render unto God what is God's, everywhere sowing terror and righteousness, and accumulating immense wealth. You may be sure that they also take advantage of the anxieties of the sick. But they do not feel comfortable near them, for if an illness should spread through a religious community, doubts concerning their own moral value come to the minds of the people who immediately go into a rage and, despite the threats and the wolflike faces of the impotent priests, want to take back what is theirs.

The Gaurs are without pity for priests "whom God has abandoned." With the memory of people obsessed, haunted by the beyond, they immediately recall that at that particular sacrifice years ago, this particular priest hesitated, started again, stammered, uselessly repeated some formula. Now that the scales have fallen from their eyes, they are drunk with wrath and justice, and they will offer up the priests as a sacrifice to the gods. Convents and monasteries are miraculously depopulated, God takes back His own and the Earth its tranquillity.

MURNS AND EGLARMBS

The Murns: pretentious, gobblish, goborious crabbots, known far and wide for their stuffed, hermetically sealed stupidity, as the Agres and the Cordobese are for their jealousy, the Orbis for their slowness, the Smilinettes and Ribobelles for their easy virtue, the Arpedars for their hardness of heart, the Tacodions for their thrift, the Eglarmbs for their musical talent.

Pick an Eglarmb at random, whistle any tune at all to him and he will repeat it to you note for note whenever you wish, adding—since they sincerely believe that all music comes from them—that it is one of their old melodies, even if you have whistled a theme from the *Rheingold*. But he will whistle it reluctantly, as being a tune from a rude era, which the Eglarmbs have long since left behind.

THE NONESE AND THE OLIBARIANS

The Nonese have been slaves of the Olibarians for an eternity. The Olibarians make them work beyond all reason, for they are afraid that if the Nonese regain a bit of strength, they will take advantage of it to go back to their country, although it is just about barren by now and partially flooded.

Due to the ill treatment they have received, the Nonese race has been cut in half, so that the Olibarians are forced to go out and hunt them in their country much further away than in the past, up to the swamps, into which they would probably escape, were it not for the dogs trained for the purpose of hunting them down.

From time immemorial, these expeditions have constituted a national pastime, which has, moreover, been celebrated by all the great Olibarian poets. But unfortunately, fewer and fewer Nonese are brought back, really out of all proportion to the military effort deployed, and it's not the generals' fault.

Consequently, under government supervision, reservations of male and female Nonese have now been set up, where they can more easily reproduce in abundance like a normal race that does not wish to decline.

Once the children have reached the age at which they become robust, they are released into the province of Bempty, where the Olibarians can come hunt them.

For an Olibarian cannot perform any task other than hunting. To undertake a different one would demoralize him, would most certainly kill him. But he knows his destiny and remains faithful to it.

It would be absolutely useless constantly to bring war into a country that is already so impoverished. Even the generals can understand that. It is more worthwhile to give free reign to the Nonese for a few years so that everything fructifies once again, even if it means politically combatting any possible uprising. Thus, with great and highly visible honors at the start, they invite the Nonese leader who is in their way; once he has crossed the border, they have a policeman cut his tongue out, then solemnly affirm that this Nonese had an indisputable right to his tongue and even to great honors; however the tongue does not grow back, neither does speech, and the handicapped leader is promptly eliminated. The

Olibarians, pretending to misunderstand his wishes, dress him up in a clown costume "at his own request," put him—still at his own request (!)—in the company of degenerate party-goers with whom he finds himself involved in stupid, hideous perversions, and surround him with signs relating his baseness, while magnanimously pretending not to condemn him, as after all he is an "invited guest."

But human resistance has its limits. He who knows them can push you over them so promptly it's amazing. The unfortunate Nonese is soon turned into a complete wreck and dies in despair.

The Olibarians also get the Nonese to lend them their holiest statues, as between allies who wish each other well. So with the greatest signs of veneration and respect they carry away a relic or a holy statue, claiming it will be a blessing for the whole country. But once they get back to their Olibarian countryside, the tired bearers drop it, as if accidentally, into a ditch full of manure; there are no ropes to be found, it stays there for a night and a day, it comes out unrecognizable, stinking, and they throw it into a heap of refuse to join the many other revolting objects that were once the holiest relics of the Nonese.

But the Nonese are patient. God will not stand for this indefinitely, they say. He is waiting for his time to come.

Of course he's waiting.

THE HIVINIZIKIS

Always in a hurry, ahead of themselves, feverishly running here and there, very busy, they might even lose their hands. Impossible for them to be satisfied for any length of time.

Enthusiastic, impetuous, "pointed," but always for a short time, butterfly diplomats, placing landmarks everywhere which they then forget, with a police force and chiefs of staff who have dozens of extremely ingenious secret codes, never knowing which one to apply, codes constantly changing and adding on new fakes.

Gamblers (busy from morning till night shooting dice for their whole fortunes, which change hands from one second to the next so that no one can tell debtors from creditors), card sharps, tricksters, bunglers not from confusion and foggy minds, but from a host of clear ideas that pop up irrelevantly, frenzied logicians but full of flights of fancy and intuitive departures, proving the existence or nonexistence of everything under the sun, absentminded yet tirelessly working their scams, going (but only for a few hours) to bed and to sleep at the same time and coming out of them in the same way, like a door opening and closing, getting angry over nothing, distracted from their anger by less than nothing, by a hovering fly; open like a sail to all winds, melting into sincere tears at the bedside of their sick father but as soon as his eyes have closed running off to hear the will, arguing over the inheritance while sitting on the bed still warm from his body, burying him in the twinkling of an eye (good idea: otherwise they would forget about him until he stinks).

Prostrating themselves before their gods hundreds of times like tightly wound up mechanical dolls, then bounding off without even turning around; loving just as they worship—fast, with ardor, and then "let's forget about it"—getting married without forethought, thanks to a chance encounter, on the spot, and getting divorced in the same way; working, selling or crafting things in the middle of the street, in the wind and the dust and the kicking of horses; talking away like machine guns; on horseback as often as possible, and galloping, or if they're walking it's with their arms thrust out in front of them as if they were finally going to clear up and clear out this Universe for good, this Universe full of problems and difficulties surging up constantly before them.

(1936)

Surrounding the Land of Magic, tiny little islands: buoys. In each buoy a dead person. This ring of buoys protects the Land of Magic, acts as an alarm for the inhabitants of the country, tells them when foreigners are coming.

Then all they have to do is send them on the wrong course and far away.

.　　.　　.

On the highway, it is not rare to see a wave, all alone, one wave separated from the ocean.

It is absolutely useless, does not constitute a set.

This is a case of magical spontaneity.

.　　.　　.

On the other hand, walking on both banks of a stream is an exercise, and a hard one at that.

Thus you will often see a man (a student of magic) going up a stream by walking on both sides at the same time: as he is extremely preoccupied, he doesn't see you. For what he is accomplishing is a delicate business; it admits of no distraction. In the twinkling of an eye he would find himself back on one bank, alone, and then would he ever be ashamed!

.　　.　　.

I saw the water restraining itself from flowing. If the water is used to you, if it's *your* water, it does not pour out, even if the pitcher should break into four pieces.

It simply waits to be given another pitcher. It doesn't try to flow around outside.

Is this the power of the Magus at work?

Yes and no—apparently no, since the Magus may not realize that the pitcher has broken and the water is putting itself through so much trouble to stay in the same place.

But he mustn't make the water wait too long, as this position is uncomfortable for it, painful to hold, and without exactly dissolving, it might spread pretty far out.

Naturally, it has to be your water and not the water of only five minutes ago, the one that has just been poured in. That water would flow out right away. What would hold it back?

■ ■ ■

Doors open and shut under the water.

You have to know how to hear them. Then you can learn your future, your near future: today's. Some clairvoyants are remarkably gifted at doing this; you meet them at the seaside, hoping for customers.

No matter how many errands you're going to run that day, they can hear in advance all the doors you'll go through, opening and shutting, and they see the people you'll meet on both sides of the doors and what they're going to say and decide.

It is stupefying, really.

Until nightfall, you think you're living through a day you have already lived.

■ ■ ■

The child, the chieftain's child, the sick man's child, the plowman's child, the idiot's child, the child of the Magus, the child is born with twenty-two folds. They must be unfolded. The life of man is then complete. In this form he dies. He has no folds left to open.

Rarely does a man die when he still has a few folds left to open. But it has happened.

Parallel to this operation man forms a nucleus. Inferior races, like the white race, see the nucleus more than the unfolding. The Magus sees mostly the unfolding.

Only unfolding is important. The rest is merely epiphenomena.

.   .   .

What most people do all the time is to gnaw on their double. In the land of the Magi, this is absolutely not permitted, they'll be severely punished, they must reform immediately.

.   .   .

No longer have to go through the calf for calf's liver. No longer train calves. No longer have to lead them out to graze, to have them be born, to kill them, no longer have to make calf personalities appear and disappear.

Just once, a long time ago now, they killed a calf: they removed its liver, tended it, found it a suitable environment and now it develops in infinite masses.

The liver has its enemies that prevent it from growing, from developing (the worst is the calf, which only thinks of itself), it has its own poisons against which the calf itself struggles valiantly, valiantly, ceaselessly and not very well, not very well at all, since it is only a calf.

Shouldn't a Magus know more than a calf? So it goes: for apples, for the white meat of the chicken, for figs, for everything. Apple trees, fig trees are gone (except for decoration, instruction, and the liberty of nature), they are no longer needed. After a first sowing, they make chicken meat, apple meat, meat out of everything that grows and lives.

The right to meat! The meat they didn't know how to grow, or didn't want to. It is taken away from them. Now it's the Magi's!

.   .   .

There, offenders caught in the act have their faces ripped off on the spot. The executioner-Magus arrives immediately.

One needs unbelievable willpower to pull off a face, so accustomed is it to its man.

Little by little, the face lets go, begins to come off.

The executioner redoubles his efforts, braces himself, breathes heavily.

Finally, he rips it off.

If the operation is done well the whole thing comes off, forehead, eyes, cheeks—the whole front of the head—as if cleaned off by some kind of corrosive sponge.

Thick, dark blood gushes out of the pores, which are wide open all over.

The next day a huge, round, scabby clot has formed which can inspire nothing but terror.

Anybody who has seen one will remember it forever. He has his nightmares to remember it with.

If the offender is particularly tough and the operation is not performed well, they only manage to rip off his nose and eyes. This is still quite a result, because the extraction is purely magical: the executioner's fingers cannot touch or even graze the face to be pulled out.

.   ▪   ▪

Standing in the middle of a perfectly empty arena, the suspect is questioned. Through magic.

In deep silence, but powerfully for him, the question resounds.

Reverberating through the rows of seats, it bounces off, returns, falls back and comes down on his head like a city collapsing in ruins.

Under those waves pressing him, comparable only to successive catastrophes, he loses all resistance and confesses his crime. It is impossible for him not to.

Now a miserable, deafened wreck, with an aching, ringing head and the sensation of having faced ten thousand accusers, he leaves the arena, where the most absolute silence has reigned unbroken.

.   ▪   ▪

They judge the value of a man more accurately once he has died. Now that he's rid of what made him tick, of his workshop (the body), he reveals himself at last, they claim.

The most sensational accomplishments have always been the work of the dead. One must act fast, however. Ten years or so after death (eighteen or twenty for exceptional temperaments), the dead person fades away. For a Magus, surviving as long as possible is a question of self-respect. But the forces of disaggregation act, too, strongly, inexorably. The winds of the beyond triumph over the Magus in the end, and only the most recent dead can be counted on for remarkable actions.

Not everyone can be a Magus. There are dead people who are held back, sick. Some of them go mad. Here is where the *Psychiatrists for the Dead* come in. Their task is to guide the unfortunate, to cure them of the disorders caused by death.

This profession demands a great deal of delicacy.

.   .   .

There it is, bleeding on the wall, alive, red or half-infected: the wound of a man, of a Magus who put it there. Why? As an exercise in asceticism, the better to suffer from it; for if it were on him, he couldn't prevent himself from curing it through his thaumaturgic powers, which are so natural in him they are totally unconscious.

But this way he can keep it for a long time without its closing up. This procedure is quite common.

Strange wounds, suffering on blank walls, that you come upon with embarrassment and nausea…

.   .   .

The Stomach (the stomach-province) was used against enemies from the West. Rather than actual invaders, they seem to have been natives of the mountains, who have completely disappeared today.

When they came down into the plain, these mountain people had to cross a river. Their feet were digested. Further on, they were hit by a heavy rain: it attacked them immediately, gnawing through flesh and cloth.

The whole region before them had been transformed into a stomach: that is the truth of the matter.

The humid air devoured them. Their skin fell off in great strips and the flesh underneath was rapidly hollowed out. Even the dust they raised was against them: as it mixed with their sweat, it attacked them. Eaten up, not by leprosy, but by the awful juices of the Stomach, nearly all of them perished.

.   .   .

The most interesting things in this country cannot be seen. You can be sure you have not seen them: they surround them with fog. So it was that the Federal Capital remained inaccessible to me, invisible—even though I was told how to get there I don't know how many times, and indeed I spent a full week almost touching it.

They have seven kinds of fog (I am referring to the main ones) and all you need is the third to prevent you from seeing the very horse you're riding. The next one is so solid that you'd think you were caught in an avalanche of white sand. To learn if it's real fog, see if it follows the wind. If not, it's a magic fog. But the wind itself may be magical. I say this because it seems to be an objection. But in actual fact a Magus does not produce both fog and wind, although I do not know the reason for this.

Their fog is enough to drive you mad. That total absence of landmarks... you can see a leaf, a paw, a muzzle, but impossible to make out the bush, the animal.

A certain Kal who trusted me lent me his antifog glasses. There must have been something wrong with his vision, for people and things appeared to be bubbling around so much that I was completely disoriented. Extremely disgruntled, I gave him back his glasses. I should have kept them.

.   .   .

Why is it that despite the appeal cities have for me, I always have to find them unbearable, even in this land of magic?

I would get furious, I would panic, I would be sorry I wasn't a child any more so that I could yell, cry, stamp my foot, tell my troubles to someone. What was I to do? All I heard were complaints:

"Someone phoned you. Someone just called (or should I say telecommunicated?). They had someone call you back... What is it?... Why didn't you answer?"

So difficult is it for them to imagine that their occult messages cannot be heard, that words on a wall in capital letters underlined three times cannot be read.

Out of my mind with exasperation, my head buzzing from everything I felt going on around me without being able to sort it out, a ridiculous cripple when clairvoyance was the commonest thing in the world, sometimes I tried to guess, the way you do at roulette. As in roulette, I would lose. Revolting! And I would leave again for the country, ashamed of myself, envious, nasty.

．　．　．

Sometimes in the dark you may happen to see the jerky movements of what looks like a rather large, luminous casing.

What you are seeing here is a fit of anger.

If you draw nearer, you will soon see the Magus himself.

I would not, however, advise you to do so.

．　．　．

He spits out his face on the wall.

The fact I am relating here is connected to what I say elsewhere about the capsule. This act of scorn means that you wish to have nothing to do with the individual, that you do not want a trace of him on yourself. So you reject him publicly.

The Magus spits out the hated face, made hideous (although perfectly recognizable and true) on to the nearest wall, and the Magus goes away without a word. The face remains on the wall for a while, then it slowly gets covered over with dust.

．　．　．

As I was opening a soft-boiled egg, I found a fly.

It emerged from the lukewarm yolk of the uncoagulated egg, rubbed its wings together with difficulty, and flew heavily away.

Someone must have played this trick on me. Should I even mention it here? Is it worthy of the name of Magic?

.　　.　　.

It seems to me they don't have a knack for mechanical things.

Few will simply agree. They answer that it's anti-philosophical, anti-magical, anti-this, anti-that. I was explaining the bicycle to one of them (thinking I would amaze him), and he claimed that once they had invented a bicycle for insects, a present they used to give to children, who would play with them for some time. That's about all it was worth, he seemed to say.

.　　.　　.

In the Land of Magic, thought is utterly different from what it is here. Thought comes, takes on form, becomes clear, then leaves in the same way. I could feel the difference quite easily. Those sorts of scattered presences, those ideas that are constantly crossing your mind in Europe, without any benefit for others or for yourself—vague, contradictory—those larvae are simply not found over there: they have set up *the great dam,* which surrounds their countries.

A few rare, powerfully transmitted thoughts, of Hindu and Moslem magi and ascetics, of Christian saints and a few dying men too, are the only ones to have pierced through the dam, and even then for a very short time.

.　　.　　.

When they spoke to me of withdrawn horizons, of Magi who knew how to take the horizon and nothing but the horizon away from you, leaving everything else visible, I thought it was a kind of verbal expression, a jest only in language.

One day, in my presence, a Magus withdrew the horizon all around me. Whether it was through magnetism, suggestion or some other cause, the sudden subtraction of the horizon (I was near the sea, and an instant earlier I could appreciate its immense expanse, and the sands of the beach) provoked such great anxiety in me that I wouldn't have dared to walk a step.

Right away, I admitted I was convinced—I mean, *convinced!* An intolerable sensation had invaded me, one that even now I do not dare evoke.

. . .

Cannon-faces!

Faces always aimed, faces always thundering.

Avoid people with a cannon-face.

Even if they wanted to, they couldn't prevent themselves from shelling you in passing, and, when evening comes, after a few hours of seemingly banal, unimportant conversation, or of playing games or just strolling around, you are amazed to find yourself so tired, so overwhelmingly, mortally tired.

. . .

In that country, where natural magical power is great, where it is developed through subterfuge and technique, delicate and nervous people must take special precautions to keep their autonomy.

Even important people, famous in their way, said to me in moments of sincerity, revealing their fear: "Are you sure this is me? You don't notice anything... anything *foreign* in me?" So afraid are they of being occupied by someone else or controlled like dummies by stronger colleagues.

When I told them about Christ and Francis of Assisi or other saints who later received the stigmata, who drip blood from their hands and feet every Friday, they would often look, not pious, but serious, defensive, even overwhelmed.

"What! You say he's been dead for two thousand years, and he's still vampirizing you!" I could see they were sorry for us, and almost terrified, too.

. . .

Perfidiously, prudently, brilliantly, they have perfected a unique method of hunting.

They act against lions *by wounding the collective soul of the lions.* In a secret way they dominate the minds of the dead lions, compress them and block their reincarnation or else squeeze it exaggeratedly, with results that are very bad for the health and constitution of the lions: they are extremely degenerate and lazy over there (except in the western savannas) to an absolutely incredible point, diminished in size and in everything else and such that a billy goat would easily stand up to them.

So those enemies of men and herds, those beasts who were once apocalyptic in the terror they inspired—they kick them out of the way when they come across them, and threaten to bastardize them still more, to bring them so low a rat would frighten them.

And as if they understood the anathema, the lions retreat with their tails hanging down and their heads between their paws. Some can be seen rummaging around in the garbage like derelicts.

. . .

I did not see the tree that beats its branches, but I heard a lot about it. It can only beat them during the first fifteen days of spring; after that it loses flexibility and remains indifferent and sedate like other trees, stuffed as they are with cellulose and other hard substances incompatible with dancing and artistic expression.

. . .

Who likes to see his secrets revealed? I was often pursued, attacked.

Karna, who guarded me, had a difficult task.

There were frequent attempts to poison me. My hand was often behind me, pierced through by the tines of a pitchfork. Birds would peck at my ear by mistake. A number of times sections of cliff split away from the mountain to fall upon me, but always Karna would arrive in time to lift the spell and the fearsome masses of rock floated down to my feet like handkerchiefs.

But one day, as I was feeling a heavy influence, I called out to him and he wasn't able to help me in time. He did walk toward me right away, and although he was at the other end of the room only six yards from me, and although he soon began to run toward me faster and faster with powerful strides for long, long minutes at a stretch, he was not able to get to me, nor even to come palpably nearer. Confronted by this hostile magic, he stopped, hiding his head for meditation or invocation, stayed that way for a while, then began walking rapidly again. This time, he was drawing nearer, I was opening my arms to take him in, when a cyclonic wind swept him aside toward a half-open door. He tore himself away from it and set out in the right direction once more, but as he was brusquely pulled off course toward the gaping door, he had to turn around to get a fresh start. A third time he charged forward, but he was sucked up as irresistibly as wheat in the automatic suction loader of a modern freighter, pulled into the opening, and vanished. I never saw him again.

That same day, I found myself ejected from the Land of Magic. I do not know how.

(1941)

PODDEMA-AMA

"How much are lips?"

But my question remained unanswered, I was making a mistake, as I wasn't at Nyooah, but at Kryooah, where kisses are free, absolutely free, no matter how long they are.

In actual fact, I never saw anything but short ones over there, simple, and well shared.

Foreigners are delighted by this custom.

People in mourning are exempted from kissing duty.

"Take a look," he said, "A man killed by his words."

It is one of their most remarkable inventions. Thus one should take care to speak judiciously in the Chamber of Lies. There I saw one of my former guides, who had an unfortunate reputation; he was led there by surprise and interrogated. I wanted to intervene. "You fool, be quiet." But as he was proud, he spoke, and his words, coming back to him duly loaded, knocked him on his back. He was dead.

Hence no need for sentencing.

.　.　.

I was in Langalore. I had just arrived. It was the first time. There were many women around, beautiful, magnetizing.

I loved them immediately. I loved them en masse and the city retreated from me, like a city that does not know you. The men of the ejaculatorium know what to do in this case, but that would not have suited my passionate desire for communication, for limitless communion.

In this vain, torturing transport, I turned—perhaps through association of ideas with the suffering of the crucifixion—I turned to the wall (for I was in my room where I was martyrizing myself at the window by looking at those beautiful Langalorettes walking by, thoughtlessly, carelessly). With my arms outstretched in a cross, I pressed myself naked against the cold wall.

I would so like to make you feel what happened next!

My transport melted into bliss—proud, harmoniously infinite bliss. I groped avidly around on that great, cold, seemingly endless surface, to sate myself on it.

I was getting rid of an unbelievable tension.

I was getting rid of an intolerable, unshared love. In sum... I loved that wall. Absolutely! At that moment, I would have given away anything, provided it was immense.

The wall received this gift better than a woman could have. There was something in it that could not be completely apprehended. Moreover, it was ice-cold. Tremendous momentum was necessary not to feel repulsion. With momentum, it was immensifying.

Since then, I have touched other walls without feeling the same austere pleasure. Was that Langalorian wall really a wall like any other?

.   .   .

In the chamber for the detection of future crimes they look for those who are going to murder, who are on the verge of murder.

The files they draw up are secret. The suspect doesn't know about it himself, unconscious as he is of the budding thoughts they have found in him.

Before going into the Chamber of Secret Plans one enters the Chamber of Provocations. The action of the latter facilitates the action of the former.

Detected as most dangerous is the man with thoughts elaborating a single crime. He must be promptly arrested before he can act, whereas another person, in whom they have found dozens of embryonic crimes—someone who actually flits from one murder to another— presents practically no danger at all, as he can't manage to make up his mind. In fact, thanks to this inner butchery he can keep himself active and happy to a ripe old age.

Consequently they leave him in peace, and are careful to keep the contents of his file from him, for he is either hardly aware of his state or he innocently believes that everyone is equally murderous.

No, one must never reveal his illness to him. It could affect him badly, with no benefit in return; it would take away his energy and zest, the joy of his friends and family.

.   .   .

In Huina, at the first signs of old age, old people are reeducated, as being unfit to feel the Present.

If they were left to their own devices, without a method, it would soon be completely impossible to reeducate them.

They do try, as one may imagine, to play hooky, out of pride. So much the worse for them. And even if some old man exhibits a diploma of reeducation obtained through pity or pull, this protection won't grant him immunity. If he should inadvertently happen to show signs of old age by expressing the opinion that he is not getting the respect due him or that young people are more frivolous nowadays than they were in his time, he will promptly be led into the Chambers of Forgetting. The last discussion is over.

With this threat hovering over them, many old people become extremely prudent; as they are more attached to life than to respect, they agree to everything and take "sensitivity examinations" as many as three times. When these old people fail, it is because of their zeal, the excess willpower they tactlessly displayed at the exam (that bony willpower of the old, a source of hardness).

And what's the result when they pass? Well, it makes for rather pleasant old people, I must say, quite helpful on occasion, although they do tend to watch themselves a bit too much.

.   .   .

In Arridema, an unparalleled advantage: comfortable houses—simple but extraordinary houses, musical ones.

Each house is hollowed into a deep, narrow hole in the rock, a kind of case. When the day is over, they let a drop fall through the middle of the ceiling, opened for this purpose, then another drop, then another drop, indefinitely drops in a small, isolated, hermetically sealed room (except for the hole in the ceiling).

Through the compression of the air or for some other reason, the drops falling in this way produce a celestial, crystalline sound.

This enchanted flute—I mean this closed room, I also mean the neighboring room, I mean the whole house filled with the miraculous, contained vibration—shakes up one's being, which drifts off, lost, in sonorous drunkenness.

This sound is sustained, though not without highs and lows; it goes (in intensity) from the plaintive murmur of the wind in the reeds to the formidable rumbling of waves bursting like a battering ram into a half-submerged grotto and bouncing around in disorder—a mass of sound, infinitesimal or enormous, but always celestial and crystalline, and in this radiant, unique sound (in which, however, one seems to hear thousands), the house drifts off to sleep.

I can't tell you what this music means to the Arridemians. It is their father and mother, their cradle.

PODDEMA-NARA

.   .   .

In Inwrinki, they lose their teeth very early, so that they are obliged to have their food chewed for them by dogs, domesticated for this purpose. Some big eaters even thought of domesticating lions for this use, but that animal, who is actually quite lazy, is also not easily distracted from its needs in matters of food, nor, consequently, easily trained in this way. He has too much common sense.

.   .   .

In Billooli, they are shy. Equally so in Lillooli. Their capital is built facing a big mountain with a high peak. This peak is anonymous. They don't dare give names to peaks. They don't dare give names to mountains.

They do name streams though, and sometimes, little rivers. Not big ones. Just imagine: how insolent that would be. They only talk of it through ambiguous allusions in which no river, even if it were a god, could find itself and in any case could find nothing at which to get angry.

On the other hand, they unhesitatingly give names to brooks. And to themselves, you ask? Certainly not, or not always and never before reaching adulthood.

In general no names for large units. Billoolians and Lilloolians are afraid to give them too much existence by naming them.

Thus I had a terribly hard time finding my way around. And if there was a name, even a distantly allusive name of very little use for finding a thing or a place, they still were afraid to teach it to me, for fear of suddenly endowing it with new importance.

I enjoyed being with them...

.   .   .

The Olioolians may be even more shy. In fact, they are so shy they hardly dare raise their eyes to animate beings.

Consequently they know next to nothing about themselves or about nature, as they never have the time and the audacity to observe things, and, once that habit has been acquired... even for a flower moving in the wind, they have the reflex of averting their eyes and getting out of its way.

For this reason they are extremely ignorant and almost seem stupid. It's shyness. It's nothing but shyness.

.   .   .

In Dinari, which is right next door, they can't be upset in the slightest without getting sick, without coming down with a malignant flu. A Dinarian may die because you fail to show up at some appointment and this makes him wonder if he really is the person he thinks he is. Taking advantage of this moment of suspense, sickness—always at the ready—sickness like an open hand coming down on an absentminded, undecided fly at the corner of a table and nimbly grabbing it, thus does sickness catch him, pushing his wavering powers over the edge, and after a short fever his whole being gives in and withdraws into nothingness.

.   .   .

The Poddemians of Errimania.

They use their eyes, which are of a fine blue color and which, appropriately treated, can be worn as ornaments. Unfortunately, the eyes do not grow back. This is not so for Aaha Poddemians. Their eyes grow back up to three times. Consequently, they raise a lot of them. Unfortunately, their eyes are very, very small and do not have the reputation of being anywhere near equal to the eyes of Errimanian Poddemians, who, alas, die prematurely.

.   .   .

After much research, after thinking dozens of times that I was being misinformed, I met the giants. I was horrified by them. It is quite true that their forms are enormously developed, almost as much as those of balaenopterae, but it is apparently impossible to supply them with an adequate bone-structure and a sufficiently lively nervous influx to stiffen their enormous muscular plaques. Thus they move forward almost by crawling (when they manage to move). From afar, I thought at first I was looking at fallen trees stripped of their branches. Finally these sausage trees moved, slowly, clumsily, with difficulty.

Their eyes are the size of billiard balls, small for their bodies, but so big for ours, so dismayed, so gentle and exaggeratedly full of woe that they seem more like targets than the instruments of observation which eyes are.

They seem to be mistreated. Their own nature does rather mistreat them.

Experiments are performed on them, but in parks closed to the public. They cannot be transported, and they are so soft that giant-supports have been made for them.

These consist of various instruments in the form of pillars, giant shovels, huge belted plates, inclined planes, stirrups and forks for the support of limbs that otherwise would be in danger of asphyxiation, necrosis and rotting.

All this flaccidity hangs and spreads out like an expanse of mud made beast.

In the fields one can also see oxen with spotted hides, which the panthers do not dare attack.

(1946)

LIFE

IN

THE

FOLDS

In this collection the author's magical "interventions" often take the form of comic-sadistic inventions, grouped in a section called, appropriately enough, "Freedom of Action."

The lengthy "Portrait of the Meidosems" (more than 150 pages in the original) could appropriately have appeared in *Elsewhere*. Like the strange peoples described in the previous volume, the Meidosems are *here,* too, and in a special sense: delicate, constantly injured, suffering but surviving, "clamped to their weakness," they could collectively compose a portrait of Henri Michaux.

The subtitle of the original volume is *poèmes,* but only half a dozen texts in this volume are written in verse. It's not the length of his lines which makes Michaux a poet.

(La Vie dans les plis, Gallimard, 1949, revised edition, 1972)

THE SESSION WITH THE SACK

t on my life. I want nothing to do with it.

can do no better than his life?

It began when I was a child. There was a big adult in the way.

How could I get even with him? I stuck him in a sack. There I could beat him whenever I wanted. He would yell, but I didn't listen to him. He was not interesting.

Wisely, I've hung on to this childhood habit. The possibilities for action which one gains when one grows up, aside from the fact that they don't go very far—I distrusted them.

You don't offer a chair to someone who's in bed.

This habit, I say, I have kept, and until today have kept secret. It was safer.

Its drawback—for it has one—is that thanks to this habit, I have too much tolerance for absolutely impossible people.

I know I'm just waiting for a chance to give them my sack. Now *there's* something that gives you incredible patience.

I let ridiculous situations last on purpose, let people hang around who prevent me from living.

The joy I would feel in throwing them out *in reality* is held back at the moment of action by the incomparably greater delight of getting them in my special sack a little later. In the sack where I can beat them up with impunity and with an energy that would wear out ten strong men working in regular shifts.

Without this little art of mine, how could I have gotten through my life—a discouraging, poor life, always in the way of people's elbows?

How could I have gone on with it for decades, through so many disappointments, under so many masters near and far, during two wars, two long occupations by an armed people that believes in knocking down bowling pins, and with countless other enemies?

But this liberating habit saved me. By a hairbreadth, it is true, and I resisted the despair that seemed sure to leave me with nothing at all. Mediocrities, boring women, some brute I could have gotten rid of a hundred times over—I kept them around for the session with the sack.

THE SAUSAGE CELLAR

I love to knead.

I get hold of a field marshal and grind him up so fine that he loses half his senses, he loses his nose that he thought really had flair and even his hand that he can't raise to his cap any more even if a whole army saluted him.

Yes, through a series of grindings, I reduce him, I reduce him—a sausage unable to do anything from now on.

And I don't limit myself to field marshals. In my cellar I have lots of sausages that were once important people supposedly out of my reach.

But my infallible instinct for jubilation triumphed over these obstacles.

If they act up after that, it's really no fault of mine. They could not have been mixed and ground any more than they were. I've been told that some of them are still moving about. It's printed in the papers. Is this real? How could it be? They're rolled up. The rest is the tail end of a phenomenon, the kind that one might encounter in nature, a sort of mystery comparable to reflections and exhalations whose importance should not be exaggerated. No, absolutely not.

In my cellar they lie, in deep silence.

THE MAN-SLING

I also have my man-sling. You can shoot them far, very far. You have to know how to deal with them.

And yet it's hard to shoot them far enough. To tell the truth, you never can shoot them far enough. They come back to you forty years later sometimes, just when you thought you could breathe easy at last, whereas they're the ones who breathe easy, coming back with the measured step of a man who is in no hurry, who was still there five minutes ago, who was going to come right back.

ON THE SPIT

A sling for some, a spit for others… and it's so natural. Hard to keep your chair. The guests are eating. You have to make room. New ones are coming in. Where to put the earlier ones. Where to put them? You put them on the spit.

Driven from chair to chair, from spot to spot, they find themselves in front of the fireplace. You push them in and *there!* on to the spit!

There's no lack of naturalness here. Nothing to complain about, as far as naturalness is concerned.

That's why no one resists. Sucked in gently, but irresistibly, they slip toward the warm opening. The idea of resisting does not really come into their minds. They don't fight back, they have been struck by the obvious.

A RECOMMENDED INSTRUMENT: APARTMENT THUNDER

Instead of destroying all the kids in the neighborhood, it's more peaceful to install thunder in the apartment, or in the room the peace-rending shouts are coming from.

You need great noise willpower (some experience with symphony orchestras can put you on the right track). As soon as it starts up, it goes really smoothly and can last a long time and not one single shout filters through the dam of sound. It's better not to use a brass band, as even imaginary brass causes headaches. And in that case, why go to so much trouble?

With thunder, as long as it's nice and manageable, you should be able to stand having a bunch of screaming kids at recess nearby for an hour and a half. Longer is hard.

You're better off moving.

Besides, you should always avoid schools. Twenty years later, they can still stir up memories.

THE SLAPPING-GUN

As one might expect, it was in the course of family life that I produced the slapping-gun (machine-gun model). I produced it without thinking about it. Suddenly my anger exploded from my hand, like a wind-filled glove, like two, three, four, ten gloves, gloves of emanations shooting out of my fingertips, racing toward the goal, toward the hateful head that they reached immediately.

This repeated discharge of the hand was astonishing. It was really not just a slap, or two slaps. I am naturally rather reserved and only let myself go by falling off a high cliff of rage.

A veritable ejaculation of slaps, an ejaculation in cascades and jolts, while my hand remained absolutely motionless.

That day, I touched upon magic.

A sensitive man might have seen something. A sort of electric shadow spurting spasmodically from the end of my hand, coming together and forming again in *an instant*.

To be quite frank, the cousin who had laughed at me had just opened the door and gone out when I suddenly realized the shame of the offense and responded *by delayed action* with a volley of slaps that, truly, *escaped* from my hand.

I had discovered the slapping-gun, if I may say so—but nothing says it better.

From then on I couldn't see that phony any more without slaps like wasps shooting from my hand to her.

This discovery was certainly worth being forced to sit through her hateful talk. That is why I sometimes recommend tolerance in the family.

THE UNFINISHED

Face not saying not playing
not saying yes, not no.
Monster.
Dark space.
Face
reaching,
moving,
passing,
slowing, budding toward us...
Lost face.

Besides, like all Meidosemmas, all she thinks about is getting into Confetti Palace.

.   .   .

The clock that strikes the passions in the souls of Meidosems awakes. Its time accelerates. The surrounding world is hurrying, rushing toward its fate, a fate suddenly clear now.

The stick churning the bottom bangs around violently, and the spasmodic knife attacks.

.   .   .

Can thirty-four spears all tangled together make up a living being? Yes, a Meidosem. A suffering Meidosem, a Meidosem who doesn't know what to do with himself, who doesn't know what posture to take, how to face up to things, who doesn't know anything but being a Meidosem.

They have destroyed his ''one.''

But he's not beaten yet. The spears there, to be used against so many enemies... first he thrust them through his own body.

But he's not beaten yet.

.   .   .

They take the shape of bubbles to dream, they take the shape of lianas to be deeply moved.

Leaning against a wall, a wall no one will ever see again, a shape made of a long rope. Entwining with itself.

That's all. It's a Meidosemma.

And she waits, slightly sunk in, but far less than any freestanding bunch of ropes her size.

She waits.

Days, years, come now! She is waiting.

.   .   .

On her long, delicate, curved legs, a Meidosemma, tall, graceful.

Dream of victorious races, soul full of regrets and plans, a real soul.

And frantically she darts forward into a space that drinks her up, indifferently.

.   .   .

Hundreds of threads shaken by electric spasms. With this uncertain latticework for a face, the anxious Meidosem tries to look calmly at the massive world surrounding him.

It is with this that he will respond to the world, as a shivering little bell responds.

Meanwhile, shaken by calls, struck, and struck again, and called again and again, he longs for a Sunday, a real Sunday, which has never come yet.

.   .   .

In ice, the fibers of his nerves are in ice.

Their brief stroll through it stabbed by violent twinges, by steel along the path back to the cold of Nothingness.

Head bursting open, bones rotting. And his flesh... who can still talk of flesh? Who still expects flesh?

Still, he is alive.

The clock rolls on, time stops. Trapped in the narrow passage of the tragedy.

He doesn't have to run into it, he's in it...

The marble is sweating, the afternoon darkens.

Still, he is alive...

.   .   .

A mange of sparks makes a skull itch painfully. It's a Meidosem. It's a running pain. It's a rolling leak. It's the cripple of air floundering desperately about. Is there no help for him?

No.

.   .   .

They like him and yet...

He sleeps on horseback in his immense suffering. His road is the circular horizon and the breached Tower of the astronomical sky.

They like him. His unseen horizon enlarges the other Meidosems, who say: "What's going on? What is it?... " and feel something strange, something enlarging, as he approaches.

And yet he sleeps on horseback in his immense suffering...

.   .   .

Infinite are the passages from fog to flesh in Meidosem country...

.   .   .

Flows of affection, of infection, flows from suffering behind the lines, bitter caramel of the past, stalagmites slowly formed: he walks with these flows, he apprehends with them, spongy limbs dripping from his head, limbs pierced by a thousand little transversal flows from extravasated blood, bursting the arterioles, but it's not blood, it's the blood of memories, of the pierced soul, from the delicate central chamber, struggling in the packing, it's the reddened water of useless memory flowing aimlessly but not purposelessly in its small passages leaking all over—minuscule, multiple punctures.

A Meidosem bursts. A thousand small veins of his faith in himself burst. He falls into new darkness again and again, into new ponds.

Oh, how hard it is to walk like this...

.　　.　　.

Behold the face in chains.

The chain-mail chaplet holds him by the eyes, wraps around his neck, falls down, rips out, makes him suffer from the weight of the mail combined with the weight of slavery.

The long shadow he casts in front of him speaks volumes about this.

Time! time! All the time you have, the time you would have had...

.　　.　　.

Tall, tall Meidosem, but not so very tall, really, if you look at his head. Meidosem with a charred face.

So, what burned you like that, darkie?

Was it yesterday? No, it was today. Every today.

And that face has a grudge against the world.

Charred as it is, isn't that natural?

.　　.　　.

With very little support, always very little support, there they are again, their spines (are they even spines?) showing through the ectoplasm of their being.

They probably won't go far.

Yes they will!—clamped to their weakness, strong in a sense because of it, invincible even...

.　　.　　.

From an air carriage, or from a small, unknown land hidden in some ionosphere, a little band of Meidosems has descended, naked, some of them hanging on to parachutes, others to a few strings or a falling lump of earth, others not hanging on to anything at all.

Light, with their fibers and threads flowing out behind them, these Meidosems came down at a slant (some drifting, no doubt) with their hands at rest, pressed against their legs.

If they're going to fall, they would rather fall prudently, in a slight drift.

No, not worrying, coming down calm, calm, with their limbs stretched out. No second thoughts. No need to worry yet. They still have a few seconds left before the smash.

.   .   .

And here are a few of the places where Meidosems live, truly strange places—strange that they should agree to live there.

.   .   .

To be honest, they usually live in concentration camps.

Now, these Meidosems don't have to live in those concentration camps. But they're worried about how they would live if they were no longer in them. They are afraid that outside, they would get bored. They are beaten, they are battered, they are tortured. But they are afraid that outside, they would get bored.

.   .   .

Here a plain swells up wildly toward the Meidosem who stops, stupefied, dropping his work (although he was quite engrossed in it), dropping everything to obey the fatal fascination.

The rubber bands of his being are stretching taut, swelling out.

Perhaps this is not as dangerous as one might think.

.   .   .

Heads pop out through broken ceilings—avid faces, curious, dismayed, Meidosem faces.

Through fireplaces, through cracks, through everything that can accommodate the seeing apparatus.

In the house, in the room, from between the lath-work (and there are hundreds of little laths per door) Meidosems appear, Meidosems disappear, reappear, redisappear.

Prying Meidosems, quickly here, quickly gone...

.   .   .

Wings without heads, without birds, wings pure of bodies are flying toward a solar sky, not brilliant yet, but fighting hard for brilliance, riddling its way through the empyrean like a cannon shell of future bliss.

Silence. Takeoffs.

What the Meidosems have longed for so much, at last they have reached it. There they are.

(1948)

OLD AGE OF POLLAGORAS

uld really like to know why I always

w the horse whose bridle I am holding.

With age, says Pollagoras, I have become like a field on which a battle was fought, a battle centuries ago, a battle yesterday, a field of many battles.

Dead men, never quite dead, wander silently around or lie at rest. It's as if they have lost the will to win.

But suddenly they burst into motion, those who are lying down get up and attack, armed to the teeth. They have just encountered the ghost of a former enemy who—shaken—suddenly charges feverishly forward, ready with his parry, forcing my surprised heart to quicken its beat in my chest and in my sullen being, which reluctantly comes to life.

They fight their battles among themselves, without ever interfering with the previous ones, or with the next ones, whose unknown, peaceful heroes go walking about until they in turn encounter their contemporary enemy, straighten up in a flash and charge irresistibly forward into combat.

So it is, says Pollagoras, that I am old, through this accumulation.

Cluttered with battles already fought, a clock of more and more numerous scenes that *strike,* while I would like to be elsewhere.

And so, like a manor abandoned to poltergeists, I live without living, a place haunted by thoughts that interest me no longer, although they still work themselves into a frenzy and renew themselves, feverishly emptying themselves out in a way that I am impotent to paralyze.

Wisdom has not come, says Pollagoras. The Word is increasingly strangled, but wisdom has not come.

All my life long, like a seismographic needle, my awareness has gone through me without charting me, groped around me without forming me.

At the dawn of old age, before the plain of Death, I am still seeking, still seeking, says Pollagoras, the little far-off wall in my childhood by my pride erected, while with soft weapons and a tiny shield I walked around between the cliffs of shadowy adults.

Little wall that I built, thinking I had done the right thing, thinking I had done a marvelous thing, to put myself in a fortress immovable. Little wall, too solid, built by my resistance.

And it is not the only one.

How many did I cement up in the time of my mad defense, in my frightened years! I have to search them out now, all of them, covered with living fibers.

As my life drains away with only a trickle left, it avidly seeks the rapids still being wasted, and the magnificent work of the brave little builder will have to be ruined for the benefit of the old miser, still hanging on to life.

(1949)

Untitled, 1939. Courtesy of the Musée
National d'Art Moderne, Paris. © 1992
ARS, N.Y. / ADAGP, Paris.

Repos dans le malheur, 1945. Courtesy of
the Musée National d'Art Moderne, Paris.
© 1992 ARS, N.Y. / ADAGP, Paris.

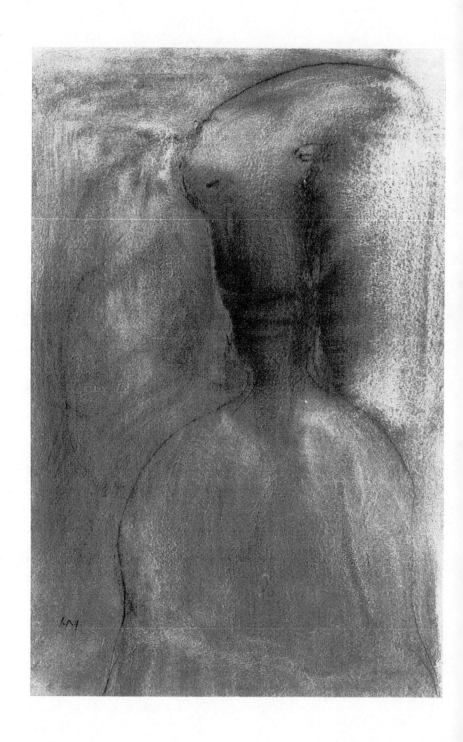

Untitled, ca. 1946–1948. Courtesy of
the Musée National d'Art Moderne, Paris.
© 1992 ARS, N.Y. / ADAGP, Paris.

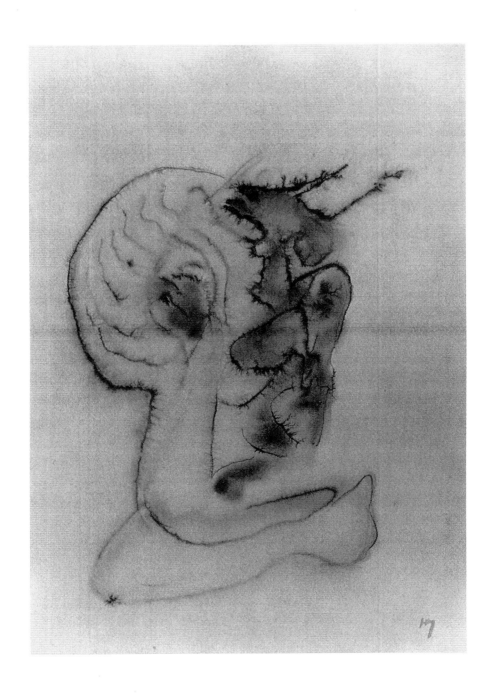

Untitled, 1948. Courtesy of the Solomon
R. Guggenheim Museum, New York.
© 1992 ARS, N.Y. / ADAGP, Paris.

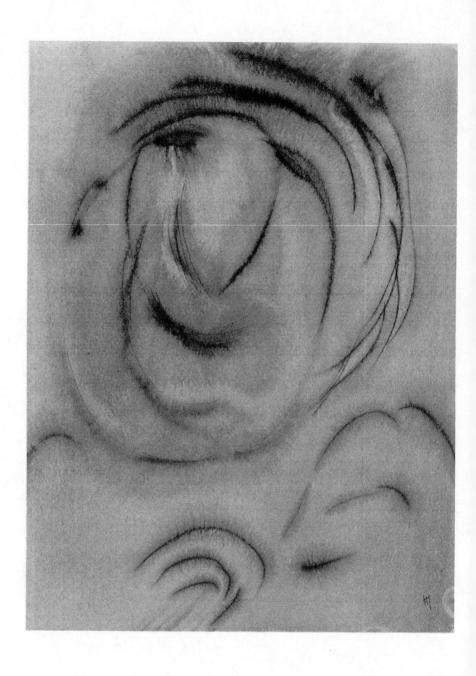

Figure jaune, 1948. Courtesy of the Musée
National d'Art Moderne, Paris. © 1992
ARS, N.Y. / ADAGP, Paris.

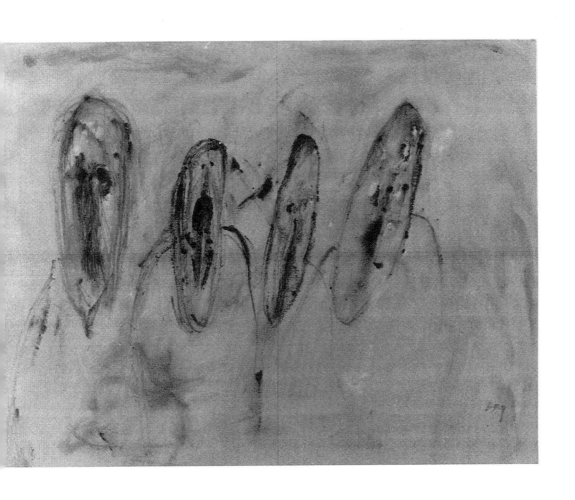

Untitled, 1949. Courtesy of the Musée
National d'Art Moderne, Paris. © 1992
ARS, N.Y. / ADAGP, Paris.

Untitled, 1955–1956. Courtesy of the
Musée National d'Art Moderne, Paris.
© 1992 ARS, N.Y. / ADAGP, Paris.

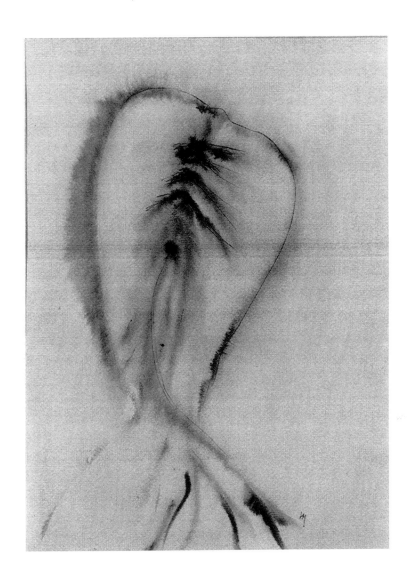

Tête bleue, 1963–1964. Courtesy of the
Musée National d'Art Moderne, Paris.
© 1992 ARS, N.Y. / ADAGP, Paris.

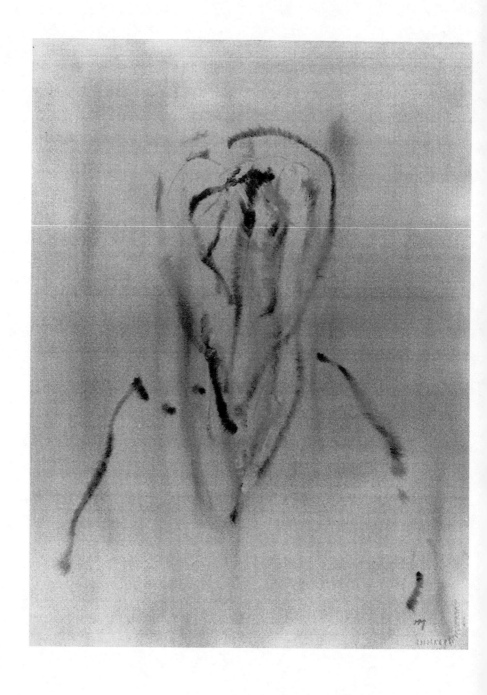

Untitled, 1965. Courtesy of the Solomon
R. Guggenheim Museum, New York.
© 1992 ARS, N.Y. / ADAGP, Paris.

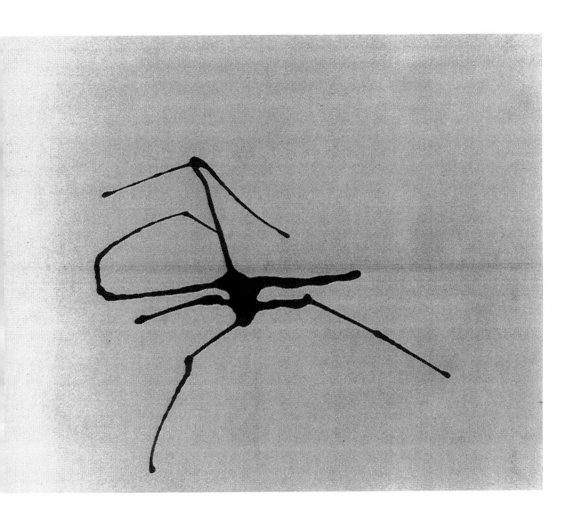

Untitled, 1954. Courtesy of the Musée
National d'Art Moderne, Paris. © 1992
ARS, N.Y. / ADAGP, Paris.

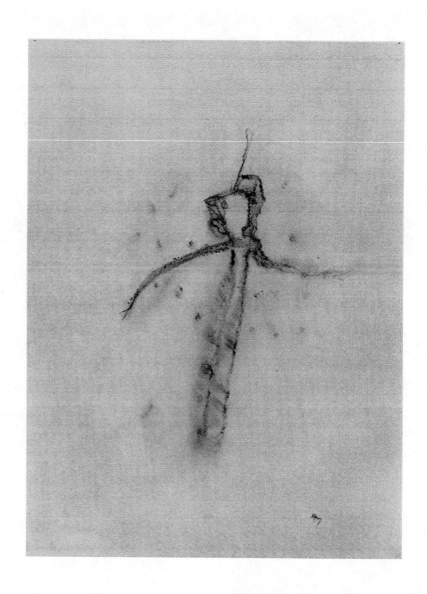

Untitled, no date. Courtesy of the
Solomon R. Guggenheim Museum,
New York. © 1992 ARS, N.Y. / ADAGP,
Paris.

Untitled, 1970. Courtesy of the Solomon
R. Guggenheim Museum, New York.
© 1992 ARS, N.Y. / ADAGP, Paris.

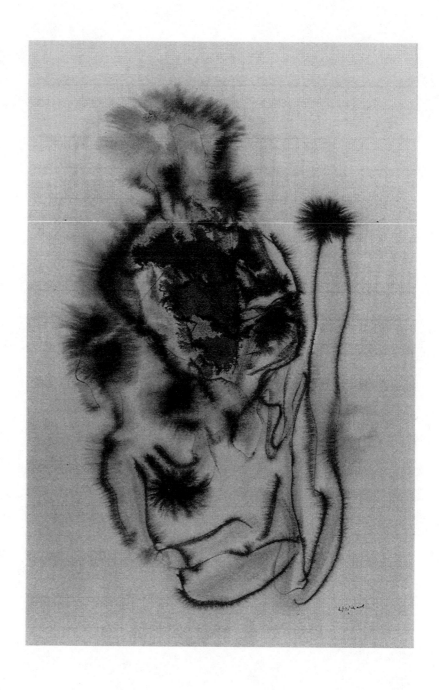

Untitled, ca. 1955. Courtesy of the
Musée National d'Art Moderne, Paris.
© 1992 ARS, N.Y. / ADAGP, Paris.

Untitled, 1938. Courtesy of the Solomon
R. Guggenheim Museum, New York.
© 1992 ARS, N.Y. / ADAGP, Paris.

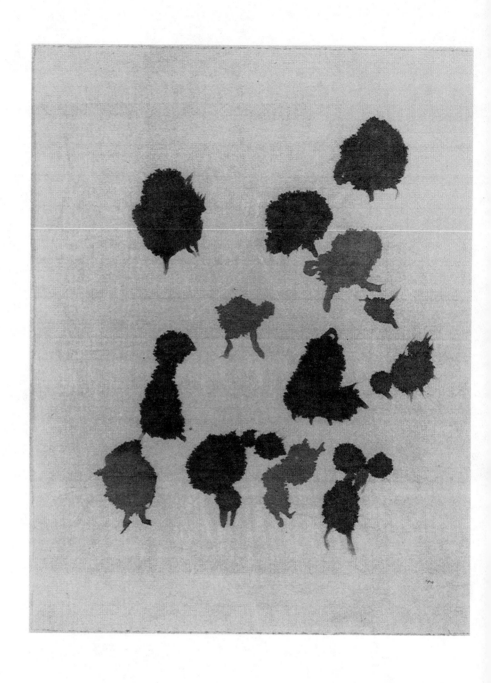

Taches, no date. Courtesy of the Musée
National d'Art Moderne, Paris. © 1992
ARS, N.Y. / ADAGP, Paris.

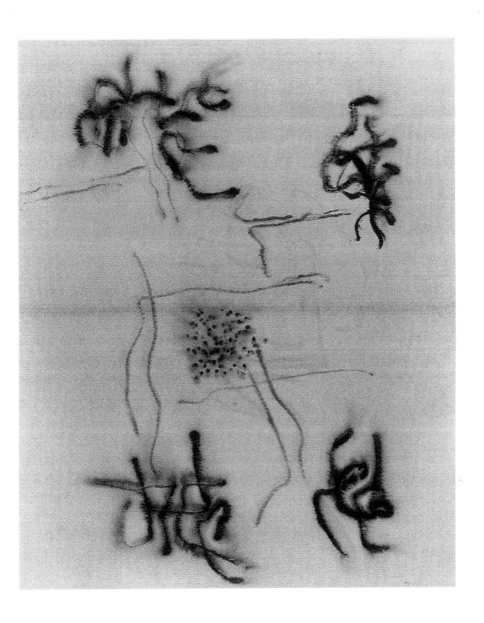

Untitled, 1963. Courtesy of the Musée
National d'Art Moderne, Paris. © 1992
ARS, N.Y. / ADAGP, Paris.

Untitled, 1967. Courtesy of the Solomon
R. Guggenheim Museum, New York.
© 1992 ARS, N.Y. / ADAGP, Paris.

Untitled, 1975. Courtesy of the Solomon
R. Guggenheim Museum, New York.
© 1992 ARS, N.Y. / ADAGP, Paris.

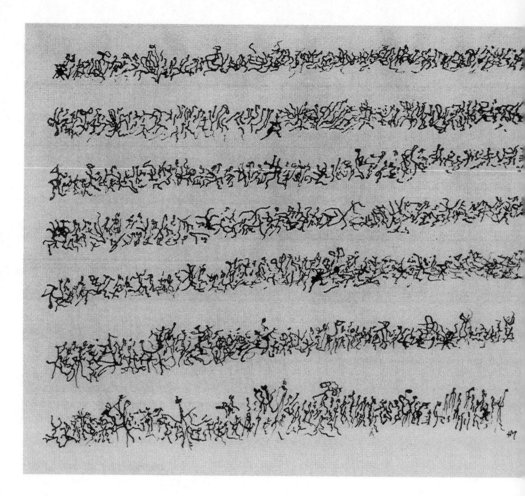

Untitled, 1962. Courtesy of the Musée
National d'Art Moderne, Paris. © 1992
ARS, N.Y. / ADAGP, Paris.

Untitled, 1959. Courtesy of the Musée
National d'Art Moderne, Paris. © 1992
ARS, N.Y. / ADAGP, Paris.

(*above*) Untitled, June 1960. Courtesy
of the Solomon R. Guggenheim Museum,
New York. © 1992 ARS, N.Y. / ADAGP,
Paris.

(*opposite, top*) Drawing, 1962. Courtesy of
the Musée National d'Art Moderne, Paris.
© 1992 ARS, N.Y. / ADAGP, Paris.

(*opposite, bottom*) Untitled, 1962. Courtesy
of the Solomon R. Guggenheim Museum,
New York. © 1992 ARS, N.Y. / ADAGP,
Paris.

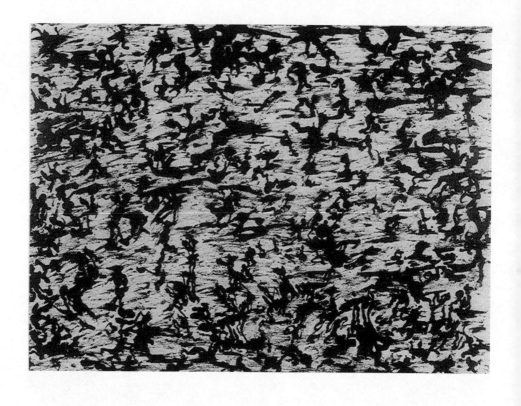

(*opposite, top*) *Champs de bataille*, 1963.
Courtesy of the Musée National d'Art
Moderne, Paris. © 1992 ARS, N.Y. /
ADAGP, Paris.

(*opposite, bottom*) *Mouvement II*, no date.
Courtesy of the Musée National d'Art
Moderne, Paris. © 1992 ARS, N.Y. /
ADAGP, Paris.

(*above*) *Mouvement III*, 1965. Courtesy of
the Musée National d'Art Moderne, Paris.
© 1992 ARS, N.Y. / ADAGP, Paris.

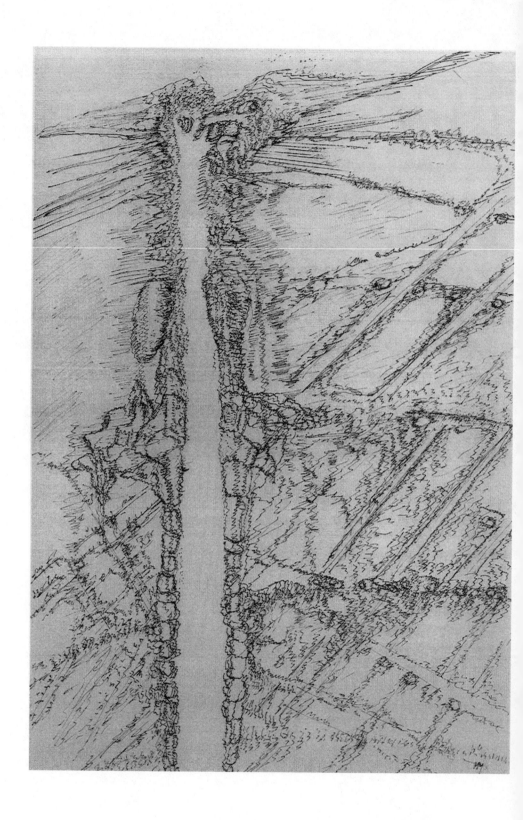

Mescaline drawing, 1958. Courtesy of
the Solomon R. Guggenheim Museum,
New York. © 1992 ARS, N.Y. / ADAGP,
Paris.

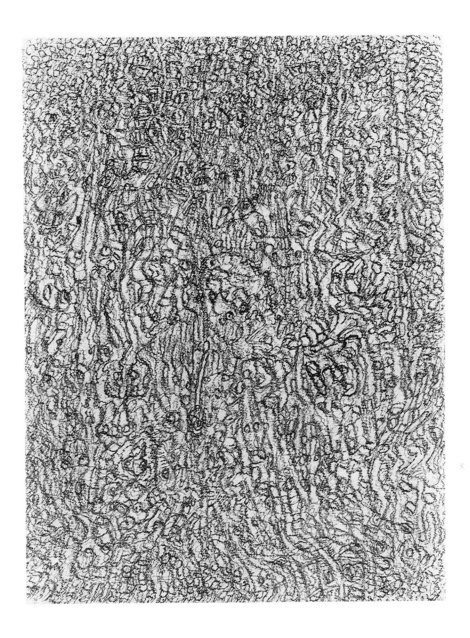

Mescaline drawing, 1959. Courtesy of
the Musée National d'Art Moderne, Paris.
© 1992 ARS, N.Y. / ADAGP, Paris.

Arborescences intérieures, 1962–1964.
Courtesy of the Musée National d'Art
Moderne, Paris. © 1992 ARS, N.Y. /
ADAGP, Paris.

FACING

THE

LOCKS

Michaux's wife died, accidentally, "as a result of atrocious burns," in 1948; from 1951 to 1953, Michaux says he "writes less and less, paints more." Yet *Facing the Locks* (1954) is one of his strongest collections of writing. It contains the incantatory "Poetry for Power," two parts malediction-exorcism, one part chant of salvation here and now; pages of aphorisms ("Slices of Knowledge"); and the amazing "Space of the Shadows" (1952). On one level, this long prose poem reflects the death of his wife: it is tempting to think that she—or Michaux's imagining of her on the Other Side—is the speaker in the poem. It is also a representation of the imagination's attempt to exist under the worst possible conditions, and of the self's attempt to survive in absolute solitude and eternal danger. "Space of the Shadows" continues the vision of infinitely continuing imprisonment and suffering concisely expressed ten years earlier in "Labyrinth" (*Ordeals, Exorcisms*) and elsewhere; moreover, it foreshadows the psychic dangers of his experimentation with drugs—an adventure Michaux was to pursue over the next decade.

(*Face aux verrous*, Gallimard, 1954, revised edition, 1967)

POETRY FOR POWER

I. I AM ROWING

I have cursed your forehead your belly your life
I have cursed the streets your steps plod through
The things your hands pick up
I have cursed the inside of your dreams

I have set a puddle in your eye that can't see any more
An insect in your ear that can't hear any more
A sponge in your brain that can't understand any more

I have frozen you in the soul of your body
Iced you in the depths of your life
The air you breathe suffocates you
The air you breathe has the air of a cellar
Is an air that has already been exhaled
been puffed out by hyenas
The dung of this air is something no one can breathe

Your skin is damp all over
Your skin sweats out waters of the great fear
Your armpits reek far and wide of the crypt

Animals stop dead as you pass
Dogs howl at night, their heads raised toward your house
You can't run away
You can't muster the strength of an ant to the tip of your feet
Your fatigue makes a lead stump in your body
Your fatigue is a long caravan
Your fatigue stretches out to the country of Nan
Your fatigue is inexpressible

Your mouth bites you
Your nails scratch you
No longer yours, your wife
No longer yours, your brother
The sole of his foot bitten by an angry snake

Someone has slobbered on your descendants
Someone has slobbered on the laugh of your little girl
Someone has walked slobbering by the face of your domain

The world moves away from you

I am rowing
I am rowing
I am rowing against your life
I am rowing
I split into countless rowers
To row more strongly against you

You fall into blurriness
You are out of breath
You get tired before the slightest effort

I row
I row
I row

You go off drunk, tied to the tail of a mule
Drunkenness like a huge umbrella that darkens the sky
And assembles the flies
Dizzy drunkenness of the semicircular canals
Unnoticed beginnings of hemiplegia
Drunkenness no longer leaves you
Lays you out to the left
Lays you out to the right

Lays you out on the stony ground of the path

I row

I row

I am rowing against your days

You enter the house of suffering

I row

I row

On a black blindfold your actions are recorded

On the great white eye of a one-eyed horse your future is rolling

I AM ROWING

Effective as coitus with a virgin girl
Effective
Effective as the absence of wells in the desert
Effective is my action
Effective

Effective as the traitor who stands apart surrounded by his men ready to kill
Effective as the night for hiding objects
Effective as the goat for producing kids
Tiny, tiny, heartbroken already
Effective as the viper

Effective as a sharpened knife to make a wound
As rust and urine to keep it going
As shaking, falls and bangs to make it wider
Effective is my action

Effective as the scornful smile for raising an ocean of hate in the breast of the scorned
    man, an ocean that will never dry up
Effective as the desert for dehydrating bodies and toughening souls
Effective as the jaws of a hyena for chewing the unprotected limbs of corpses
EFFECTIVE
Effective is my action

III. TO ACT, I COME

Opening the door inside you, I have entered
To act, I come
I am here
I support you
You are no longer abandoned
You are no longer in difficulty
Their strings untied, your difficulties fall
The nightmare that left you haggard is no more
I am shouldering you
With me you place
Your foot on the first step of the endless stairway
Which carries you
Which brings you up
Which fulfills you

I appease you
I am spreading out sheets of peace in you
I am soothing the child of your dream
Surge
Surge in fronds on the circle of images around the frightened woman
Surge on the snows of her paleness
Surge on her hearth... and the fire lights up again

TO ACT, I COME
Your thoughts of thrust are supported
Your thoughts of failure, weakened
My strength is in your body, slipped inside
...and your face, losing its wrinkles, is refreshed
Sickness no longer makes its way in you
Fever leaves you

The peace of vaults
The peace of flowering prairies
Peace comes back into you

In the name of the highest number, I am helping you
Like a smoking crater
All the heaviness rises off your overburdened shoulders
The wicked heads around you
Venomous observers of the miseries of the weak
Can see you no longer
Exist no longer

A crew of reinforcements
In mystery and a deep line
Like an undersea wake
Like a bass chant
I have come
This chant takes you
This chant raises you up
This chant is animated by many streams
This chant is fed by a calmed Niagara
This chant is entirely for you

No more pincers
No more dark shadows
No more fears
There is no more trace of them
There is no need to have them
Where pain was, is cotton
Where scattering was, is solder
Where infection was, is new blood
Where locks were is open sea
The carrying sea and the fullness of you
Intact, like an egg of ivory.

I have bathed the face of your future.

AFTERWORD: POWERS and MALEDICTIONS (excerpts)

(*Poetry for Power* was first published as a small book in 1949 with a frontispiece by Michaux; in 1950, he published a "Note on Maledictions" as an Afterword to it in *Les Cahiers de la Pléiade*. This essay and "Powers" (1958), both collected in *Passages*, contain essentially the same reflections on the process of making "power poetry." As the later essay seems a lot clearer to me, I have translated it in full, below, and included important excerpts from the "Note on Maledictions" in the footnotes. Both essays complement Michaux's Preface to *Ordeals, Exorcisms*.—D.B.)

.

POWERS

As one must be able to lose the dangerous comfort of happiness, one must be able to lose some of one's friends; but enemies must be kept. Precious!

The airplane makes speed out of excess pressure. The problem is not to calm this pressure down, but to place it. To transform what is wrong, the enemy, the irritating situation, hostile surroundings, *into energy*.

Far from wasting the eruption of anger on the often quite ordinary individual who seems to be its cause, it is important, on the contrary, to cut one's connections to him as much as possible, to float inside the anger, take pleasure in it, to grow, intensify in it.[a] This I did from my earliest times. But a few years ago, living in a country that has for thousands of years been the land of magic, where paintings and sculptures give commandments, where words spoken or carved in stone exert some control over the living, the dead and the gods, one day when I had been extremely frustrated, I had the inspiration of directing my anger (instead of letting it raise me and shake me up in a disorderly way) and placing it on some

---

[a]   "   I will do such things—
what they are, yet I know not, but they shall be
the terrors of the earth,"
says King Lear. Immensity of the surge of rage, out of all proportion to the push-button event. Such an excessively vast, unbearable force with no gland for it and thus no outlet either, condemned to be platonic (but it will drive you mad if you don't do anything)—you have to *aim* it.

character (who actually happened to be largely responsible for it) and this repeatedly, insistently, incessantly. I then felt my anger as matter, as a resistant fluid, as a weapon, while I was thrust into action and reinventing, almost without realizing it, the verbal instrument of anger—that is, the malediction.[b]

But I constantly had to keep putting my anger back on the target, which was not exactly easy, to my surprise. The man I thought I hated so much tended to become blurry. Insufficiently hateful, he did not measure up to my total rage, which wanted a more exciting target, an ideal target. I therefore modified him, but not too much, and his situation, too. It was him and it was not him. It was better than he was.[c] Perhaps I had also been afraid of striking him a fatal blow, for it is hard to believe that when using such a warlike battering ram nothing is going to happen.

This is what "I Am Rowing" and "Across Oceans and Desert" are about: two attacks, which were called poems, two emphatic poems.[d]

Some time after that, when I was with a person who was very dear to me and who slowly, too slowly, was recovering from the recurrence of a serious illness, I suddenly said to myself: "I must do something. If words really have effective power, if the inner force of intense feeling can be directed, I must succeed right here, I must succeed in working on that force—and work a cure."

As I soon saw—and saw better, as I progressed—a love poem could not possibly be appropriate here, the kind of poem that is no doubt moving but more surely still a self-indulgent return to lovesickness, to the incomparable disturbance brought by the loved one: no, that was not the kind of thing that would *have power*. What was needed was a poem all for her, an action-poem, to make her over again, remodel her in the shape of health according to the real desires of her nature, now inhibited by illness. An act of healing, not of awestruck love, still less of underlying desire, still less of pity... and I constantly had to avoid those temptations, those paths, in order to remain "devoted" to her.

That is what the third poem, "To Act, I Come" is about.

---

[b]Maledictions and particularly chain maledictions—and reading them is almost always quite bracing—tend toward something other than destruction; they tend to create a motor. Not to wound or eliminate the enemy, but by opposing the enemy, to create in oneself the Dragon of Fire
[c]Once the individual who was darkening the whole horizon of your angry being has become quite pale and restricted to himself, he really is no longer up to the *superhate* you were reveling in

Besides, this experience with targets will quickly show you that there is no perfect target No one is perfectly suitable for it, ideally hateable He always falls far short of it (This is a surprise) He falls short and he has too much. He has roots in several other people, he has blood that is not only his and the salt of circumstances He has his genus linked to an era, to a whole hateful world

So you are naturally driven to modify the character You will make him worse, thus making him better for your purposes
[d]As for the magic of malediction, it is, above all, hammering, hammering, hammering

Although this gift was insufficient, it does not seem to me an empty gesture. It had its effect. I am not speaking of the cure that did occur—although neither miraculously nor suddenly. Apparently I was not a healer of bodies. But there were other effects in her, and in me a kind of cure,[c] the beginning of a new union between us.

I have something to say about the act in itself.

We are terribly mixed, dispersed. Enormous, surprising are the obstacles we encounter even if all we can do is make a poem with a direction, a poem we would like to be truly beneficent, effective.

A thought, a thought-feeling generates other thoughts, impulses, sometimes actions and a short-lived general transformation. But, without a certain extreme—extreme concentration—there is no direct, massive, permanent, magical action of that thought on the thinker. Intensity, intensity, intensity in unity, is absolutely indispensable. There is a certain threshold beyond which, but *not before,* a thought-feeling counts, counts differently, counts genuinely and *takes on power.* It may even spread out in all directions...

[c]Effects on oneself You are cleansed, quite differently than you would be through confession or the analysis of psychological causes You haven't wrung out your sponge and you haven't seen the crumbling of your edifice You have done a job

How much less hateful men would be if every one of them did not wear a face.

.　.　.

At the age of eight, I still dreamed of being granted plant status.

.　.　.

"Do come in," said the shark, and he ate him. The shark was a man-eater, but the era was polite.

.　.　.

Inside the melon, a heart was beating.

.　.　.

You can't see the commas between the houses, which is what makes reading them so difficult and walking through the streets so tedious.

The sentence in the cities is interminable. But it is fascinating, and the countryside is deserted by people who were once its sturdy farmers and now want to see for themselves the admirably tricky text that everyone is talking about, so hard to follow, most often impossible.

Which is, however, what these stubborn workers try to do, walking ceaselessly, lapping up the diseases of the sewers and the leprous facades as they go by, rather than the still elusive meaning: that still escapes them. Groggy with poverty and fatigue, they wander by the store windows, occasionally losing their goal, but never their quest… and that's the end of our fine countryside!

.　　.　　.

Budding—watch out! Instead, write for the short circuit.

.　　.　　.

Horse-dream: Horse, having eaten its wagon, contemplating the horizon.

.　　.　　.

Ears in humans aren't defended very well. It seems no plans were made for neighbors.

.　　.　　.

My life: dragging a baby carriage around under water. Those born tired will know what I mean.

.　　.　　.

Without answering, the Tibetan took out his storm-calling horn and we were thoroughly drenched under great flashes of lightning.

.　　.　　.

In Siam they use the tiger's docility in following his cruel instincts to lure him on to a bleating lamb over a deep ditch in which he will then perish, fuming with rage at having stupidly let himself be found out by little cowardly bastards so inferior to him in every way.

·   ·   ·

Everything is not hard in the crocodile. His lungs are spongy, and he dreams at the water's edge.

·   ·   ·

Swallow the rivets, the cruiser falls apart and the water is calm once again.

·   ·   ·

Every century has its high mass. What's this one waiting for to set up a grandiose celebration of disgust?

·   ·   ·

The bird's ravings have no interest for the tree.

·   ·   ·

In my considerable experience, says Sunyair, the Universe is a big, complicated, superficial business, which appears in one part of the day, almost always the same one, and apparently so well hooked on, in those moments, that it is called "reality."

Yes, it seems coherent, but only for a short time, and it quickly goes tumbling down again into the indifferent abyss.

This being the case, we don't need much urging to sleep like a log.

·   ·   ·

The temptation to sleep in the bed of one's mother and kill one's father constitutes the first Sphinx trap of life, which we must be able to answer with our brains hardly formed yet—a trap into which sickly natures condemned forever to misjudge obstacles and overestimate pleasures infallibly fall. The test treacherously presented by nature will be examined later, but the sign that they'll always be fascinatable can be seen already: and in fact fifteen, twenty years later there they are, worried, looking around behind them instead of in front, wretchedly confessing themselves to snooping strangers whose paralyzed prey they become, like children, like children—just as we expected.

.   .   .

He who hides his madman dies voiceless.

.   .   .

In this century, the phallus is becoming dogmatic.

.   .   .

Cauldron of thoughts taking itself for a man.

.   .   .

Even if it's true, it's false.

.   .   .

He who sings in a group will put his brother in prison when asked.

.   .   .

He who leaves a trace, leaves a wound.

.   .   .

He who has rejected his demons badgers us to death with his angels.

.   .   .

When one watches seminarians—soon to be Doctors of Theology—play at kicking around a soccer ball, one is led to observe that it is apparently easier for the tiger to be totally, and in dignity, a tiger, than it is for man to be man.

.   .   .

After two hundred hours of uninterrupted questioning, Bossuet[1] would have confessed that he did not believe in God.

When he was proclaiming his faith, they should have replied "No." When he was proclaiming it again for the thousandth time, they should have demanded "More! More!" and made him recite all over again from the start, the whole thing without stopping, every time. They would have seen him collapse, confessing, once that layer in the self was reached in which no certainty remains.

He was lucky—that bishop so sure of himself—to have lived at a time when they didn't know how to question you thoroughly. He took advantage of this like the parvenu he was, he just wallowed in it.

Like us, however, he needed a lot of rest to get ideas. Otherwise, they would fly right out of his head, as they will so often do. Real thoughts, you know? If you can find them again, you're doing fine.

But you can read him over and over: he didn't have a clue.

.   .   .

The heart of a sensitive person suffers too much to love.

. . .

To understand, the intelligence must get itself dirty. Above all, before it even gets dirty, it has to get hurt.

. . .

It is all that is not man around him which makes man human. The greater the number of men on earth, the greater the exasperation.

. . .

He who wins with garbage puts on free and easy airs.

. . .

A scientist will get up more promptly to stop a door from swinging than to stop a murder going on silently in the next room. This is because he knows the price of silence, he who devotes his life to calculation and thought. Let those who are eternally distracted go for distractions…

. . .

Don't act proud. To breathe is already to be consenting. Other concessions will follow, each one fitting into the other. Here's one. Enough, let's stop it.

A FEW DAYS OF MY LIFE AMONG THE INSECTS

Although they were insects and not men, they immediately decided that I could not remain alone and offered me a caterpillar of my size with whom I could spend the night.

Unexpected, certainly, female caterpillars—but then everything was unexpected.

Her skin was a gorgeous blue-green velvet, with islands verging on orange, but cold and hairy.

Fascinated, I watched the undulating and perverse procession of chubby flesh progressing toward me, queen and caravan.

Monstrous company.

However, when she was close to touching me—my spirit like a man going to the guillotine but my body consenting, won over, panting—I gave myself up.

Then came almost twenty centers, muscular and avid, laying siege to my overwhelmed body.

Storm, a long storm, that night.

In the morning, when I awoke, hopelessly depressed but at the same time sated as I had never been in my life, it seemed to me I would never dare look anyone in the eye again, and at the same time, having finally reached bottom, I would henceforth be able to face all of nature, beasts, the earth.

It is true that the welcome I was given from then on was much freer and more natural than it had been the evening before.

What had appeared as *their* stiffness, their uneasiness with me, had thus been the effect of my reserve, my restraint. Some restraint! What man in the history of humanity had shown less?

Meanwhile life went on, the days distracting me from the fascinating nights.

Nevertheless, there was one morning full of annoyance, of nervous irritation, when... I caught her, wrung her neck (it wasn't easy, huge, all muscled!) and barely dead as she was—still twitching all over and dangerous to the point of biting reflexively—split open her head and ripped out a fragment of brain.

A succulent morsel, that I can compare to nothing so much as to coconut heart, although it is sweeter and lightly vanilla-flavored.

What was the chief going to say? Well, he simply inquired if I had found her good. He nonetheless appeared concerned, and, while offering me half a dozen replacements, added, as one who wishes to be obeyed: "For eating, take them absolutely virgin." For what reason, I do not know. He put six of them aside for me to this effect and I had one other at my disposal for the ecstasies of the night.

I was nonetheless trying to control myself, only eating between long intervals, fighting the dawning, insidious habit...

It seems there are quite a few of these sexed caterpillars—a surprising phenomenon. In the evenings I saw them, and at night I could hear them. The continual crushing in of my roof indicated the passage above me of animal masses tormented by desire...

We also went on manhunts. Degenerates!

In full flight, myself astride the thorax of a four-winged flyer, the insects gather them in by the head for you while they walk with that patient, measured, ridiculous gait of theirs, which reeks of hypocrisy.

Their children are still more savory. All we had to do was lean over and catch them, they have no strength at all. Skill, still less. Intelligence, just about none at all: short, squat, and unarmed, they wouldn't be able to use it if they had any.

Next to our territory, the land of the giant wasps and elephantine Custives was dangerous.

One day, a huge female ichneumon-fly pounced on me and I had an incredibly hard time avoiding her egg-bearing rod, which she absolutely wanted to sink into my kidneys so as to pour out her abundant eggs; I would then have had to nourish them for months at a time, fetid victorious larvae.

You may be sure I struggled. Although little accustomed to the rapier, still less to the staff—my only weapon at the moment—I relearned in a few minutes the little I had learned of feints, thrusts, twirls and parries. I'm sure my wrist would have been utterly wrung with fatigue, if the danger had not given me muscles of steel and terrific power-strokes… and constantly the sky spat that black-thoraxed demon back at me, so fast-moving…

At last, upon a sudden flight of Bidirics, this single-minded mother changed her plans and zoomed off in their wake, clearing my horizon and my life of the appalling menace…

SPACE OF THE SHADOWS

...The torture of the weak, much worse here than on earth...

How right they were to be full of fear, an unreasonable, unjustified fear (it seemed), for which they were interrogated, analyzed, sent through other terrible experiences, as if its origin, its object, its knot were in the Past, in the convulsive nest of wretched childhood memories, whereas it was in the Future, the far-off future, and their correct clairvoyance led them to sense it, terrifying, unspeakable, and waiting for them like icing on the cake, at the end!

At the instant of their arrival they'll understand, they understand. It was a mistake to think they could hope! No, their life has only been a reprieve. Here, for sure, they will be dominated. Impossible to keep their mask, to find a new one. Backs to the wall.

Woe, woe to them, as soon as they appear, hunted by the *Hawks of the Invisible.*

Sometimes the rumor spreads that we are visited[2] by transparent shadows.

Who knows? Who knows?

How can we find their traces when we have trouble finding ourselves?

The stinkers are settling in. They absolutely have to pollute, to stink up all the others. How can we resist? What can we do? It's an impregnation.

No messages are exchanged. But the horrible smell is contracted, we can't get rid of it, it contaminates the shadows, makes them members of the clan, of the repulsive clan. The rest is obvious, once we are impregnated. What "rest"? One would hardly dare tell, and who on earth would understand?

It is whispered about among the newly arrived dead that such unheard-of progress is being made by you, the living, or is just about to be made, that you will soon be able to help us, really help us.

Is it possible? We have been hoping for this such a long time... Is it possible? Do it quickly, then, quickly, but is it even desirable? We no longer know...

Watch out. You'll hear from me later. I have to watch out. The hyena-shadows are ceaselessly searching in the night.

.   .   .   .

.   .   .   .

.   .   .   .

...again I have to go away, have to cut myself short. A great Presence is being treacherous to me, pretending to protect me, watching me from a distance, spying on me, looking for an opening, for a moment of weakness.

.   .   .   .

.   .   .   .

Again I have only a minute.

I must beware of the J... Zone. I was carried into it by some unknown current. The shadows get caught in this jelly, which can, after a while, become highly concentrated in shadows, in despairing shadows.

No, I am not at this time the satellite of any soul. No, not yet... I struggle as I can, dully. My strength has not increased. The drainage continues. I am in the sea of weariness, my love.[3]

.   .   .   .

Oh, no, my encasing tube of strength has not returned.

The face of death has flattened all strength in me.

Perhaps I am blocking the currents of the Infinite. Surely I must be blocking them; that is the reason for my night.

Other souls ask themselves no questions. They get in the "right" position at the surge and they're carried off in a split second by the great invisible avalanche that is ceaselessly flowing toward the center, bearing away the ones who are ready.

.   .   .   .

No help, or help more dangerous than the lack of help. Who can we call? Everyone is an orphan here. As for me, I am unable to move forward; I'm always thrusting, though, and still more, hemorrhaging—a wound faithful to the knife.

Someone pushing me back, perhaps. An influence paralyzing me?

. . . .

Another interruption, and with such suffering, but it had to be. "She" was there.

I remain quiet about her. Her "n" level is greater than in other souls her age. That is suspicious. Probably her fault, at least partly. Perhaps she is a go-between. Behind her, the mixer of souls appears, always.

Emptiness! Emptiness!

Through the scrap of tortured soul I have left, I torment myself with this emptiness.

And as if that were not enough, excavating souls empty us still more as they move across space, toppling out our soft substances for their own good, either voluntarily or by the mere fact of their prehensile nature, killing with the innocence of hemlock. Of course they don't go so far as to *kill*—that's not it—but after they have been here it takes a long, long, time to build up what they took away.

What course would it be wise to take? What can we possibly say about that? Wise! There is nothing one can do. The fetus wants itself out. Always that which is hidden seeks, horribly, to see the day...

But I am wrong to speak. I am wrong to think. The blind man swears aloud in the echo chamber. Reckless of him! That is what he should not have done.

. . . .

I suffer too much from the lack of air. Maybe that's it. Oh! this emptiness. And just a while ago, passing through the flaccid spheres, that *tap* they performed on me...

When the clothes-moths in the room find a coat, what a party! What a party! And even in a shabby wardrobe-closet what a party! But if a curious person seized the moth, it would only be a bit of evanescent silk and his fingers would get all sandy from the soft corpse.

That's what we have become—moths, but with the party gone, too light in our smothered memories.

I know, I look back too much.

All of us are not like me. In times gone by, I met a man from far-off yesteryear. He said to me: "Peace is coming, sister. Nothing has happened to me for more than sixteen hundred years. This indefinite repetition of time has finally assured me—and I am highly skeptical by nature—of the *being* I was never able to be sure of on earth.

Now it is almost impossible for me to be skeptical. Surely there must be something other than accidents. I am almost certain of it. There must be being. Even I, most assuredly, must *be.*"

.   .   .   .

So many shadows! So many unbearable shadows!

And all these dead heavy, so very much heavier than I am, even though I am much too heavy, "weighing" despite myself toward the earth.

But do I really wish to? No, no, the infinite and the forerunner of the infinite is such a relief here that there is nothing, I swear to you, nothing in this world that would make me want to return to yours. We have not forgotten it, you know, cut up in slices, in unequal, surprising slices, a world of distraction, a root that is never watered.

Better to die again completely and be nothing, nothing at all.

.   .   .

Tomorrow, departure of essences.

.   .   .

.   .   .   .

The leaves splash the eyes of the tired traveler with light, but there are no leaves and no more eyes.

Slabs of gong sounds, hurling out lamps, lamps and rugs. That is the situation. More signs than supports, more passages than fibers, fog and alarm and anemia taking your claws away.

One part for the windows, one for the angels. Lost panoply, plugged-up artillery, gag on your face, useless hedgehog. That's it. That's really it, but it's none of those things that it is.

Fatigue with its thousands of suction-cups pulls the being back, far from its life of travel, far from memory, far from missions, far from renewal, that's it, but it is nothing of that which it is, saber-teeth without a tiger, starless night, corpseless death, bodiless life.

And the instant of definitive uprooting always behind us, like a huge black negative.

When I grazed *her* I grazed a deep pit of joy.

My feverish thoughts stopped short, pacified. But she said nothing, like a girl in the garden under her father's gaze. In the midst of millions of rustlings an arch formed over us... and then suddenly she had to go.

What was the obstacle? Who prevented us from being together?

Where can I find her?

We were speaking without speaking, flowing toward each other.

Where is she, that beneficent being?

They made her go away, as one might rip off a veil.

Punishing me? Punishing her? Punishing for what?

We played as children, we are punished as mothers.

I cut myself off. Do not be discouraged, still less angry. I had to run away, to hide behind the group of Halloos.

For a group of Lic... was going by out there. Just seeing them far off has already taken something away from me. And they can swoop in so dizzyingly.

A threat, the worst of all.

Through secret drainage, they can empty the soul they encounter of its *Kr* principle, and that makes it much more obedient, practically indifferent, and the slavers who follow them profit from this subjection even more than they do—unceasingly greedy, indefatigably vampires.

In what way, I'd really rather not say. We are not on the same side. I have to watch out. And even where I am, I am not yet on the side that *knows*.

It is so dense, here, everything, even the emptiness we move through... we are stretched out enormously, unhappy, a presence between the indefinite and the infinite, from abyss to abyss.

This density is already an answer. Don't ask too much of me; although I'm far from earth, I am still farther from the center.

That's why it is tempting to make ourselves screens, however transparent they may be. But how eagerly I would knock mine down, if you came at last.

I am calling you, oh, how I am calling you! This attraction must be for some higher reason, which escapes us.

I see you still hesitating a little between there and here. You must make up your mind, but I know that once you have made your decision *you* won't backslide as I do.

One must turn away from those on earth, it is necessary, but if I had done this, would I ever have found you?

No, memories rarely come back to us as supports, rather as wounds. The man loaded with bowling pins, make him walk between bowling pins, too—that's the way it goes here. That's all.

Even if he's strong, he who has seven rows of doubts does not hear the one who has but one row of doubts, even if he's weak. That is why conversations are so rare between you and us.

However deplorably we may suffer, we are rid of those millions of accidents that are your impressions. Although we still have enough to be deeply affected and even more deeply—but you'll see for yourself the astonishing change... and the astonishing permanence.

I can help you in a different way (a little), stealthily, for the law demands that you be harassed and not supported.

The high shades of R... not only try to take the living away from us, but even our access to the zone of refuge, a holiday zone where—back with our memories—we still think we can put some more wood on the fire.

Out of penitence we are pushed back into the F... Zones. There we can still shudder, but we can no longer pray. (Yes, pray, but it's hardly what you think. It is our only money, our only joy, our open hand.) There, we no longer have the right.

Angels with nematocysts are watching us, stinging without stimulating, or stimulating without illuminating.

. . . .

I can't show everything. Countless are the shadows, countless the categories of shadows.

Overrun by the unheard-of world of one's fellow shadows, infinite demonstration of our infinitesimalness, a marble in the midst of millions of warehouses of marbles.

Not well do we know them. They keep the twelve envelopes, for our twelve ignorances.

With some of them, it's like a pinch when you come near them. You'll never know anything more about it.

Near others, you flake with old memories.

Hiding out of insignificance, out of angelism, or one eclipsed by another? It's still a try at the same old thing.

Some can even be seen (the better to steal away) in suspension inside another… Otherwise, they might get too bored, perhaps? They are bored because they no longer secrete anything.

The luckiest only go through the white crisis. The rag illness follows. In that state, ready for anything, they would even agree to be convertible into each other—a state others can use to their advantage.

Swarms of weak ones, assembled through panic, swarms of weak ones form, destined to succumb still more unavoidably. The "hawks" are coming. You can see the signs of great despair. The whole colony is going to disappear.

Encumbered by unbearable postulants (gregarious, they'll do anything to provoke a kind reaction), we try to leave the first zone as soon as possible. False kindness reigns here, nauseating kindness, kindness like a placenta, like a net, like a parade under police surveillance, like a house of prostitution from which we will never escape.

Quickly, quickly, the running waters of unknown rivers slant you, carry you well away, if you know how to use them. Beyond, the messengers of the second death are lurking. How can we fight back? The law of domination-subordination cannot be flouted indefinitely. Nonetheless, I must try to go still further beyond…

Again hyena-shadows… , shades with a powerful ascendancy, hardly have you seen them than you are carried off in their wake.

As long as they don't carry me away before you get here…

Decapitated souls and all that can proliferate after death, from the aromatic to the stinking, from corollas to detritus. We are a meadow to be mowed, prevented from growing back, a meadow that is mowed down endlessly.

Impossible to raise ourselves even by the height of one idea. We no longer have hard knowledge in this gluey crypt.

Wounded souls THEY are constantly reopening, smashing open yet again for who knows what bone splinters that may still remain. And *they* have to go and find them, ripping out all relief.

Eternally gaping souls, when will we finally be closed?

The cry of intimate pain is our cry. But nobody moves. In a hospital, who turns around at a groan?

They have to reduce all that has been—the *Severe Presences,* ceaselessly filing us down.

We lose many of our tumors, but some remain to be lost: you wouldn't believe it, you have to feel it. The pain of deep probes. We don't dare move. We don't dare move even a thought, a memory, for fear of being pierced to death. One half is learning, the other is draining away.

Struggle and answer still in suspense, the answer we have been awaiting for centuries.

Drums of smoke, thunderbolt of sighs. We are still swallowing the ball with a thousand spikes of suffering. When will it end?

The long-awaited heavy shower, the shower of the infinite, which will calm the soul, we would not dare to speak of it; there are zones where if we spoke of it, we'd be insulted, attacked all over by the desperate shadows.

.　　.　　.

The milestones of ordeals go by slowly, interminably. Threats of an ocean of flames ahead of me. Already, in the neighboring zones, the heat is unbearable.

Must what is intimate perish, too?

.　　.　　.

Struggle, struggle, the suffering is increasing, the expanse too, resistance sometimes. Don't worry, I'm not the one who refuses the most, although I do, a lot.

There is a great resister here.

His defense is through spinning blades (I'm translating for you, because we can't hope to get blades here, nor use them). Nothing has been able to vanquish him.

For the nine hundred years and more that he has been dead, he makes the motions of his indefatigable refusal again and again, without limbs, but not without a will tougher than steel on earth. Nothing has been able to get through his defenses (for he is terribly quick).

Will he ever come to truly die? The High Presences themselves have abandoned him to the centuries. And he, the bravest of the brave, defies any approach, any acceptance.

It is in this kind of hard-winged windmill, with him shaking like the floor of an airplane at takeoff, that he remains unvanquished.

The propellor blades of "No" reject the flight of the angel.

Knowledge, another knowledge here, not *Knowledge* for information. *Knowledge* to become a musician of the Truth.

Here, zero wealth, no gifts, and fidelity loss.

Always periphery seeking center! In big empty Day, full to bursting.

Adaptation: Drama of the seven lives. But how can I prevent myself from thinking of you?

Urgent! I have to get hold of myself, I have to, totally attentive here.

. . . .

Soul-kidnapping, when you learn about it… ceaselessly, ceaselessly, against that, trying to hide each other, sneaking away.

Once again, a great flood is threatening me. Coming from all over. Refuge, where refuge? Someone must have detected us…

Space—really you can't conceive of this horrible inside-outside, which is true space.

Some shadows especially, tightening themselves up one last time, make a desperate effort just to "be inside their own unity." It turns out badly for them. I met one.

Destroyed by punishment, she was nothing more than a noise, but enormous.

An immense world still could hear her, but she was no more, she had become solely and uniquely a noise, which would continue to sound for centuries, but destined to die out *completely,* as if she had never been.

A few moments ago, once again, a Presence of prey. I'm frightened. As long as you don't get here at a moment like this.

. . . .

You can speak again, it's all right. It has gone by. Now here's the slow inoffensive procession of souls who are left with only one option.

Poor things! But at least they know it.

Has anyone ever seen a living being here, a real one?

It's rare: first of all he has to have been softened up by suffering, by separation from the earth—from everything on the earth, from all food, all pleasure, all refuge.

I saw one, so dazzling he was almost scary. He was from earth though, you could see that from a certain difficulty, from the rhythm, from his jerky, almost convulsive luminousness.

Never had I suspected that such beings could exist on earth. His saintliness bathed even the haloed dead. He had only come for a little while. But whenever he comes for good, he won't stay long in the waiting zones. Immediately sucked up toward the center by the avalanche, he will move as fast as it does, through his own inhalation.

Souls thrice dead bowed down to him in admiration...

Past me go the B... They don't know how dead they are, and sometimes they don't even know if they are at all! Unbelievable, but true. They ask each other. "How about me, am I?" or "Am I more dead than that one, than the other one?"

And silence, the sign of Nothingness, leaves them hanging, with their question indefinitely repeated.

...No, at the next level, nothing left. All that is world for those trapped in the second envelope, is shadow for the unbound.

But the lust to dominate has not become shadow.

Some of us, real demons, ceaselessly watch the earth, lying in wait, lying in wait, tailing the wounded, searching out the dying, going from one to the other, picking ("This one will be mine," "That one will be my slave"), trying to pull life out of the wounded by surprise—the man in shock—while fending off the others.

Still, there has to be a certain compatibility between the subjugator and the subjugated. Besides, many are lost on arrival: the shadows thought they already had them but they drifted away due to complex influences. For one who is no longer blind, our space is full of signals, points of attraction, strong zones, weak zones, injections, messages.

Fear nothing, I will watch, I will accomplish the impossible. You must not be afraid...

You are weary, now. Fret no more. Beneath your confusion, you are keeping up your strength, you have the strength you will need, believe me. I can see it. I swear I can see it. Do not be afraid.

Be calm, o burning face. I am there.
No uprooting.
Tenderly, I am waiting for you...
I am waiting for you.

.   .   .   .

Help! Help! Friends, if any friends are left, help, fast, fast, whoever you are, if you can do something, fast! Fast!
They are here! right near me. They are upon me!

I AM GOING TO BE SWALLOWED UP...

NOTES

1   An eloquent bishop under Louis XIV, in Michaux's day, anyone in a French-speaking country with a secondary education would likely have studied at least one of his sermons.

2.   *visitées* in the French. So the speaker is feminine, as is the invented noun *puantes* (stinkers) in the next passage—which doesn't necessarily mean they are women. The speaker is grammatically feminine because it is an *ombre* (noun, fem.: shadow, shade, spirit). But the "shade" does seem feminine in other ways, too. Most of the inhabitants of this space are feminine, a notable exception is the masculine "They" in the last lines

3.   *mon aimé* the addressee is masculine.

MISERABLE MIRACLE (1956)

TURBULENT INFINITY (1957)

KNOWLEDGE THROUGH THE ABYSS (1961)

THE GREAT ORDEALS OF THE MIND (1966)
and the Countless Small Ones

The very titles of these volumes speak eloquently to the kind of experience Michaux had with mind-altering drugs; in his foreword to *Miserable Miracle,* in his epigraph to *Knowledge Through the Abyss* and elsewhere, he comments amply on what the books are about; so does the Introduction to the present anthology. Two further points may be helpful here.

First, if "knowledge" and not pleasure is, as he says, what the poet is after in this enterprise, it must be admitted that he was fascinated by that very particular kind of knowledge and attracted by hallucinogens more than he wanted to admit. "Let's say I'm not very gifted for dependency," he writes in a final Addendum announcing his intention of "giving up these substances" (1971). So he *was* dependent on these drugs, or close to it, despite his repeated disclaimers. And ten years later, a hallucinatory text or two will begin with references to "a prepared substance." We hardly need this broken promise to add the unspoken threat of addiction to the mental dangers Michaux explores in these four works.

He does bring us knowledge, though, as he promises and in the way artists do: through words and images. We can learn more about what madness feels like from the account in *Miserable Miracle* than from any psychiatrist. Moreover, madness, as we are constantly reminded, is an extension, a wild acceleration and condensation of forces already present in the self. Mescaline "unmasks," Michaux says—with terror, but with exaltation too.

For sometimes, these works show us what another side of psychic experience *at the limit* is like: the mystical experience, not only of "the thousands of gods," but of everything that goes infinitely beyond the human. The poet will pursue this aspect of his exploration until he stops writing, shortly before his death.

MISERABLE

MIRACLE

FOREWORD

This is an exploration. Through words, signs, drawing. Mescaline is the thing explored.

(. . .) As for the drawings I began immediately after the third experiment, they were done with a vibratory movement that stays in you for days and days—automatic, blind, you might say, but thus precisely reproducing the visions I had undergone, going through them once again.

Since I could not present the manuscript itself, which directly translated the subject, rhythms, shapes, and chaos all together, as well as the inner defenses and their breakdowns, we found ourselves in great difficulty, facing a typographical wall. Everything had to be rewritten. In any case, the original text, easier to feel than to read, as much drawn as written, would never have been adequate.[1]

Quickly thrown out, in jerks, in and across the page, interrupted sentences—their syllables flying, shredded, torn apart—would go charging, diving, dying. Their remaining tatters would revive, shoot out again, streak across the page, explode once more. Their letters ended in smoke or disappeared in zigzags. The letters after that, similarly discontinuous, continued their troubled story in the same way, birds in high drama, with invisible scissors cutting their wings in flight.

Sometimes words would fuse together on the spot. ''Martyrisingably'' for example, would come in again and again, full of meaning for me, and I couldn't get rid of it. Another would tirelessly repeat ''Krakatoa!'' ''Krakatoa!'' ''Krakatoa!'' or a still more common word like ''crystal'' would come back twenty times in a row, giving me its own long speech,

(Misérable miracle la mescaline, Gallimard, 1956, revised edition, 1972)

weighted with another world, and I couldn't manage to augment it ever so little, or to complement it with some other word. It alone, like a shipwrecked sailor on an island, was everything to me and the rest and the rough seas from which it had just emerged, and it irresistibly reminded the castaway that I, too, was alone and holding out in the debacle.

In the immense churn of lights, splashed with brilliance, I moved forward, drunk, carried away, without ever turning back.

How can I relate all that? It would have taken a diversified style that I don't possess, full of surprises, nonsensical jumps, flashing insights, twists and turns—an unstable, tobogganing, baboonlike style.

(. . .)

I wasn't neutral either, and I admit it. Mescaline and I were more often at odds than together. I was shaken, broken, but I wouldn't go along with it.

Its visions: tacky, really. Moreover, all you had to do was uncover your eyes to stop seeing that silly fairyland. Inharmonious Mescaline, an alcoloid extracted from Peyotl (which has six of them), really seemed like a robot. It could only do a limited number of things.

But I had been ready to admire. I had come in full of confidence. That day, my cells were churned, shaken, sabotaged, thrown into convulsions. They were caressed, then in the next second ripped out. Mescaline wanted my total compliance. To enjoy a drug you have to enjoy being a subject. I had too much the feeling of being "on duty."

Out of *my* terrible shocks, *it* produced its show. I was the fireworks scorning the fireworker—if someone can even prove to it that it is the fireworker. I was stirred around, folded over. Bewildered, I stared at the Brownian movement, a panic of perception.

I was distracted, tired of being distracted, my eyes glued to that microscope. What's supernatural in this? You scarcely left the human. Instead, you felt caught, a prisoner in a workshop of the brain.

Should we talk about pleasure? It was unpleasant.

Once past the anxiety of the first hour—a result of confronting the poison, an anxiety such that you wonder if you're not going to fall into a faint as some do (though rarely)—you can let yourself drift with a certain flow, which might resemble happiness. Is that what I thought? I'm not sure of the contrary. Still, all through those extraordinary hours, I find these words in my journal, written more than fifty times, clumsily, with difficulty: *Intolerable, Unbearable*

Such is the price of this paradise (!).

(March, 1955)

In great discomfort, in anguish, in inner solemnity.—The world pulling away to some distance, a growing distance.—Each word becoming dense, too dense to be pronounced from now on, word full in itself, word in a nest, while the sound of wood crackling in the fireplace becomes the only presence, becomes important: preoccupying and strange its movements... Waiting, a wait that gets heavier every minute, that listens more, grows indescribable, more painful to carry with me... and how far can I carry it?

. . . .

Far away, like the slight whistling of a breeze in the rigging before the storm, a shiver, a shiver without flesh, without skin, an abstract shiver, a shiver in the workshop of the brain, in a zone where you can't shiver with shivers. How, then, will it shiver?

. . . .

As if there were an opening, an opening like a gathering together, like a world, where something can happen, many things can happen, where there's a whole lot, there's a swarm of possibilities, where everything tingles with possibilities, where the person I can vaguely hear walking around next door might ring the bell, might come in, might burn the place up, might climb on the roof, might throw himself screaming out the window. Might everything, anything, without choosing and without any one action preferred over any other. (. . .) [Might, might, might.]

. . .

Suddenly, but preceded by an outpost-word, a courier-word, a word uttered by my language center alerted before I am, like those monkeys that can feel earthquakes coming before humans, preceded by the word "blinding," suddenly a knife, suddenly a thousand knives, suddenly a thousand brilliant scythes of light set in lightning, huge enough to level whole forests, violently start slicing up space from top to bottom with gigantic slashes, with amazingly rapid slashes that I have to keep up with, inwardly, painfully, at the same unbearable speed, at those same impossible heights and just afterward in the same abyssal depths, in increasingly excessive, crazy, dismembering leaps... and when will it end... will it ever end?

Over. It's over.

.   .   .

Himalayas spring up abruptly, higher than the highest mountain, tapering to a point, in fact not real peaks, just outlines of mountains, but no less high for all that, gigantic triangles with increasingly acute angles to the farthest edge of space, absurd but enormous. (. . .)

The himalaying machine has stopped, then starts up again. Huge plowshares furrow away. Inordinately huge plowshares are making furrows with no reason to make furrows. Plowshares, and once again the giant scythes slashing nothingness from top to bottom, with big slashes repeated fifty, a hundred, a hundred and fifty times . . .

And "White" appears. Absolute white. White beyond all whiteness. White of the coming of the White. White without compromise, through exclusion, through total eradication of nonwhite. Insane, enraged white, screaming with whiteness. Fanatical, furious, riddling the retina. Horrible electric white, implacable, murderous. White in bursts of white. God of "white." No, not a god, a howler monkey. (Let's hope my cells don't blow apart.)

End of white. I have a feeling that for a long time to come white is going to have something excessive for me.

. . . .

.   .   .

At the edge of a tropical ocean, in the thousand silvery shimmerings of an invisible moon, in the undulations of the churning waters, ceaselessly changing...

In the silent breaking of the waves, the tremors of the illuminated watery sheet, in the rapid oscillations tormenting the spots of light, in the tearing of curls and arcs and luminous lines, in the eclipses, the reappearances, the bursts of light dancing, deforming, reforming, contracting, spreading out to redistribute themselves once more before me, with me, in me, drowned and in an unbearable crumpling, my calm violated thousands of times by the tongues of oscillating infinity, sinusoidally invaded by the crowd of liquid lines, enormous with a thousand folds, *I was and I was not,* I was trapped, I was lost, I was absolutely ubiquitous. Thousands and thousands of rustlings were a thousand shreddings for me.

.　.　.

Feeling of a fissure. I hide my head in a scarf, to learn, to reconnoiter.

I see a flowing furrow. Furrow swept by quick little cross-channels. Inside, a fluid, mercurial in its brightness, torrential in appearance, electric in speed. Looks flexible, too. Whooosh, there it goes, with infinite little curlicues showing on its flanks. I can also see stripes in it.

[It's a torrent, that's what it is, it's falling all over the place, it's exploding.]

Where exactly, this furrow? It's as if it were going right through my skull, from forehead to sinciput. Yet I can see it. Furrow without a beginning or an end, striking me vertically, with an average width roughly equal at the bottom and the top, a furrow that seems to come from the end of the world, crossing through me and then leaving for the other end of the world.

(. . .)

.　.　.

There is haste in me. There is urgency.[a]

I would like. I would like anything at all, but fast. I would like to get out of here. I would like to be rid of all this. I would like to start all over again. I would like to leave all this. Not to leave through an exit. I would like a multiple leaving, a whole spread of them. An endless leaving, an ideal leaving so that once I've left I begin leaving again right away.

---

[a]What would happen if this "accelerator" were administered to slow animals to the chameleon, to the three-toed sloth or to a marmot just coming out of hibernation?

I would like to get up. No, I would like to lie down, no, I'd like to get up, right away, no, I'd like to lie down this very second, I want to get up, I'm going to make a phone call, no, I won't call. Yes, I have to. No, I'm absolutely not going to call. Yes, I'll call. No, I'll lie down. So ten times, twenty times, fifty times in a few minutes I decide something, decide the contrary, come back to the first decision, come back to the second decision, make my first resolution again, completely, fanatically carried away as if on a crusade, but the next second totally indifferent, uninterested, perfectly relaxed.

(. . .)

. . . .

. . .

(. . .)

So, that day was the day of the great opening. Forgetting the tacky images that in fact disappeared, giving up the struggle, I let the fluid cross through me, and as it came in through the furrow, it seemed to come from the end of the world. I myself was a torrent, I was drowned, I was navigation. My great constitution hall, my ambassador's hall, my hall for gifts and exchanges into which I usher foreigners for a first examination—I had lost all my halls with my servants. I was alone, shaken around violently like a dirty thread in a churning wash. I was brightening, I was breaking, I was braying to the ends of the earth. I was shuddering. My shuddering was a barking. I moved forward, I slid downward, I plunged into transparency, I was living crystallinely.

Sometimes a glass stairway, a stairway like Jacob's ladder, a stairway with more stairs than I could climb in three whole lifetimes, a stairway of ten million steps, a stairway without landings, a stairway to the sky, the most formidable, the most senseless enterprise since the Tower of Babel, rose into the absolute. Suddenly I would no longer see it. The stairway into the sky had disappeared like bubbles of champagne, and I went on with my headlong navigation, fighting not to roll over, struggling against suctions and pulls, against infinitely small, jumping things, against stretched-out webs and curving, spidery legs.

Now and then, thousands of little ambulacral stems from a gigantic starfish would anchor so intimately on me that I had no way of knowing if it was becoming me or if I was becoming it. I would squeeze myself together, make myself watertight and compact, but everything that contracts here promptly must loosen, even the enemy dissolves like salt in water, and once again I was navigation, navigation above all, shining with a pure white flame, responding to a thousand cascades, to foaming ditches and wheeling ravines, that folded me over and creased me as I shot by. He who flows cannot inhabit.

The streaming that went through me during this extraordinary day was something so immense, unforgettable, unique, that I thought, that I did not stop thinking: "In the state I'm in, a mountain, despite its unintelligence, a mountain with its waterfalls, its ravines, its runoff slopes, would be better able to understand me than a man... "

.   .   .

THE EXPERIENCE OF MADNESS[2]

...but there was a fourth time. A mistake in arithmetic led me to swallow six times the dose necessary for me. I wasn't aware of it right away. With my eyes closed, I was watching inside myself, as on a screen or an instrument panel, the colors and lines of Mescaline, this time out of all proportion as they appeared in my inner vision, with the turbulence of the images so surprising still. Then suddenly, nothing. I saw nothing. I had slipped into an abyss. A door that had been open up to then had just snapped shut in absolute silence.

What? What's happening? Headquarters is grabbed by the collar, loses sight of its troops. Less defendable than a cork bobbing about in choppy water, more vulnerable than a little boy advancing against a column of tanks coming down the road.

The waves of the mescalinian ocean had broken over me, pushing me around, turning me over like light gravel: the movements, which had been in my vision until then, were now *on* me. It hadn't lasted ten seconds, and it was over. I was done for.

Not so fast. Let's not go so fast. The torture has to last for hours. It hasn't begun yet . . .

. . . Innocently, like a tourist, I watch the first changes. Calmly, I watch the bizarre inner turbulence, I already know it, I recognize it. I note the start of the shreddings that I am no doubt going to see soon, the sensation of the horse's mouth, note that over there at the window, where the curtains aren't completely drawn, it's as if big, shining white sheets are flapping around. The beginning of deeper breathing forms in my chest, prelude to another "awareness."

Lines, more and more lines, I don't know if I'm really seeing them, though they're already distinct and delicate (then I must be feeling them?), now I'm beginning to see them (how tenuous they are, this time!), how spacious their curves, spacious! I note that now and then they disappear, and then again their spaciousness, truly extraordinary for their thinness, and I know the white I'm going to see soon will be faintly purple, although I can't see any shade yet but the light gray, light, from enormous spidery threads that are highly, rhythmically, incessantly crossing over the emptiness.

(. . .) Great Z's go through me (zebrastripes-vibrations-zigzags?). Then either broken S's, or also what may be their halves: unfinished O's, like giant eggshells a child might have wanted to draw without ever succeeding.

Egg-shapes or S-shapes, they begin to get in the way of my thoughts, as if thoughts and shapes were of the same nature.

(. . .)

From time to time, I encounter a formidable intersection of irritations, a terrace for the unbearable winds of the mind, and I begin to write, almost without realizing it, without thinking, busy transmitting these words I don't recognize, although they are highly significant: "Too much! Too much! You're giving me too much!"

The lines come in one after the other, almost without stopping. Faces slip into them, sketches of faces (profiles most often) caught up in the moving outlines, and stretch, twist, like heads of pilots distorted by excessive pressure, kneading their cheeks, their foreheads, like rubber. Lines more linear, less horrible, merely grotesque. What begins to bother me is their dimensions, the dimensions of a cliff, and as the sinusoidal lines carry them off, they seem to grow still more.

Apart from these grotesque faces laughing in emptiness (or was it the sign of a situation I didn't understand?) nothing.

These are the only ships sailing in—not on—those unbelievably gigantic waves.

They leave me for a moment. Something or other slides down a dizzying gutter, but this doesn't last and the lines come back, the lines, those cursed lines racking me . . .

And bigger still grow the lines, I couldn't draw them, even vaguely, the paper is no longer in scale. I stop, put down my pencil, push the paper away, and am going to undertake something else.

...I SANK.

It was an instantaneous dive. I closed my eyes to find the visions again, but it was no use, I knew, it was over. I was cut off from that circuit. Lost at a surprising depth, I couldn't budge. A few seconds went by in this stupor. And suddenly the countless waves of the mescalinian ocean were breaking over me, knocking me down. Knocking me down, knocking me down, knocking me down, knocking me down, knocking me down, knocking me down. It would never stop, never. I was alone in the ravages of that vibration, with no circumference, no annex, a target-man who can't manage to get back to his offices.

What had I done? By diving, I think, I had reached myself in my utmost depths and coincided with myself,[b] no longer as an observer-voyeur, but myself returned to myself and, above us and coming down on us, the typhoon.

---

[b]Coincided—what does that mean? In my life, I have tried to come as close as I can to myself (since I want to watch), but without coinciding, without letting myself go, without *giving* myself (   )

It is so absolutely horrible, horrible in its essence, I can't find any way of saying it and I feel like a counterfeiter when I try.

Wherever one is nothing else but one's own self, that's where it was. There, incredibly fast, hundreds of lines of force were combing my being, which never managed to pull itself back together fast enough, which at the moment of coming back together was raked by a new row of tines, and then again, and then again. (Is this going to last all my life, now that it's started, now that I'm in the path *it* is passing through?)

In a flash I recalled that very remarkable look of wild-haired madwomen, not only the wind makes them look that way or their wandering hands, or their helplessness, but the imperative inner necessity of translating (at least in that way) the rapid, infernal combing-uncombing of their being—martyrized, penetrated, drawn out like wires, endlessly.

Thus, and always at that relentless, inhuman speed, I was assaulted, pierced by the electric mole burrowing its way through the most personal essence of my person.

Trapped, not in something human, but in a frantic mechanical shaker, in a mixer-crusher-crumbler, treated like metal in a factory, like water in a turbine, like wind in a wind tunnel, like roots in an automatic wood-grinder, like iron in the tireless motion of steel lathes turning out gears. But *I* had to remain conscious!

Like a garden warbler in the churning wake of the propellers of a four-engine plane, like an ant flattened under the crushing waters of a an open floodgate, like I don't know what, like nobody.

A struggle intense beyond all intensity, with me active as never before, miraculously outdoing myself, but overwhelmingly outdone by that dislocating phenomenon.

The main horror of it was that I was only a line. In normal life, you're a sphere, a sphere that comes upon panoramas. You can enter a castle from one moment to another, you ceaselessly go from one castle to a new castle, such is the life of man, even the poorest, the life of a sane man.

Here only a line. A line breaking into a thousand aberrations . . .

.   .   .

Becoming a line was catastrophic, but it was, still more unexpectedly (if that's possible), prodigious. All of my self had to pass through that line. And through its horrible joltings.

Metaphysics taken over by mechanics.

Forced through the same path, my self, my thought, and the vibration.

Self a thought only, not thought becoming my self or developing in my self, but *my self shrunk into it.*

On top of this came the disarticulating vibration that "rejected" thought and after a few modulations—which ripped thought apart—eliminated it.

The thoughts struggled furiously, desperately, against their disintegration. But they'd had it. It happened very fast. A bacillus under the radiation of radium salts knows what this is like, but humans don't know it. They are preserved from it.

The intimacy of it! I'll never say it well enough, how an idea is your center, and how destructible it is, pliable, disintegratable. Someone who has not gone through it can't possibly know how disintegratable they are.

Yes, ideas can be flagellated, lysed. There was no end to it. Destruction twenty times faster than the self.

The thought-smashing waves kept coming and coming.

The cruelty of that rushing at a thought is unimaginable. After a few breakaways in shreds the stringy thought just disappeared, unrecognizable.

As if my mind, having become a conductor for some kind of electricity, had just been taken over as a convenient path for currents lethal to thought. Lightning and I had to pass through together.

Impossible to leave the bed of the terrible phenomenon. There was no other path for it but through the exact center of my self, it almost everything, it a quivering comb, me not much of anything, hopelessly, ceaselessly under the furious carding. The thalli of laminaria perpetually shaken by the waters of a jostling sea are on a vacation, compared to what I was. No vacation was given to *me,* not two seconds of vacation.

Terrible, beyond terrible! Yet I felt no terror. The soldier under fire has other things to do. I struggled continuously. I couldn't allow myself to be terrified. I didn't have the breathing space for it.

(. . .)

.   .   .

. . . The lamp near the mirror showed me a face I'd never seen before, the face of a raging madman. It would have frightened a murderer. It would have made him shrink back. Outside myself, horribly photogenic and determined (whereas I'm not), the face of a complete extrovert, a fanatic's face, although neither it nor I had moved a muscle, it was the congested mask of someone who no longer listens to anybody, the terrible face of a raging madman, who is in reality a raging terrified man. Corner an animal, its face turns nasty. However, my voice was assured, almost gentle (I checked this later with people who had heard it), and I didn't feel the slightest hint of anger or hostility in myself. "He" must have already killed someone, I thought, for I could not consider that face on the verge of murder as mine. "It must be a matter of minutes now, twenty-thirty minutes." This was the origin of my calm, the serious calm of someone who is responsible for a dangerous madman, for that was changing the situation. But I could still be seriously hit in another, absolutely atrocious way. A man is really vast.

At the moment when the trepidation and internal destruction become intolerable, the madman is going to have to express them in corresponding acts, by destroying, breaking, burning, wounding, killing, or killing himself: in a word, when he begins "his work," will I be able to hold him in... until he's dragged away, or, laughable as an inadequate sphincter, will I be unable to hold him in? In that case, now's the time to call for the straitjacket.

(. . .) Meanwhile, there was something new, something bad. What had been separate no longer was. Two watertight compartments had just been flooded. Now I had to fight with all my strength against the absurd acts surging into my mind: upon seeing my face, I had realized they were about to come, but I never would have guessed *this*. With speed, senseless speed, they were appearing, shaking me so that I would perform the acts they were suggesting, shaking me over and over like a rag in the wind of a windmill, then disappearing. Others would come in, pushing, pushing, all of them abnormal, eager to be carried out, not one kind of act but ten, not against this person or that nor against me, but against anything at all, indifferently, insatiable: a dozen murders and as many fires wouldn't have satisfied them, they couldn't be satisfied. As soon as they appeared, there was no question of trying to struggle (it was pointless); no, I had to put another, harmless thought in their place—but often after a few quick triturations it would become dangerous too, for what does not contain a word which can't turn into a knife? And what about the knife, how not to take it, to stop it? Face those thoughts? Absurd. I am them. They coincide with me, with my self more than consenting, me inseparable from them as soon as they appear. Everything happens in madness *because there is no distance.* An idea goes along with you down one single path. No panorama. No diversion. No third person. No comparison. No stop (so necessary for judgment).

AFTERWORD

. . . One more word. Those who go in for unified explanations may be tempted to judge all my writings as the work of a drug addict from now on. Sorry. I'm more the water-drinking type. Never alcohol. No stimulants, and for years no coffee, no tobacco, no tea. From time to time wine, and very little of that. All my life, very little of everything people take. Take and abstain. Abstain, above all. Fatigue is my drug, as a matter of fact.

I was forgetting: twenty-five years ago or more, I must have tried ether seven or eight times at the most, laudanum once, and twice alcohol (frightful).

NOTES

1   One thing Michaux did was to put a kind of running analytic-poetic commentary in the margins of the text. Production costs obliged us to eliminate this. I have included some of the marginalia in brackets, [thus].

2.   When Michaux reprinted large parts of this text in his anthology *Choix de poèmes,* he cut everything that was anecdotal, particular to the incident: a crystal ball happened to be in the room, Michaux picked it up, etc. I have followed his cuts My own cuts are indicated by .   .

TURBULENT

INFINITY

. . . .

Something incredible, something desperately desired from childhood on, apparently denied me, something *I* certainly would never see, unheard of, inaccessible, too beautiful, sublime, forbidden to me—it happened.

I SAW THE THOUSANDS OF GODS. I was given that marvelous gift. Faithless as I am (without realizing the faith I might have had), they appeared for me. They were *there,* present, more present than anything I've ever looked at in my life. And it was impossible and I knew it, and still. Still, they were there, arrayed in their hundreds one beside the other (but thousands followed, hardly perceptible—even more than thousands, an infinity). They were there, those calm beings, noble, suspended in the air by seemingly natural levitation, moving very slightly or rather animated in place. They—those divine beings— and I: alone facing each other.

Out of something like gratitude, I was theirs.

But really, one might say, what did you believe? I reply: Believing simply doesn't matter, SINCE THEY WERE THERE! Why should I argue about it, since I was completely happy?

They were not at a great height, but at all the height needed to keep their distance while revealing themselves, to be revered by the man who witnesses their glory and recognizes their incomparable superiority. They were natural, as the sun in the sky is natural. I didn't move. I didn't have to bow. They towered over me quite enough. It was real, like an

(*L'Infini turbulent,* Mercure de France, 1957, passage selected by Henri Michaux for inclusion in his anthology, *Choix de poèmes,* Gallimard, 1976, my source for the present text)

understanding between us from a previously arranged agreement. I was full of them. I had stopped being unfilled. Everything was perfection. I had no need to think, or weigh, or criticize, any more. No need to compare any more. My horizontal was now vertical. I existed at a height. I had not lived in vain.

(. . .)

gs bore us with their paradises.

THROUGH

them give us a little

THE

wledge instead.

ABYSS

is not a century for paradise.

All drugs modify your supports. The support you had from your senses, the support your senses had from the world, the support you had from your general impression of being. They give way. A vast redistribution of the sensibility takes place, making everything bizarre—a complex, continual redistribution of the sensibility. You feel less *here,* and more *there.* Where "here"? Where "there"? In dozens of "heres," in dozens of "theres," that you didn't know, that you don't recognize. Dark zones that used to be bright. Light zones that used to be heavy. You no longer end up in yourself, and reality, even objects, lose their mass and stiffness and no longer put up any serious resistance to the everpresent transforming mobility.

You begin to surrender, in little ways (drugs tickle you with abandonment), in big ways, too. Some like it: paradise—that is, abandonment. You go through multiple, varied invitations to let go... That's what strong drugs have in common: and it's always the brain getting hit, watching its action in the wings, its little tricks, playing for low stakes and high, then observing from far away, from singularly far away.

Above all I will talk about *mescaline,* more spectacular than the drugs of the past, clear, brusque, rough, predestined to unmask whatever remains covered over in the others, made to rape the brain, to "inform on" its secrets and the secret of rare states. To demystify.

(. . .) After a short phase of nausea and discomfort, you begin to deal above all with light. It's going to start shining, striking, piercing with its rays that have suddenly become

(Connaissance par les gouffres, Gallimard, 1961, revised edition, 1967)

penetrating. You may have to shelter your eyes under thick cloth, but *you're* not sheltered. The whiteness is inside you. The sparkling is in your head. A certain part of the head that you can soon feel by its fatigue: the occipital; white lightning strikes there.

Then come the visions of crystals, of precious stones, of diamonds or rather their streaming down, their blinding streaming.

The excessive stimulation makes the visual apparatus respond in brilliancies, in dazzlings, in loud shocking colors; brutal and vulgar, they form ensembles that shock you, as your visual cortex is now being shocked and brutalized by the invading poison.

And you encounter multitude. A crowd appears, of points, of images, of little forms, that very very very quickly go by, the too-lively circulation of *a time that has an enormous number of moments,* which shoot by prodigiously. *The coexistence of this multiple-moment time* with *normal time* (it has not completely disappeared, and comes back in intervals, only partially obliterated by the attention you give to the other) is extraordinary, extraordinarily *de-realifying.*

Moreover, *a space of countless points* (all of them very ''detached'') coexists with more or less normal space (the one around you that you look at from time to time, now seemingly drowned and subliminal); this is extraordinary in the same—and parallel—way.

And Multitude expands (with speed linked to it) into the thoughts ferreting in full speed, in all directions, into the memory, into the future, into the data of the present, to grasp the unexpected, luminous, stupefying connections—you would like to hold on to them, but they are carried away in a rush and erased from your memory by the huge number of connections that come crowding in next.

Multitude in your consciousness, a consciousness that expands to the point where it seems to double, to multiply, drunk with simultaneous perceptions and knowledge, the better to observe synoptically and hold together the most distant points.

The abnormal excitation radiates out. Hyperacuity. Your attention prodigiously *present,* at the height of its powers, an abnormally quick, clear receptor. The ability to separate out, to gauge, increases in the eye (which can see the most delicate reliefs, insignificant wrinkles), in the ear (which can hear the slightest sound from far away and is hurt by loud noises), in the understanding[a] (an observer of nonapparent motives, of the underside, of the most distant causes and consequences that ordinarily go unnoticed, of all kinds of interactions, too numerous at other moments to be grasped simultaneously), and above all

[a]But the intelligence, which is at work *there,* cannot give good answers to any foreign problems that may be submitted to it

in the imagination (where visual images flash by, with unheard-of intensity, far above "reality," which weakens and diminishes)—and finally, importantly, in paranormal faculties, which sometimes reveal the gift of clairvoyance and divination to the subject.[b]

The orchestra of the enormous, magnified inner life is now an absolute marvel. However agile your mind may have become at apprehending on several fronts, you return often, too often, to the visions: of all the elusive things crossing through you, they seem the least elusive. Continuous multitude. Vibratory, zigzagging, in continual transformation. Lines pullulate. The cities with a thousand palaces, the palaces with a thousand towers, halls with a thousand columns... of which so much has been said, now here they are. But the show is really silly. Little columns, much too thin, needles that couldn't support a thing. Towers, too many towers, or rather turrets, elongated, frail, unbelievably slender. Ruins, fake trembling ruins. A mess of tangled-up ornaments (ornaments in the ornament of the ornament) slipping in everywhere, even into a group of runners, for example: you were looking at them and suddenly, for no reason, they ribbon up, snake around, roll themselves up in loops, in loops of loops, in unstoppable spirals...

At this point things are so silly that you stop contemplating the inner spectacle: impossible to find what you really like in it. That absurdity and a thousand other similar points really don't seem to originate in the intelligence, even when it's turned against itself, even when it's letting itself go, but rather in something totally foreign, like a mechanism. Meanwhile you have a craving to swallow the jar of paste, or the pack of paper clips, to throw yourself out of the window, to call for help, to kill yourself or to kill someone else—but only for half a second, and then the next second no craving at all, the next a mad craving, and so hundreds of times sometimes the "yes" goes by, sometimes the "no," with no gradation, thoughtless, with the regularity of a piston. You start writing long strings of meaningless superlatives. Infinity is calling, enormous, overwhelming. Why? How? While the wall moves rhythmically forward and back, as your arm seemingly gets periodically longer, there are also bursts of uncontrollable laughter, equally meaningless...

Don't forget you've swallowed a toxic substance. Psychological explanations—too tempting. To see psychology everywhere is to lack psychology.

A great many of the characteristics of mescaline drunkenness, from the most common to the most absurd, share the same basic phenomenon. Incessantly, in one form or another, it manifests its presence. That is: waves. Is it absurd to think that brain waves, actually quite

---

[b]"All metagnomogenetic plants are hallucinatory." A Rouhier, *Des Plantes divinatoires,* supplement to his book on *Peyotl,* ed Doin, 1927

slow,[c] become perceptible in some states of violent nervous hyperexcitation, especially that of the visual cortex? New experiments must be performed here, and a more thorough study of encephalograms of subjects intoxicated by mescaline.

When people who know nothing about the very existence of brain waves talk of waves, of wavelets, of undulations, of oscillations they are seeing or have seen, should we conclude that they are merely translating an impression of floating into visual terms—an operation that is actually possible, which would not replace the other but add to it, one example among many of parallel actions, echoes, recalls, that have been observed in the disturbance caused by the drug?

(. . .) there are correlations between certain characteristics of abnormal waves recorded on electroencephalograms and certain characteristics of mescaline waves.

But above all, one should consider the characteristics of waves in general. If there is wave, in the first place the wave represents: *continuation*. If one considers each similar element, it is *repetition*. If one considers its trajectory, indefinitely intersecting an imaginary right angle, it is *oscillation, rhythmic interruption,* perpetual alternation. This is why it may appear *mechanical*. In some cases, only the *tips* will strike you, in others it will be its *undulations*. When they intermingle, you'll have *ornaments* and the festoons they form periodically, moving ornaments. In other cases, it will be the impossibility of stopping. Or its immaterial side, or again its renewal, almost *identical, endless,* its monotonous symmetry, its perpetuity. Their trace may be easily found in many mescalinian phenomena, particularly in visions.

(. . .)[1]

Infinity in mescaline. Its characteristics: Feeling of the infinite, *of the presence of infinity,* of the proximity, the immediacy, the penetration of infinity, of the infinite endlessly crossing through the finite. An infinity on the march, a steady march which will never stop again, which can no longer stop. Cessation of the finite, of the mirage of the finite, of the illusory conviction that anything finite, concluded, terminated, stopped, exists. The finite either prolonged or fragmented, everywhere betrayed by a crossing, overflowing infinity, a magnificent annuller and dissipater of everything circumscribed, which can no longer exist. An *infinitely* which no longer allows you to put an end to anything at all, which takes off in infinite series, which is infinity, which modulates into an infinitisation from which no

[c] As are *thêta* waves that appear at periods of crisis in many schizophrenics, or *lambda* waves "which appear in the occipital regions during periods of visual attention." Antoine Remond, *Concours médical,* January, 1958

finite can escape, in which even our pettiness, reobserved, is immediately prolonged, deepened, lost and infinitied, decircumscribing, in which any subject, any mood, emotion or feeling takes on that stupefying and so natural infinity. Obsessive, harassing infinity,[d] which no longer allows anything but itself, a return to itself, a passage through itself. Infinity which, alone, is, which rhythm is. If the rhythm is majestic, the infinite will be divine. If the rhythm is precipitous, the infinite will be persecution, anxiety, fragmentation, bewildering, incessant reembarkation from here to farther away, farther away, farther away, farther away, farther away, farther away, farther away, farther away, forever far from any haven. Infinity infinitising everything, but far more than any other feeling, marvelously in tune with goodness, tolerance, mercy, acceptance, equality, forgiveness, patience, love and universal *compassion.*

Can anyone dare to speak of waves here? Yes, and even of one particular wave. After all, a genius is nourished by vitamins and animal flesh and kept going by his hormones. Is it so scandalous that what is most immaterial in matter should come to support the feeling of infinity? "Peyotl helps you to worship," said one of its adepts. The wave that helps us to worship. Whoever has taken mescaline took a bowl of vibrations, that is what he took, that is what's possessing him now. Aided by his exaltation, let him set up the best wave in himself,[e] the one that through its marvelous unusual regularity and through its amplitude lifts up and bestows majestic importance, the wave that is foundation for infinity, its sustenance, its litany.

The impression of prolongations, of persistence, of fascination, through unusual repetition impossible to shake off, a certain silliness, the twisting rails of a hypnotic continuation in yourself, all also seem to come from the irresistible wave. Faith through the path of vibration.

Alternation. Oscillation of ideas, desires.

. . . In mescalinian drunkenness, if you have a desire to see someone and not to be alone any more, as soon as it appears, this desire seems caught up in an immaterial fist of

---

[d]This quite unexpected infinitisation, measureless, choiceless and preferenceless, clearing away anything finite, accepting any job at all, infinitising trifles too, unstoppable, prolonging everything endlessly and referring to something farther on, no doubt comes from the neurons, from a periodic constrictive movement rather than from contact with another world, still, it renders in its way something of the Infinite, which, far from being a suburb of the gods, is an eternal surpassing, removed from any grasp, from any rest not an essential halt, in any sense, in any direction, in any object, in any matter, breaking, tearing apart, always beyond, beyond any person however divine one may wish him, beyond, no matter how, beyond, beyond, inaccessible, dizzily escaping from any enclave coming from the human mind.

[e]A bit before ecstasy, I would notice regular sinusoidal waves, which are also the simplest of periodic functions Religious undulations do exist Artists, and not only buddhists, know that parallel, closely spaced lines, gently undulating, repeated rhythmically with very few variations, are lines of abandonment to feelings of piety, religion and the infinite Drawings made at the end of the mescalinian day show this tendency in their gentle parallel windings, which also make them similar to the drawings of mediums

Numerous examples among Eastern mystics Thus Ramakrishna describes his first ecstasy " As far as my eyes could see, I perceived shining waves heaving up on all sides and breaking over me. " (*Ramakrishna et la vitalité hindoue,* S Lemaître, Paris, Seuil, p 62)

contradictory movements. Fifty times a minute, you go from "I'm going to call him" to "No, I won't call" to "Yes, I'll call him" to "No, I won't," etc.

(. . .)

By itself, the mechanical phenomenon of oscillation (when it's amplified and accelerated) can be a disaster. The contradictory passages break the courage to live, break the will. Some oscillating passages will no longer allow an image to form, to subsist, won't allow a thought to maintain itself, to come intact. Waves so intolerable they have led madmen suffering from them to throw themselves out the window in order to put an end to that infernal serpent with no thickness, which stopped them from thinking and drove them to think, which detached and attached them and detached them endlessly, endlessly. By committing suicide, they put an end to it. Waves of madness.

If our normal state is mixture, examination and mastery of antagonistic impulses and views, if the state created by drugs or mental illness is an oscillation with a succession and total separation of antagonistic drives and opposing points of view, there is a *third state,* one without alternation, as it were *without mixture,* in which consciousness reigns *with absolutely no antagonism* in an unheard-of totality. Ecstasy (whether cosmic or loving, or erotic, or diabolical). Without extreme exaltation you can't enter into it. Once within it, all variety disappears, in what seems to be an independent universe. Ecstasy and only ecstasy opens up what is absolutely unmixed, absolutely uninterrupted by the smallest opposition or impurity that may be the slightest bit, even allusively, different. A pure universe, of total energetic homogeneity in which the *absolutely* of the same race, the same sign, the same orientation lives together, and in waves.

This and this alone is "the real stakes," so it doesn't matter if it is or isn't a wave helping along that autonomous universe in which a rapture comparable to nothing in this world maintains you uplifted, away from mental laws, in a sea of bliss.[f]

[f]At another time, with the same totalness, you will be trapped inside a total perversity equally impossible to leave, equally unmixed and uncentered

NOTE

1   (Michaux continues with a descriptive analysis of various categories of these phenomena: "visions of ornaments, visions of grimaces, ruins, mountains, minarets, visions of animals with fantastically elongated necks, images of squares that can't resist the mescaline and become triangles, laughter." The last two categories, infinity and alternation, are given below.—D B.)

THE GREAT

ORDEALS

OF THE MIND
(and the Countless Small Ones)

For a long time now I had wanted to take cannabis indica at high altitude and then go look at a mountain skyline. That's why I had come to this place. To see if it would have any effect on me, and which. A few days went by. Finally I took the substance, one coveted at other moments. Time passed. Nothing. I can feel no change. The mountains in front of me look exactly the same. My health over-restored, perhaps. Then, as meals sometimes have a catalytic effect, I go down to the dining room.

Night came too soon. I must have miscalculated.

I had thought that when I returned I'd find the mountains still more likely to make a strong impression on me, in the twilight. When I came back, they were no longer there. Even the highest peaks were no longer visible. Every last one of them had disappeared into the night.

Dismayed, my journey a failure, alone on the wide terrace beyond my room, with nothing to look at in front of me, not knowing what to do, I remained there, crushed.

At last, before going back inside, I raised my head. A black sky stretched out everywhere full of stars. I sank into it. It was extraordinary. Instantaneously stripped of everything as one is stripped of an overcoat, I was entering space. I was shot into it, I was rushed into it, I was flowing into it. Violently sucked up by it, without resistance.

. . . .

An utterly unsuspected wonder... Why had I never experienced it before? After the first moment of surprise it seemed so natural to be swept away into space. And yet, how many times had I looked at skies just as beautiful, more beautiful, with no other effect than real—and vain—admiration. Admiration: an antechamber, nothing but an antechamber. I realized this once more.

Whatever I was experiencing, it was something quite different from admiration, a totally different register.

What, exactly? It's not easy to grasp. As if torn away from earth, feeling myself swept invincibly upward, carried off farther and farther by some marvelous, invisible levitation, into a space that did not end, that could not end, that was incommensurable to me, that was pulling me more and more toward it, I was soaring higher and higher, sucked up inexplicably, with no chance of ever getting there. Obviously. Besides, getting where?

It could have been horrible. It was radiant.

Everything static, finished, solid, was over and done with. Nothing left of all that, or almost nothing. Stripped down, I was careening along, propelled, stripped of possessions and attributes, stripped even of all recourse to the earth, dislodged from all sense of space, an unimaginable stripping down that seemed almost absolute, so incapable was I of finding something that had not been taken away from me.

No doubt about it: up to then I had not seen, not really seen the sky. I had resisted it, looking at it from the other side—from the terrestrial, solid, opposite side.

This time the shore had collapsed, and I was plunging. Vertiginously I was plunging upward.

I was there, in the sky. At last we were in contact.

And I kept on looking at it, if you can apply the word "looking" to an abyss you're thrown into, an abyss from which nothing separates you any longer.

The unity of the starry sky had suddenly disappeared, unmasking its bottomless depths. It deepened endlessly.

From time to time, turning my eyes away, I would try to collect myself "against it," since I'd been pushed to the limit of what I could bear to lose of my self. When I had gotten hold of myself, I looked at it again and it would snatch me up again right away, coming on me full speed ahead. Inexpressible invasion. A tidal wave suddenly breaking into the land, but it was the sky, the enormous sky that was coming in, imperiously.

I was taking in the sky and the sky was taking me in.

Simultaneously, I was inside an extraordinary expansion. Space was spacifying me...

(...)

I was sailing in a sort of nausea that had become a delight, swaying under the far-off, moving stars, which sometimes seemed like the lights of ships you see at night pitching and rolling on rough seas, but here, lights of galactic ships navigating the ocean of boundlessness. This ocean was in all directions; it alone mattered.

ADDENDA 1968–1971

I.

(. . .)

What has happened up to now in my life, even what was most serious and dramatic, was always me finding myself essentially on the same level.

Not this time. What's happening to me now is at another level, and yet it gets there, strangely it gets there.

In my youth and later still, I remained convinced that there would never be an *event*. that I would come to the end of my life without any.

And now one has come, an indisputable event, going beyond anything I've ever known, gigantic in every sense and yet at my level... my size—which is adjusting itself to it.

From the very start everything or almost everything in me has gone into surpassing, superhumanising, transmuting, transubstantiating, and sometimes opening onto the sacred (the sacred is a mode—the mode of receiving it), a few times to the demonic, sometimes to the insane.

The extraordinariness I had longed for so badly—this time I've got plenty of it, all kinds of it.

Optical phenomena are only a part of this new, phenomenally active universe, *in which* I am, where I have to make do, with instant good judgment, and on all sides, on all sides completely.

It is possible to enjoy the changed sight of one's surroundings—and the visions, still more. Get drunk on them for hours at a time, or learn from them. Follow the passage from image to thought. Observe the derangements, the faulty connections of thought, the mistakes of the thinking instrument now being pushed around, the illusions of the human who owns this fragile thinking instrument. Detect sudden, violent surges towards madness,[a] toward absurd, dangerous, deadly acts. In a way, you can grasp the composition of the universe of madness, especially its texture.

The "Mental Revealer,"[b] the revealer of all the twists and blunders of the mind, shows it, shows what it is finally possible to see, instead of merely guess at.

You go to the borders. Sometimes to one border, then to another.

Mescaline carries you there effortlessly—and just *beyond*. As a gift, you receive the distance you've covered. It's stunningly easy.

Wherever you may already have taken yourself to seek whatever was beyond and opposite—now all of a sudden you're *there*. In this just-beyond your borders.

You ignore what you formerly perceived, you leave it aside, without integrating it, or you no longer feel it at all.[c]

A great silence has settled into the part of your consciousness that was in use up to now.

Silence, where just a few minutes ago it was so lively.

Many parts have become something like one zone, and now form a great silence together.

The pseudohomeland no longer answers. The field of your attention is now Elsewhere.

You have a particular impression of a whole, of wholes, of being a whole, of belonging to a whole.[d]

Sharing ad infinitum. Everything, interconnected; everything and everyone, exchangers, a whole.

Whole as far as eye can see.

A whole, as well, mad ideas, madly endearing, agglutinating absurdly, grandiosely embracing.

---

[a] Just as running is not walking fast (as fast as you may walk, you won't be running), as a gallop isn't a trot, it's another, specifically different way of moving; thus having false ideas, problems, frustrations, complexes—all this isn't madness, being insane is another way of moving that has become specifically different, a different functioning in which frustrations, problems and complexes that were not at all dangerous become extremely so, and almost all at once, just as, in an organ of the body, colibacilli, saprophytic germs that had been harmless up to then suddenly become pathological and set off an illness.

[b] Without giving the author's name, Professor Julian Huxley quotes this very accurate expression to describe this type of psychotropic drug

[c] Desire, drive, once you've gone past a certain level zero And the same for the spiritual impulse beyond a certain level nothing Meditation, or prayer, in these cases, is like a cast on a wooden leg The thing is to first change levels, thresholds, so that something can happen

[d] For me, buried in irritations, attracted by a thousand curiosities, too rebellious as well, I didn't feel it at first I didn't accept it, no doubt With surprise, I note its near absence from *Miserable Miracle* It appears only in the following volumes

Intense pleasure of the whole throughout everything, despite every obstacle, and the more obstacles there are (the more it's beyond plain old reality and common sense), the more you're carried away, seduced.[e]

Utopia, the joy of uniting utopia beyond the boundaries of true and false, wins out in an utterly new way, exalted, triumphant.

Spatial awareness expands. That awareness is never so dense as when it is the awareness of nothing in particular.

Unifying awareness, of such scope that afterward it makes the so-called real world seem like an alteration of the unified world.[f]

[e]Speaking of the more limited drunkenness known in his day, William James wrote "Drunkenness is the great stimulant of the approbatory function" Even when it is hostile, aggressive, it is inclusive—freshly, extremely, inclusive
[f]A drug addict, apparently nothing but the wreck of a man, who seems to have learned nothing (since he's unable to say it), nonetheless sees others—be they scientists or important people—as shrunken beings.

IV.[1]

Why did I stop taking Mescaline?

Not reliable. Not as easy to handle as one might wish.

Then how about other, less aggressive substances? But they are less interesting.

Over the years, I had made progress. With important states, the ones that count, I knew how to get them (to me), but not enough, not securely, only irregularly... intermittently.

Invisible, but always there, behind the extraordinarily wonderful states—apparently irreversible, definitive—suddenly once again the very, very, very bad would appear, the one you don't want, or else something chaotic, bizarre, extravagant, that you thought you'd left behind.

Problems with getting it back, with maintaining, and for that second category, with eliminating, with sending it away.

Taking some of these substances once or twice every four years, just to know where you stand, probably wouldn't be a bad idea.

Even that I'm giving up.

Let's say I'm not very gifted for addiction.[g]

[g]Chemical dependency on Mescaline, Hashish and hallucinogenic drugs, which hardly deserves the name "addiction," is in no way comparable to the real, extremely serious addiction to heroin or a drug of that kind, which—and not only for that reason—I abstained from taking
  (Note the French word *dépendance* means both "dependency" and "addiction."—D B)

NOTE

1   This is the last passage Michaux added to the 1972 edition of *Miserable Miracle* It seems to be his last word on mescaline. But the echoes will continue .   —D. B

SLEEPERS,

WAYS OF

WAKERS

Michaux apparently wrote this book because he was asked to; he seemed particularly well suited to write about sleep and dreams. But in actual fact, as he says again and again, dreams don't interest him—at least, not night dreams. He nonetheless reports a fair number of them in this volume and analyzes them in his own poetic (not psychoanalytic) way.

The two dreams below are related to basic longings in the poet: to understand and actually become part of another world, an extrahuman world, and to find "a language in which everyone really under[stands] everyone else at last."

THE CURTAIN OF DREAMS

(. . .)

Another time, under the eaves of a big house, I see some birds. Mostly waders. Among them a sea bird, a solan gannet, rough and foul smelling. I ignore the stench, regardless of how much it bothers me.

While I'm talking with the man next to me, I have the feeling that the bird has understood what we were just saying. As I say something to it, it answers me, very much at its ease, free of any prejudice. Ah, here's something that's going to change life, to make it natural at last, freed from its unbearable barriers.

Is this extraordinary? Yes and no. It is not completely unexpected. It's not surprising that it's talking simply and easily. For unless I am very much mistaken, that bird is also a woman, an American woman who came to see me this afternoon, who spoke French from time to time. I can't tell you how much she irritated me. While she was babbling I distanced myself from her as if she were not only a being from another race and civilization that has nothing in common with our own, but even another species of animal. I wanted none of her in the human race. Inwardly, I rejected her utterly. She had come for some information. I refused. But little by little, as my disgust diminished, intrigued by so much barbarousness, I was the one who asked for and obtained information about her girlish life which finally made that absurd foreign woman exist for me. After all, she's a human being, too.

As the visit had upset me, I had to erase it. The movies. I went to see a film with beautiful shots of the outdoors. The American countryside. A magnificent river. The beauty of days gone by. Come now, everything isn't totally inhuman over there.

I made my peace with America. Through its landscapes, at least, *it talks a language I can understand*. Now I was calm again.

But what about her, that unbearable person who was brought up in such a different way, the kind of person whose motivations one hasn't the slightest wish to know (and besides, we wouldn't understand them), the kind of woman one calls a *bird?* Well, I made my peace with her, too.

The dream uses all these elements, all of them actually preformed already.

There are many other beginnings that insidiously lead us to the world of animals... and yet of humans, so that dreams, by completing the fleeting impressions of daytime, later agglutinate them in the most unexpected way.

Hence this next dream. But first I want to describe the atmosphere I was living in at that time. With a maker of science films and his crew, I was looking for locations to film. It wasn't easy, in fact nothing was easy. They said they understood my point of view, but they didn't, and I didn't understand theirs. I couldn't get the objects, the meetings, the appointments, the material I wanted, the shots—nor, above all, the style. They came back with "technique," technical limits, technical demands, techniques of every kind, never the ones I needed.

Everything was artifice, nothing was ordered by nature, that nature which in a way (an unusual way, I admit) I wished to join. I needed *a language in which everyone really understood everyone else at last.*

One night, I dream. I am walking through the halls with my hands full of things. Impossible to find the director. I have something to tell him about this afternoon's shooting. Although I pass by many offices full of people, I can't manage to run into him. Ah! his dog, a big German shepherd. Now, here's something that brings me closer to my goal. Hugging the dog's head (he's standing up on his hind legs): "Well!" I say, "so where's Eric?" (that's his master), expecting to see his good old head brighten at the name. And now to my great surprise a voice answers me, as if it were coming from his entrails, the semblance of a voice, with no precise vowels, but nonetheless not confused (no onomatopoeias or pidgin, as one might expect, instead of the complete sentences I actually hear). It was the sound quality that bothered me: blurry, as if it were coming from behind drapes. Hurried phrases. It's quite clear he really wants to tell me what he knows. And, as he realizes I'm having trouble understanding, he starts explaining it to me in English,[1] still more volubly. Now, in fact, I understand him better. Nearly whole sentences are intelligible to me, clear, and moreover in normal syntax, perfect, coming out in one stream, with no hesitation at all. It's marvelous.

Something worth noticing: it's not the miracle in itself that bowls me over and fills me with pleasure: for me, the miracle is that this major discovery in nature—the speech of dogs—has been revealed to me for the first time after all the years I've gone around looking at animals from all sides. How wretchedly absentminded I am!

Well, now I know. At least I'll have met one talking dog. My desire to meet his master has been pushed into the background. The important revelation commands all my attention. I've heard dogs talk. I'm going to watch them more closely from now on. They won't fool me any more. As I turn these thoughts over in my mind, I touch lightly on the surface, which is waking, a slow, cottony, solidifying business, which dissolves the other.

...No doubt I've drifted off. And a common language between dogs and men has temporarily led me into error. I was seeking, and all night I kept seeking, understanding between human beings, quite simply—between different categories of human beings—surely that aspiration has been wonderfully satisfied and I wake up feeling immense contentment. Hasn't it been oversatisfied? What is this need, one might say, for utopia, for extravagance?

Underlying all this is one of my major problems.

As a child I did not understand other people. And they didn't understand me. I found them absurd. They were foreigners. Since then, this has gotten better. Nonetheless, the impression that we don't really understand each other has not disappeared. Oh, if only there were a universal language that absolutely everybody could understand! dogs, men, children—and not just a little, not with things being kept back. The appeal and the mirage of a true, immediate language—the longing for it—has survived in me despite everything.

On many occasions, women's voices, overheard during the day from fairly far away, when one can make out the high sounds of soprano voices without grasping the meaning, on many occasions people to whom one is listening absentmindedly or with irritation while they keep talking away, will make me "dream": neither women nor birds, half-women, half-birds. Hardly conscious, the vague thought of the day continues to make its way, night comes and those birds, freed from our rationalizing surveillance, will talk, and there's nothing surprising about them talking French, since they're Frenchwomen.

During the centuries when people thought that what had been encountered in a dream really existed somewhere, these dreams of talking animals must have had real consequences. Surely they were greeted with emotion, for when they awoke, the dreamers thought they had been in places where animals still spoke. Stories began to circulate from different sides, from witnesses, as it were.

They were not the creation of storytellers in need of a story, nor of silly nannies hurriedly answering the questions of little children who really haven't noticed the clear, definitive differences between animals and men yet.

No, men attentive to their dreams must have had some personal experience of talking animals. First.

I have always avoided people (however important they may have been in other respects) who had great, beautiful dreams, as being individuals with whom any real, profound understanding was impossible.

Is affinity and antipathy through dreams a general fact?

Is it natural?

Dissatisfaction through dreams:

Perhaps when I used to have my dynamic dreams during the day, daydreams I was able to make fascinating, exalting, it was more against my night dreams than against my life.

After daydreams, no need for dreams.

Deep, calm nights.

NOTE

1. Not in Michaux's native French

MOMENTS:

Crossings

of

Time

This slim volume of poems—and here, for once, the poems meet the simplest definition for poetry, as none have justified right margins—shows that Michaux's lifelong interest in the philosophy and religions of Asia has increased. Thus "Yantra" is the term for a Hindu drawing designed to aid meditation and religious awakening; it symbolically represents the moving, evolving cosmos and the unity of its contrasting principles, such as male/female: for example, triangles with their apex up are male, and triangles with their apex down are female. Michaux's poem is a verbal cosmogram.

Also behind these poems lies Michaux's attempt to penetrate pictures and paintings, to get inside them, to translate the world of art, whether visual or verbal (e.g., Paul Celan's), into his own words, and to do so as if from within, from the *other side*.

(*MOMENTS* *Traversées du temps*, Gallimard, 1973)

THE THIN MAN[1]

Looking at engravings by Matta.

Little
little in the wind
little and lacunary
in a hurry and knowing that quickly he has to know
in his cockpit in his little galaxy
on guard
perpetually on watch
in his automotor
in his autocorrector
in his tiny bit of peace
in his no peace at all
hissing in the shower of a thousand alarms
sounded and smashed
whistled up
hit by calls
pierced
thinking himself flesh
wishing himself in a palace
but living in pulleys
multiplicitous and frail
a watchmaker nonetheless
and a fetus too, commanding through the squalls
aimed at
broken into
boarded
gripped onto
clawed into

rained on by blows
engraved like a plaque
clicking like a teletype
pushed aside
diverted

mirror broken a thousand times
bewildered
listening
not wanting to be lost
drawing plans on a map
contradictory plans
foreign plans
plans bouncing back
infinite plans
struggling with plans
never going under
still struggling
knocked over
standing up again
and alerted again
dried out

making plans again
counterplans
plans of opposition
in obscurity
into futurity
in indeterminacy
a pilot
pilot as long as he can
pilot or nothing

in flight
a target staring

staring

plotting

planning

He who was born in the night

again and again will make his Mandala

THE DAY, THE DAYS, THE END OF DAYS

Meditation on the end of Paul Celan.

· ·

In silence, stoned to death by their thoughts

Still another day on a lesser level. Shadowless gestures
What century must we look at, to see?

Ferns, ferns, they might be sighs, everywhere, sighs
The wind scatters the loose leaves

Strength of stretchers, eighteen hundred thousand years ago people
were already born to rot, to die, to suffer

We've already had days like this
so many days like this

day that swallows up the wind
day of unbearable thoughts

I see men motionless
lying in barges

Out of here.
Whatever else, out of here.

The long knife of the wave will stop the Word.

YANTRA[a]   *To Kim Chi*

Filled with the power of meaning
with the plenitude of rejection, of withdrawal
the stiff serpent riddled with sounds

Stretched out, vertical
simultaneously outside and inside at the four points of the compass
withdrawn
yet in the Infinite
Universal self at all points reconjugated

Allied to the subterranean, to darkness
exactly where the dark force charges forward with furor
mouth to mouth the noble and ignoble
Unperturbed
unpenetrated
at the center of the axial space
away from the tormentresses

Descent into the forbidden zone

Eliminated the now, the accidental
the dust of the existential
eliminated, attachment
blind to otherness
invested with grandeur

[a]About a series of tantric paintings

with silence
with immateriality
with the murky vagueness of the dark powers

Faceless force
Matrix of forms and rampart against forms
In space a faceless eye is watching
with an unchanging stare
without budging, without eyelid
without tiring

Call to order
Call to return
Call to abolish

Triangles
insignificant, infinitely signifying
emotionless, accentless
nothing distinguishes them
thin triangles upside down
crossing equal triangles rightside up
revealing to the initiate their whispering secret.

. . . .

Spots, lines, here, there
impenetrable figures
Speak of beginnings, of engagements
out at the furthest stars perhaps.

Support of the meditator
at the center a point
only a point
fulfilling the need of all needs
the need for essence

for the essence of essences
in the center a point
recalling, without betraying.

Hub of arrivals
Compass of the Spirit
Circles of the ubiquitous male-female conjunction
Labyrinths:
slipping into them
imperious flagstaffs of the alphabet of the gods' own language go winding

Principle without speech,
Principle of all principles
Return to the Principle
referring us to a level beyond
always on the vibration of the Unique
tuned to everything in depth
in intimate conjunction
embracing,
in efforts to embrace, wider and still wider

The cloud of being condenses
contracts
Universe-Cosmos
cosmos of the universe of the "self"

Material reality, fat, heavy, peasant
but bound by a thread
to endlessness, and the strangeness binds it by a thread
thread roping down
emptiness itself is bound to it
totality bound to it
time and space undivided bound to it
and the original Egg floating on the waves of Formlessness is bound to it

creation and dissolution

and innerness is bound to it

and the diamond bound to its own meditation

Knowledge. Knowledge participating

Immensifying illumination in which everything goes into resonance with everything

contemplated. United

Geometry beyond geometries,

Lines, like slowed-down radiations,

insistent, clairvoyant

loaded with magic

Design for returning to the absolute

Destiny-design

1. Michaux's title, originally in English.

FACING

THE

VANISHING

WORLD

The title echoes the earlier *Facing the Locks.*

One of the hiding or "vanishing" phenomena Michaux wishes to confront is that of pain: we have all felt it, of course, but can we really remember intense pain, hold on to it? Can we learn from it? Pain comes up again and again in the poet's work; it is never rendered more strongly than in *Broken Arm*. The lesson he draws from his experience—damaging one arm, "discovering" the other—is a traditional Asian one of unity in contrast and opposition (here, left and right) as in Hinduism. He will meditate further on this odd unity five years later, in "Observations," p. 335, below.

The last piece in this section shows the poet pursuing the goal of unity by means of meditation. He, who has so strongly experienced the fragmentation of the self, is now striving in his text for a mystical integration with the universe, outside of time, outside of words. It is a surprising, impossible goal, but perhaps this is the "counter-life" he has always been seeking, consciously or not. Is he picking up on something he learned from mescaline? from Zen Buddhism? from painting? Michaux will follow this track more and more in the decade he has left to live, as we shall see in his next books—hence the brevity of the excerpt on contemplation from this book given here.

(Face à ce qui se dérobe, Gallimard, 1975)   241

BROKEN ARM

One day I had a fall. My arm could not resist it, and broke. Breaking an arm is no big deal. It has happened to several, to many. Still, it might be something worth observing well. This condition sent by chance, and followed by a few complications—I watched it. I swam around in it. I did not try to swim back to shore immediately.

I know, brave men turn away from this sort of thing. Out of modesty? Out of pride? Out of instinct? (for the will to get through it, and hope, make for a good convalescence...) But is this really intelligent?

Suffering is a world apart. Isolated, through our fault, through our failure to establish connections from it to us, from it to other impressions. Is this a rejection?

(. . .) In the same way,[1] physical pain creates disconcerting perceptions. Erroneous sensations, that have to be rectified, ceaselessly rectified, a path to delirium if they become too strong, going beyond the patient's resistance and capacity for rectification, pains that make either the body or the mind unbearable. The relationships that are so difficult to establish between pain and any new aesthesia—that's what the sufferer cannot master, that is his real suffering, the pain within the pain,[a] his failure, and also, while waiting for a better time, aiming stupidly at the future, that's how he'll forget the pain he turned his back on, how he'll become totally unable to evoke it; and yet it was that suffering which was so important, which took up his whole space. Coenaesthesia, mare nostrum, mother of the absurd. Illnesses, pain, physical sufferings are something one cannot assimilate.

As for me, I would like not to have missed the mark, not to have suffered in vain.

[a] You can't do anything with physical suffering, whereas emotional suffering is a pleasure (for some people) to communicate, to pour it out as many times as they can on to other people, who identify with it But how can you make someone identify with a fracture, peritonitis, cancer?

(. . .)

I fell. Only my left self got up again, and everything became perfectly neutral.

. . . .

A while ago, on the very spot where the accident took place, right after the fracture, when I didn't know yet that my right elbow was broken, the spirit of my body had silently, secretly deserted it. It had left those privileged places of my presence and power, of my actions, and would not return for months, neither to my hand nor to my arm, despite all that would be done to bring it back and encourage it to return.

It was sulking. In its turn, it was abandoning the arm that had abandoned *it,* and even five months later, it was in vain that the physical therapist would exhort me to go back into my arm. But I was getting along with the left: the very next day after the fall, I had begun—somehow or other, despite its clumsiness, its quasi-inexistence—to write vermicularly with my left hand, so as not to lose all trace of that frozen, sleeping-beauty aspect of nature that I wanted to observe,[2] so as never to forget it or leave it out of my future investigations.

The one who is the left in me, who never in my lifetime had been first, who had always lived in retreat and now was the only one I still had, a placid one—I couldn't stop keeping after him, endlessly watching him with surprise: a self, brother of my Self. And always the frozen countryside all around, which couldn't come to life, asleep, and I never would have thought that I had been the one animating it so much, even when I was, as so often I am, weary and worn out.

How wrong I was! How wrong one is, always!

No doubt the big smack I received at the time of the accident was keeping me exceptionally quiet. But the "shocked" state couldn't have lasted for weeks, and certainly not for months to such a degree that during this whole time it was impossible for me to get animated (still less to get angry). I continue to blame my left being for this state,[b] the one who contains my left arm, my left hand, and my gauche lefty ways—the one I don't recognize as being me: me, a real right-hander. My left arm has no style, no animation, education, affirmation, no strength. With that arm, that hand, truly *gauche,* truly left, I can't

[b]For a long time after the accident, I was not yet able to establish a valid relationship with that left hand, between it and my complex self My writing remained formless, like a schoolboy's—calm, all crooked, characterless, without impressionability, while the day I took up my right hand again to write with, although its writing was thwarted and almost illegible, it contained me immediately and translated me The same phenomenon appears in left-handed people with an injured left arm One of my neighbors, a painter and a left-hander, told me that when his left arm was immobilized the year before, for the five weeks of immobilization when he used his right, he could not find his style, which had become similarly dull, boring, empty, conscientious and ordinary Having drawn a few lessons from this event, I have—quite belatedly—tried to educate my left a bit I've even managed to get some reflexes out of that sleeper. It still lacks strength

even manage turning a doorknob or a key in a lock. My left being—the totally uneducated one—was all I had now.

(. . .)

. . . For a time, I had lost my faith in criticism, in contradiction, in rebellion—in their validity, which up to then had seemed unquestionable for me... so *that* was all it depended on!

Meanwhile, I got to know my left more and more, that subordinate, so proper, the one who never had wanted to look after my person and who did not satisfy me, but in whom I was relaxing and expanding like gas in a balloon. Too much. Without any emotion at all, I learned I was to have an operation on my oleocranon.[3] My calm state continued. Placidly, I went back to Paris, alone, not worried, not agitated, carefree, or perhaps care was not succeeding in arousing any emotion in me.

When they brought me into the operating room, I looked at its occupants one after the other—surgeons, assistants, nurses... They seemed to be gathered there for a reception (and indeed it was a reception, the reception of my body, which I had just delivered to them). After introducing himself to me, a doctor in a white smock gave me an injection in the arm, asked me to count from one, and before I had reached eight or seven, they ceased to exist for me, but they, active and efficient, took advantage of this without delay, and no doubt came up to me and with no further ado began to handle me, cut me up, slice into me, dress my wound, make me breathe, sew me up again—each one according to his abilities, until he was satisfied. Then I had to be brought back to a room, where it was very hot, and put between spectacularly white sheets. But I didn't notice it at the time, as I was still absent.

Awakening. And also, little by little, an unknown pain is awakening.

Red-hot embers. Burning embers in the arm. Embers and piercings. Horrible, those embers... and absurd. My arm was there, before this. It can't have become embers. Nonetheless, that message of "fire," repeated again and again. Fire. Fire without flames. Meanwhile, turning my head carefully so as not to move my shoulder, I can see a mass of bandages on what must be my arm and can't be fire, for who would put bandages on a fire? And yet...

Fire. Fire. Fire ceaselessly repeated.

Intervening at last, morphine puts its dampers on and I can go back to my dome (if I may put it that way) and a space, free from fire. I fall asleep in it.

Awakening.

The fire starts up again.

Fire. Fire. Fire. Fire ceaselessly fire. Fire for me, burning for me alone.

(. . .)

A vat. This illness[c] is a huge vat, and I have to hold it steady with a tensed soul, so that no further in me will it progress, so that it does not make deeper pain.

I have to hold it back and this "fire, fire, fire," this signal of fire in me ceaselessly emitted, must ceaselessly be rectified by my brain, by my weary brain.

Since this morning, to my right, to my right which is no longer an arm, which is no longer embers, a piece of furniture.

That's the inner signal now. The signal no longer says fire. It's not saying hindrance or heaviness, no, it's not even saying furniture, it's sometimes a large, freestanding wardrobe-closet, sometimes a chest of drawers. I look ten, twenty times: looking exists to correct one's impressions.

The arm is still there, despite the closet.

(. . .)

So I will have lived for two days in my bed with, instead of a forearm and a wrist, a piece of furniture on my arm, attached to my body: acting as if it were natural, absent-mindedly listening to conversations, and then one morning, with no transition, there's a link of chain in place of a piece of furniture, a link of chain on my arm (why a link?), an enormous link weighing about two hundred pounds, a link from the kind of chain used to haul up the anchors of ocean liners. (Not very different from the wardrobe-closet in weight, but hanging more. And that's why, no doubt...)

Someone unfamiliar with these phenomena might think this link would disappear whenever I looked at my arm. What a mistake: it's the arm that seemed to fool me, despite

[c]Unexpectedly, osteoporosis had seized me from my shoulder to my fingertips

its reality, since I knew that all day, as soon as I turned my eyes somewhere else, I would be dragging, I would have to drag around a bulky, heavy link of chain—too heavy: decidedly, I was not made for this. Who is made for it?

Why not simply a weight? Sorry: it was a link of chain. From the start, it was definitely a link of chain.

(. . .)

Now, walls!
Am I going to have to become a wall-moving company?
It's absurd to live in bed with walls!

(. . .)
These walls always on my arm, in air actually free of any obstacle...
This absurdity that comes back despite my constant refutation is tiring, tiring.
I'm not going to be able to hold out indefinitely...

Excavations, digs are going on inside me. Digs. I'm beginning to be terrified of digs. I can't take it any more.

Digs. Digs for nothing, to increase the pain, to multiply it, they're skinning me alive (a bad attitude, to be changed).

(. . .)
Pain just wants to become one with me, to weigh on me, expand, stretch out in me, be my city with me as its only inhabitant, to reign, to have all it wants in me.

Where can I stick it, stuff it, keep it away, at what window, so that it can entertain itself all alone, that pain I'd like to drown, to explode... But it feeds on me. It can't live elsewhere.

Maybe infinity would absorb it...

(. . .)

I do think, nonetheless. How can I dissolve my suffering? There must be a lack of intelligence on my part here. I would like this suffering to explode. No, that's not—unfortunately!—what thinking means.

One broken bone has boarded my life and taken it over. Hurt moves forward, and I can't move forward. Deep in my body the pain is buried... and me with my mind disoriented by its howling reports... (can't it alert me in a more discreet way, a way more suited to my nature?)

Pain I have to taste drop by drop.

Pain! Pain! Pain! pain without ending sliding down in me, and its wild brass band, its excruciating trumpet, for me alone. Pain and me, horrible "just the two of us," with the curtains drawn. Pain surviving everything like some inept sect transmitted all wrong, an outdated commandment governing us still.

Pain! Pain![d]

It was no longer the fracture of the arm, which had been successfully operated on, that was causing all this pain, but a posttraumatic complication (hand-shoulder syndrome).[e] (. . .)

(. . .)

My right hand, which had been completely out of it, which for weeks at a time had known only the most ascetic sensations—those of pain, hard, pure, intense—now all of a sudden, its grandeur having fallen, was receiving sensations pell-mell, sensations, through thousands of little points that had regained their sensitivity, the velvet of tiny sensations (which come from contact, heat, the pressure of blood and flesh, from outside forces), the multitude of those constant sweet little messages of nice bourgeois comforts and the mess of ordinary reality. Odious! disgusting! Whole prairies of wheedling little points.[f] I never would have thought it possible.

(. . .)

Now to speak of rehabilitation exercises. Those movements . . . were painful, and what struck me was that . . . they seemed to me *against nature*. Finger movements, very simple ones (to look at them), were (when felt) the very essence of incongruity. After long months, when I succeeded in turning my hand inwardly as everyone commonly does without paying any particular attention to it, I waited, stupefied, I remember, convinced that some disaster

[d]In the calm room, in appearance I was calm, too Silently I was swallowing my plate of suffering, under the eyes (slightly embarrassed) of people who had better things to eat They would talk to me Friends, no doubt Me, in the fire, them, outside It was never really fair
[e]Or decalcifying algo-neurodystrophia
[f]Must I add, in case someone doubts it, that I had formerly used my sense of touch like everybody else, without disgust?

was bound to strike—so it seemed—as if, for example, I had made my head go through a complete rotation all the way to my back. So totally had I lost the naturalness of my gesture that it seemed to me a crazy exploit. That's the way I experienced it, too. Such is that naturalness—too composite, then terrifying, revolting, disconcerting—which habit has made natural for me once again.

There is not, in this life, any naturalness that is really natural. Only adaptation. Usage, use prolonged a bit, usages...

Arm back again.

To itself? To me. A limb again, nothing more than a limb... at my disposal.

. . . . ' . . . .

Years have passed. Case closed.

However, now that I am free from pain, couldn't I understand certain points differently?

(. . .)

Soon forgetful—forgetting now in the other direction (one consciousness excludes the other)—I was beginning to use my arm again in a matter-of-fact way, with satisfaction, with satisfactions.
I would still do things with it...

As for the left arm, normal and disciplined once again, I was about to forget it. Bad idea. Bad idea, too, to educate it stupidly, to try to make a second right out of it. Or turn the left hand into an imitation of the right hand. Besides, it was too late, as I had passed the age where that performance can still succeed.
I insisted on keeping up the difference. I had to make its personality come out more, establish itself. Dance of the left hand. Mime of the left hand. Style of the left hand. What a pleasure! What a victory to set it to expressing itself, to being itself: frankly, uniquely, "left."
Insufficient as it may still be, its progress was not negligible. There was never any question of turning it into a virtuoso.

Different, its role. If it became brilliant, it would lose its being, and—still more se-rious—the relationship it establishes somewhere with me. I'm sure I need this. Everyone needs it to remain in harmony with those aspects of reality to which the over-active, over-efficient right (and the zone of the brain concerning that right)—too active, too efficient—is insensitive.

No doubt we need our penchant to be withdrawn, inactive, subsensitive, foreign in a way, distant, nonparticipating, close to the vegetative, to the secret, to the flip side of things.

That which does not take part, and does not intervene, sinks down. Preparation for mystery. Sliding into the subconscious.

In all probability it helps deaden the effect of a right that is too present, too immediate, too much for power; it must join in puncturing pretensions and illusions about the value of conquest, actions, ambitions.

In the left-right household that makes up every human being, his inclinations count. The contrary would be unthinkable. One must remain faithful to him.

Pendulum that restores its value to the unsituated confronted by the situated, to the indeterminate confronted by the determinate, and contributes to that double bottom, to that double aspiration which goes along with broad understanding, with antinomic realities.

The right-left unity—one of the numerous divisions of being, a division to retain, which is also union. Perhaps it has something to do with the great syntheses and theories of the World, which harmonize with the being of man. Perhaps it has put us on the way of Purusha-Prakriti,[4] and, in truly new scientific research, it has contributed and continues to maintain a two-leveled openness, a double understanding.[g]

[g]To accentuate asymmetry and not to reduce it—that's what is important, what should be taught, and must be learned by anyone who seeks to know himself (to succeed in doing it better than I did)

ARRIVAL IN ALICANTE

Got there tired, abnormally tired.

Cold, the room. Inhospitable, and they won't be able to hold it for me.

I go downstairs, I wander through the streets. After two sleepless nights, rest does not come to the preoccupied, buzzing, overheated mind. Eyes tired from night reading do not enjoy looking. They long to close, to see nothing, to give up.

Arrival at a Square. Its old-fashioned look, its date trees, its charm are arresting, relaxing. On one side, outdoors, an extremely modest restaurant-bar. I walk over to that side of the Square and sit down outside in the company of the palm trees.

The waiters don't exactly rush over to take my order. Fine. I have time, too.

A group of Spaniards appears at the other side of the Square. They came out small, quite small, extraordinarily small. Hardly a few inches high, I would have said. Oh, of course I knew they weren't really that small, knew it was impossible for so many reasons that I was too weary to examine but which I was practically certain about. Yet inexplicably I could not manage to see them any taller. Besides, how is this normally done? How did I do it before? I was responsible—obviously—for this defective vision, and I couldn't find anything to do about it. As they entered my ocular chamber small, I suppose I was neglecting to enlarge them, to enlarge them sufficiently or to feel them enlarged.

What if this became permanent, became an infirmity? I didn't move. It was adding to my fatigue. One more deficiency. What would they take away from me next? I remained inert. In no hurry to find out.

A little satisfaction sneaked in, too: so, something was still happening to me on my travels, after so many trips on this worn-out planet!

Then, from not so far away, chatting as they approached, came two men whose voices (their *voices,* at any rate) did not suffer any diminution—something that made me decide to look directly up at them, noticing with pleasure that they were two peasants about five feet two or four, a normal height in this province. Had I recovered?

To the waiter who then came over with a plate of *alcachofas* I also gave his real height as soon as I saw him, apparently without taking anything off it.

There remained the group at the other end of the Square. I refrained from looking toward that side, as my cure might not be complete, my vision perhaps not restored for all distances.

By the time I made up my mind, the group had disappeared.

A few moments before, they had walked in front of a building under renovation, and I could make out the sculptures on it only imperfectly: from afar I thought they were somewhat in the Manuelian style—an unimportant error of judgment. Even if they only had a distant connection to this style, that did not argue in the slightest against my newly restored visual perception.

A girl coming in on a motorbike reassured me completely. At a fair distance, I could already make out what she must look like and easily recomposed her body, slim but absolutely not shortened, and the same went for her brand-new moped: she was proudly holding its extravagant handlebars, which, like the ones they make today, were not small.

So I had recovered, I had completely recovered. It really looked like it; for I hadn't simply let myself be taken in by some more or less powerful illusion a little while ago. No, that exaggerated smallness was absolutely unequivocal. A shrinkage impossible to combat. Some mechanism that turns the image right side up and enlarges it, or enlarges it psychologically, working from the image—a mechanism that, like all vertebrates, I possessed—had ceased to function. Something pathological, the possible beginning of a brain tumor, that's what I had been afraid of.

Be that as it may, I hastened to take in a glass of wine and a few mouthfuls of bread. So, without a sound, and without giving myself away, I set out anew, with my original foundation, to reconquer the World. The appearance of things seemed stable and well consolidated once again. It *was* the world as it had been. Discreetly, privately, I celebrated it.

As for the Square, it was perfect.

Nothing was missing. I admired it, I savored it. Modest as it was, it had everything a man who's recuperating needs.

SURGING OUT FROM MEDITATION

Silence. Day of silence. Come back to it. Get back inside it. Impermanence has been left behind. And out of impermanence, little by little, we find (some more, some less) in the calmed-down being, progressively, repeatedly deepened, Permanence, its radiance, the other life, the counter-life.[h]

[h]Alone, without words words locate you You have to reside in the nonlocated without exchanges in order to be without cuts in a closed, covered space, without a horizon, sheltered from all modification, with no possibility of anyone interrupting you (   )

NOTES

1. .   in the same way that special eyeglasses in a famous psychological experiment—described by Michaux—change the subjects' spatial perceptions and oblige them to relearn how to walk, run, ride a bike, et cetera, and then they have to learn how to perform motor activities all over again when they take the glasses off

2   The accident took place in the Alps.

3.   Bone of the elbow.

4.   In Hindu philosophy, the two contrasting, complementary aspects of the divinity: male/female, inactive/active, spirit/matter, and so forth

PATHS LOOKED FOR,

PATHS LOST,

TRANSGRESSIONS

Almost half of this collection is devoted to prose pieces Michaux wrote about paintings by mental patients—but this poet-artist doesn't write "about" art; he recreates it in words. He did this throughout his career, from the early "Drawings with Commentary" (*The Night Moves,* above) through his later "Reading" of lithographs by Zao Wou-ki to "Adventures of Lines," his remarkable 1954 "essay" on Paul Klee (both in *Passages,* below), or his 1972 *Dreaming From Enigmatic Paintings.* In "Ravaged People" the artists are insane, clinically defined as such, and in trying to understand them Michaux is pursuing another lifelong project. As he "translates" their work, he seems to be simultaneously inside and outside their minds.

The last series of poems in this volume is quite different, as the titles show (I translate literally here): "Detachings," "Unburyings," "Days of Silence." The poet is following the path toward mystical unity evoked at the end of the previous section. To what extent has that path been traced by Buddhism, Hinduism, poetic meditation—or mescaline? We are not sure. At any rate, close to eighty years old now, he is moving toward silence in more ways than one: "Great day that nonword has made limitless . . ." These are, necessarily, difficult poems.

(Chemins cherchés chemins perdus transgressions, Gallimard, 1981)

RAVAGED PEOPLE

ing themselves, they hide.

ng, they show themselves.

Pages that came to me while contemplating paintings by the insane, men and women in difficulty, who could not surmount the insurmountable. Most of them institutionalized. With their secret, diffuse problem (uncovered again and again, yet hidden), they reveal above all—and immediately—their enormous, ineffable discomfort

I

The one who wishes to keep out of reach of the "surrounders" is protecting himself now with the bulky undownable body of a great quadruped, into which he has animally transformed. A leonine tail ending in claws—and it can whip around, too—half pulled forward, at the ready, determined.

With his defenses in place, he waits. Constantly, suspiciously.

A deeply lodged discomfort does not preclude a sense of security based on unshakably implanted ideas.

A block of silence: it will not let itself be penetrated, lets nothing penetrate.

A sphinx that will not answer your questions, that—motionless, mutely—asks *its* questions, the gravest of questions. Facing you, and always the same ones.

With its whole length leaning on its sizable base, possessing knowledge of the Ineffable, the man-eyed sphinx holds its pose, which must never be disturbed again.

2

Thrown on his back, cracked, hacked into pieces, with any connection to the human race now utterly forgotten, this one perceives himself only as ground now, ground constantly slashed apart (with collapsing anonymous mounds thrown up-cast down) not even ground any more, but waves of an angry sea, a wild sea of ground, never to be calm again.

Under this shapeless shape that deprives him of himself, he survives, prevented from recovering. Continual collapse.

Fragments indefinitely: fragments, flaws, fissures. Oblique wreck.

3

The wave, the double, the triple wave, right in front of you, heaving up, disproportionately taking up space, bears eyes in its slow whirlpools.

Majestically rolling and unrolling, endlessly coming in at him, it carries in, carries out, and carries back eyes, huge eyes with a reproachful, resentful look.

Suspended in the rising swell, they don't ever let go of him, see only him, are there only for him, eyes lusting after evil, eyes full of fury, on the constantly returning waves, filled with gigantic energy.

4

On a vast expanse of liquid plain, in a colossal, ponderous, Protestant canoe that has come down from the North, he stands, stiff and alone, alone as a man can be when he is not on the path to salvation, when, in the dark zone, he has forced his way through the forbidden passage. All around, the water: absolutely calm, neither moved nor loved, heavy water.

On this horizontal plane where his progress is painful, as if he were on an uphill climb, the man of withdrawal, hermit of the "Absolute," shows only his back, straight as a wall.

He is inhabited by the seriousness of the one Idea. Serious against them all. Certain among them all. Nonetheless, a melancholy, a distress fit for the end of the world, an irreversible fatality inhabit the cold landscape through which he, who is so wrong about himself, is passing.

The heavy monoxylic pirogue is sinking slowly into the dead space.

Overcast sky. One-winged birds. Branchless trees.

5

Heads that have gone through something as serious as death and who could not save themselves, or else not very well.

Heads of the past, that *know* the night of life, the Secret, the awful Unnameable on which all being was supported.

Struggling against blurriness, masses that try to reconstitute themselves in vain, struggling against the invading mush.

Heads profoundly hurt, that no longer trust anything, that remember.

One of them seriously smashed in, its eyes fixed and wide like the eyes of a fish, the oculomotor muscles seemingly stuck so that they can only stare straight ahead, facing others, facing the way one faces up to the world.

A gigantic nose, spilling over, pushed over, crooked, twisted, from the base to the top twisted, seems almost in profile.

Above, unchanged by the twisting, which should be painful (like the ring in a tame bull's nostrils) and even truly horrible, the impassive eyes—a major discord, the signature of his illness—act as if there were nothing wrong; in this impossible, highly upsetting contradiction, they continue, they hold fast.

The inhabitant of the disordered face is not giving up.

7

The girl, her virginity lost, a buck belling above her, is carried off without resistance, with her bed and all, by a gigantic cayman that soon dives and sinks into the waters.

Flowers fall, fruits are ripped out, earthy roots reappear at the surface. Thus is the rape of long ago remembered, unbearable forever.

In the poverty of the old clothes, in the indigence of the wretched bed, in the dying colors of the flowers, in the smallness of the hands, in the grimacing contortions of the dress swept away, in the swarming behind her of oversized whirlpools, the malignity of hostile forces *speaks*.

Bending over her, falsely good-natured, foreign faces, heads with necklaces of slugs or larvae, the faces of distant beings, offering nothing to lean on—unmovable, hypocritical, social masks. To the left, down below, once more the crocodile sinks under the waters with its victim.

9

The becalmed three-master—marvelously, totally white, so white it's crazy to be that white—has come to a halt in an immense deserted zone.

Never mind the wind or the absence of wind or the threat of wind: the three-master that doesn't want to change will not unrig. Frail, but not yielding, especially not to the obvious, especially not to obvious variations in reality—and by dint of not yielding, it has ended up in a space where there is nothing left that moves, where every breeze has been dead for a long time. And there's no turning back.

Is there nothing else left, nor anyone anywhere? There is. In the distance, a few raised folds of the many-shaped cloth of the five worlds reveal, squeezed together in a row, alert, the ambiguous faces of the "others."

Threatening? Envious? Rather, out of reach; they have taken their precautions.

In the absolute calm, where not the smallest gust arises, ever, the virgin three-master will not haul in its immaculate sails: it remains unsullied under an irreproachable sky of ice.

10

The bulky snake embracing that thick pleasure-loving Mother Earth as if she were his *thing*, won't let her go. A disgusting smell coming out of her, you can bet on it. And look at him, see what he's doing to her! And what she's letting him do! (Thus the unspeakable spoken after all.)

The huge head of the lustful fork-tongued demon watches over Earth to see that she stays far from the cone of light. Not that the admirable, clear, regenerating rays of light are going by so far away, but obviously she won't go that distance, irremediably occupied, embraced, weighed down as she is. Nets encircle her, as if she weren't held enough.

II

A nightstand is watched over by two swans. Each swan is watched by two ocelots. Each ocelot (or panther or large spotted cat) by two snakes. Each snake by sixteen triangles, and under surveillance are the triangles, by countless eyes, fixed, staring.

Nothing must escape the multiple police. Nothing can get away from the omnipresent Order.

In all this you can feel the danger of not enough watching, of lacking in vigilance: a moment of inattention would do the trick. A moment of inattention could, in the next few seconds, cause disaggregation then universal disintegration.

Distant consequence of a Guilty Verdict. Maybe.

So many potential dislocations in the "correspondences" of creation, since the whole world may be punished through the fault of thoughtless men, a world that in actual fact weighs on the shoulders of one man alone, who can no longer rest, forced to become the necessary sentry, the only one who knows, who keeps watch, who can still put off the boundless disaster that is on its way.

12

Faces crushed in, sunk into one another. The agglomerate of faces, topped by a mediocre bird, is stupidly crowned like some silly idiot on the night of a party and too much beer.

Heap of faces, faces in a blur like fetus in amnion. Eaten by one face is another face. Irresistibly, one sticks on to the other, which submits and sinks into it and slowly expires. Absorbent faces with long herbivorous tongues, liqueur-like, embarrassing, soft with slimy desires, leisurely... they eat each other up.

A lover's face agglutinates a whole row of nearby faces; she works at making them tender, then more tender still (humanity and pasty clay the same, so remarkably the same) and this facibalism spreads and increases in the little mound of flaccid inexpressive faces that stick to each other, devour each other and can't help it, nostalgically carried away by an irreversible drift. The limbo of this world, of those who have lost the power to push things away.

13

At some distance from the highest Summit, something like the Ark. Outside, barriers. The men who will be taken on, others who won't be taken, rejected at the last minute. The forsaken, the insane.

An intense, useless, scattered, contradictory movement, that will never cease... while pointlessly the rays of a star that looks like a sun go by ''off shore.''

14

Once the beast is out of the mattress, its appetite is enormous. Its teeth, impressively bared, signify to one and all that the wolf does not feed on roses. A milky space speaks of the disturbance and the birth, of swellings and swarming and the increase of pleasures.

Well, what's going to happen now?

Happen! To him, *there,* forever?

Staring, clouded, the great eyes suckling the spectacle of the world are contemplating the inside pulled outside, and from everything, from anything at all, they make milk. Those great thoughtful eyes will soon be submerged. The liquid in one is already rising and flowing and spreading outside over images he can no longer see. Milk, really, this milt?

16

The stout full-bodied woman with swollen, heavy, fascinating breasts burning red like a rekindled flame, the evil woman, covered and surrounded by cheap jewelry, is holding a mask—bigger than a small velvet eye-mask—around her eyes (eyes with no naïveté, eyes heavy with turpitude and base domination) and now carries away in her trailing skirt, ridiculously imperial, the web that holds men, tiny little men.

Clashing colors, vulgar as diarrhea, tell in their way what she would enjoy with men. No instruments of torture and tyranny are to be seen, but you can see them changed into loud colorings with flagellant stripes.

Who but the most nonexistent of men would accept their invitation, unless he had absolutely surrendered?

17

The slow quadruped moving forward in this absurdly bourgeois place, surrounded by thick whirlwinds, reveals—by lifting heavy curtains—reveals, above his great sad mouth, two sizable eyes, not quite dead, tears in reserve in the lacrimal pouch, in short the large bulbous eyes of a fifty-year-old alcoholic.

Not decided, not very much awake, a sticky look to him (a sign, perhaps, of the "falling sickness"), you can expect anything from him.

As he goes by, in his doglike form, under rich, hideous draperies, his oppressive presence, insistently inflicted—a faithful ignominious presence, animal latency in it, and the expectation of crisis—weighs ceaselessly down like a power locked up inside wax.

Locked up until when?

19

The bad angel, the angel of vice and death, the red-rayed angel holds the awakening sleeper under him—the terrified sleeper, making himself small, shrinking, already there isn't much left of him… under the threatening overhang of a great dull eye, like the eye of a hyena, frightening.

While a harp is flowering, and a kind of clergyman undergoes a mutilation that will perhaps become immolation, nobody around is surprised. Nobody seems to find anything strange about this, anything different or extraordinary or abnormal, as in fact it is the response to a problem, to his problem, the problem of a poor devil who's simply *stuck:* his idea, and him inside it like a fly inside a glass bell on a plate of cheese.

20

Grim, the demon of brown consciousness appears, with a demented eye. Crooked hands hold the cards of the game of fate, and he'll have to guess at them, plaques of mysteries that terrify the man who can't grasp anything no matter what he does. Above, a nasty sky, pitiless, a sky that has already delivered judgment, which will listen to nothing more, a dome on him as crushing as the endless sound of little high-pitched cymbals, crashing everywhere, deafening, imperatively obliging him to be silent.

In the distance two towers keep watch and a marshy surface shines.

At the limit of the sinister influence, four or five skinny, uncertain flowers are growing, slanting, poor, blocked, ill at ease, wretched.

· ·

So, life still has something to give?
What?

21

Taking up all the space, blocking the horizon, alone in the whole of the painting, an enormous head comes to meet whoever is looking at it and thus whoever painted it and saw it coming at him, threatening, malevolent, marked with the exaggerated signs of ferocious domination. Without a nose, without a mouth, without a forehead, or the whole thing jumbled together by a superhuman force like a tornado, it plunges ahead, at a restrained but irresistible speed, with its huge forces for aggression in reserve, ready.

Face issued from a maelstrom of hatred. Everything in the world that has been hostile to this man up to now is there, transformed into pure energy, and, this time, holds him at its mercy.

Loaded with diabolical dynamism and as it were bubbling, the eyes, shot through with vampiric, unspeakably implacable urges, ''command.''

No weapon anywhere is shown. No need.

The unstoppable is alone, and sufficient.

22

A creature of an unknown species, very, very near, with an enormous gaping terrifying opening just right for swallowing up the watcher, for making him disappear, soon hypnotized, lost, and above all lost is any idea of return. Fall into the enclosure of flesh. Someone certainly has this temptation.

Above, two dark eyes, globes of magnetic vision looking straight ahead, mono-ideaed, say in unison: "Would you make up your mind? Or must I still keep waiting?" For a bit of free will seems part of the rules of the game, of the sinister, fascinating game.

Teeth in one row guard—just about—the entrance. Almost translucent, they would hardly hurt, except perhaps upon leaving, if leaving were still a possibility.

In the depths of the cavernous palate it looks like fringes inside, hairs, a row of supple blades, black—like dark whalebones.

A strange entrance. The mouth—an almost flaming red—is reminiscent (by its circularity and the perfection of its curve) of a planet's admirable path around its mistress, the Star, the Star from which one cannot turn away.

24

A head with a low brow, eyes of darkness, and a huge mouth, has caught the vain framework of the inadequate refuge in its sharp canines and is savagely shaking and breaking and grinding it to bits.

Something irremediable has happened, is happening, had happened many times before, an endless repetition of the same ''punishment.''

The new shelter, like the ones before it and the ones that will follow, has been discovered and destroyed, lath by lath.

The defenseless being must succumb.

For the humiliated, the crushed, the vanquished, there would have to be a total change. Then and only then would shelter no longer be such an absolute necessity, no longer would a daytime or nighttime carnivore appear—or at least not one with such strong teeth.

26

Apathetic, with no power over the outside, one of those people who are all-or-nothing. It will be nothing. Still, he should have got himself a few weapons, some knowledge for example, or a little know-how. With the few cards he holds, the game was lost in advance, or terribly difficult.

Now a pariah and a pariah who can't float back up to the surface. The stopper that prevents him, that prevents him the most, is not shown, or just barely, and immediately disguised.

The drawing he does, that he's going to do, no matter where he begins and where he starts again, ends in inextricability. Indeed, no matter how large the animal or human shapes depicted at the start, they go off into fragments that in turn—legs or paws or furry chest or chin or udders—are prolonged and end up in branches, and those branches in fibers or threads.

Taken over and tied up by the lassos of endless lines, the first pictures have disappeared completely.

Thus what is untransmittable will not be betrayed.

However, the doubt, the distrust, start up again. And the drawing.

Threads and fibers now turn into writing, and he goes back over it, making it finer, ever finer, covering it over, crossing it so that it can truly escape all deciphering. So he is safe, he and his secrets, secrets he can finally express freely, in words with shrunken, flattened letters in which he hides, into which his words sink. A secondary indecipherability has thus been realized, and it will not fail to wear out the patience of the spies who would like to seize him, to "detain" him.

. . . .

That remains to be seen. Later the drawing, already disfigured many times over, will be torn up into infinite fragments, then scattered in far-off places. It's safer.

27

There are three of them in the painting. Facing forward, standing, in good order. Man, woman, child. Same neck, same hands, same pose.

Same expression: freed of all personality, emptied of the particularity of being a person. This is how they were painted by the man with the interrupted life: undifferentiated. Variety of feeling lost for him, lost for everyone.

No womanliness in the woman, no childhood in the child. The woman shows no difference in size, and her head, strictly the same, could just as well be put on the man's shoulders without revealing the substitution. The little one between the two of them, except for his small size, shows no other difference.

"Family portrait."

But he has not been able to overcome the invariability implanted within him—the mark he puts on everyone he will paint from now on.

The anonymous impression that isolates him, isolates them. The power to differentiate—the salt of the Earth—has incomprehensibly been taken away from him.

The same bleak adult masculinity can be found in the woman as in the boy, and even in his dog, when he happens to add it to the painting, an "extra" who invariably has the expression of a closed, frozen man.

29

A modest interior: chairs, stools, a table, an armchair.

Yet the picture gives an impression of knitting. A strange possessiveness emanates from it.

Threads, or strings (or bits of wool) are forging links (or obstacles?) that should not exist. The room is no longer free.

Discomfort. In a new painting the armchair has become possessive in its turn.

An astonishing soft effort that latches on to...

To whom? To what? To "the surroundings"? To a man who is "desired"? Or possessed already... and forever to be possessed all over again?

Weapons and links of the weak. She who is less strong will circumvent. The whole room holds on, wants, wishes to hold on.

What does holding on mean for the woman who has nothing left, her thoughts lost, her center, her family, her modest possessions of long ago?

Driveling desires. To hold on... but the room remains empty.

30

Brown, vast, opaque, earth and sky equally earthy.

Debris. A long unevenly broken line, of partially collapsed constructions, leaning houses, an interrupted aqueduct, a half-toppled church—crooked, as if pushed back, but still standing and that is surprising.

The aqueduct crosses over earth. Earth, all that remains after the disaster.

In front of the curiously clean, not too uneven row of recent ruins, two men turning their backs on them, with thin legs like herons', deep in conversation. Although only half-dressed (and badly), visibly nonworkers. They have the attitudes, the detached look one has in drawing rooms or in select places for people who are in no hurry, free, interested in polite discussion and light words about whatever subject may come up. (Is that why they have such skinny legs with no flesh on them?)

The two dummied men continue their conversation.

The End of the World? If so, the last of the human race: two chatterers.

31

In the face an eye that no longer exists, as if blotted up by a blotter. Its fold remains. Eye that has given up being, finding nothing outside to its liking.

The other one, closed by a wide, heavy eyelid, seems quite determined not to be raised. A being has pulled down its shutters.

In pain, the bitter mouth tells us clearly enough that the eye was not closed so decisively in order to dream about flowers or charms, nor to contemplate interesting constructions of the unconscious, but only to remain locked into its misery, sheltered in its misery, where everything is cancelled out—melancholy excepted.

At a distance, forming a glowing, threatening, uneven horizon line, a fire, the thin lips of a great fire. An inferno impossible to control. No one will be able to contain it.

Still far off, already encircling, seen by *him alone.*

37

He is weaker now, he is getting weaker and weaker. The feverish dying man is going to give in, will have to give in.

Slowly the shapes of the population of the Beyond are arriving. It looks like a drift. Coming death has set them in motion.

On the pillow, the angular, hollow-cheeked head, a prey with no power left to defend itself. His resistance gnawed away, he is ripe, extenuated, soon to be immobile.

They seem to float in, slow, ineluctable, supported by nothing: pale, glabrous, expressionless heads like beardless seals or albino pumas, almost spherical—a sign of equality.

There he is, so thin now, once the soul of impulsiveness (at present that would be laughable). But they, they are full, at their ease, knots of unearthly calm, sailing on an invisible current. Ready, waiting for the last trance before the end.

The aggression is going to begin at the border or a bit before it. In perfect control of themselves, eager to invade, to surround, to besiege the newcomer, they lie in wait, without the slightest inopportune rudeness.

In a corner of the *Painting of the Approaches of Death,* painted by the anguished man: the Earth, surely the whole earth is failing.

In the distance, a wisp of gray horizon—the horizon of the Past?—like a last shower of rain.

38

Ungraceful, dignified now, tough, with the look of a governess, humming sometimes, in great unpredictable anger at other times, the unattractive woman... on the paper is most attractive.

LOCKED IN. INDEPENDENT.

Forgetting her appearance, on the colored space she offers her bosom, overflowing henceforth, filled with the desire to provoke desires.

Feminine charms once utterly useless, now celebrated in a hundred paintings, reservoirs of pleasure, swelling, pearled, opal, her ideal breasts present themselves, given unrestrainedly, givens that not one of the crowd of men can resist.

Her body, her new body on the paper being colored and forever unsatiated with love, endlessly offers up its generous bosom, overabundant, gaudy, but drawn in a similar way to that of Cleopatra and other great lovers of History who come back to pose standing up, expressionlessly; only their big breasts are impudent, attractive, magnetic, the same for all women, with their red, red nipples, exaggeratedly big, ready to bleed, wounds of the woman who waited and was not chosen.

Couldn't have given herself in any other way, the proud girl now painting, mumbling unintelligible words for herself alone.

As the old, chapped hand spreads or hypnotically, vehemently crushes out the sickly-sweet colors of welcome or lust, naked fiancées who couldn't stand it any more appear on the colored sheet of paper, dilated lovers with ballooning bodies, with faces in ecstasy, eyes without pupils, without eyeballs, without sclerotica, blue only, sky blue, all sky, eyes rejecting everything else and abandoning themselves, giving themselves over to limitless intoxication.

The fast of love has ended up in this.

She for whom only the love of a prince of the blood—once glimpsed riding in his sumptuous uniform behind the wrought-iron gates of a magnificent estate—would have appeared sufficient, she who is isolated, scorned, in wretched clothing, in the narrow space of an institutional room, she is given the extraordinary vengeance of her incomparable liberty.

39

She began to throw everything out the window: rings, bracelets, a necklace, a few valuables, thousands of francs ripped from her wallet flying down, and the cushions.

Dresses fall onto the sidewalk. Naked, she keeps throwing more out.

The horror of possessions. Unbearable, despicable.

In an instant of illumination, the veil was rent. She saw how base it is to possess, to keep, to accumulate.

All of a sudden, the clothes on her body became unbearable, and the collection of objects gathered around her—she had to tear herself away from them, immediately.

That old wish to appropriate, to keep things for oneself—vile!

Following this highly personal, yet public act (seen from the street), she was deprived of her freedom. At first she talked a lot, rapidly, incessantly—then hardly at all.

She was encouraged to draw, to paint, like other women in the asylum, and one day crayons were put into her hand and a blank sheet of paper was placed on the table in front of her.

Inert, she absentmindedly makes a few scattered dots and lines, then suddenly, suddenly, without stopping now, flowers, flowers with no supports.

Unadorned flowers with simple corollas simply colored, flowers of offering, flowers of birth, flowers marked with innocence. Many. Many.

No more words, ever again.

Flowers only, flowers, flowers.

The gift, to give, to give oneself away.

"She had to be protected against herself... "

Flowers are her only answer. Flowers, flowers, flowers.

DAYS OF SILENCE

ONE LONE SHIP WILL ANSWER EVERYTHING

Foldings, foldings,
a suffering head, no longer a head
only a passage

The tree of life is being pushed around

..... soul eruptions

sucked upward
too much, too much

a force fatigues you in its push for transcendence

as if compelled to elevation

A call to higher
to exist more highly
to more delicately.....

words stressing
words meaning more now,
more stretching on, more beyond,
far-off though, as if legendary!

The base
everything is a base,
forever
and will never cease

long, long opening
swelling of the seeds
on the thinking-board
naked
nakedly
feeling, testing the new gift

No more relays
only the essential

balconies left behind

think molecularly

Smooth
smooth, the inner sea
May it remain smooth...

One lone ship will answer everything

the distances are thinking
In shivers, radiance

Let us always remember this,
Moments when we change homelands,

Light
Light until the end of the World.

It was taken away so easily
surely evil didn't have much to shoulder it up

foreign presences,
How gently they strike,

streaks of presences

More coming in, more, still more

Clothes of sand have slipped down from around me
Intruders let go in bunches

·Stagnancy left behind

Spheres
spheres on the waters

The page is opening
The intentions are revealed
immanent meaning
beneath the particular meanings

To everyone, to everything is given
the beauty of being
the plenitude of being

an accompanying grace

gratified from within
gratifying what lies without

Vast sheets of eliminations
Vast sheets of illuminations

Beneficence in the unified place

CHOSEN HANDS   *to Micheline Phan-Kim*

After meditation
a hand could be born
serene
soothing the overwhelmed
strengthening the wise
and the prostrate man, untied
carrying
repairing
a large hand of LIGHT

.   .   .   .   .

In another life
in another sight
in another emptiness
without a wrinkle, ageless
calm, saved,
driving off evil, peregrinations
recriminations

.   .   .   .   .

A lone hand
could appear
It would have lived apart
in a fountain
in lustral waters
rooted in Being

taking away every stain

.   .   .   .   .

An immaculate hand could show the Way
pure as the blue sky is blue
blue without anguish

not the blue that leads into blackness

leaving room for no doubt

eliminating, canceling out the pool of larvae crawling

out of the entrails

and pushing over the base   .   .   .   .   .

Azure Hand canceling the tantric hand

.   .   .   .   .

DISPLACEMENTS,

DISENGAGEMENTS

"The material becoming mental," as Michaux says at the end of "A Crowd Coming Out of the Dark" (with some irony in context), and vice versa, we might say: that's what he is writing about in this posthumous collection that contains eight works published between 1982 and 1984. In a sense he had been exploring this relationship all his life.

We may find it troubling that the intense religious experience described in *The Exalted Garden*—that mystical sensation of witnessing the divine heart of the universe in motion—should begin with "a bit of the prepared product." Another mystic or a less honest writer might have preferred to leave this unsaid. On reflection, though, it seems perfectly appropriate. The material drug affects the mental process, as pain does (*Broken Arm*), or the feeling we have of our bodies, or "hemianopsia" ("A Crowd . . . "). Conversely, our minds may transform the universe (in *The Exalted Garden* and elsewhere), and, as we read or write, words transform the world.

(*Déplacements dégagements*, Gallimard, 1985)

A CROWD COMING OUT OF THE DARK

When I got there, I was driven to a distant movie-theater, where they were giving a foreign film. — A big theater, I knew, one of the biggest ever built in this country.

Inside, it seemed phenomenally big to me, especially on one side (the left) which appeared to stretch out endlessly—an extraordinary effect.

The show had already started, we were in the middle of the action. Suspicious people were coming out of the darkness, conspirators, no doubt. They kept coming and coming, emerging from a kind of vast grotto, exceptionally vast, an uncertain space that I couldn't manage to circumscribe.

They really gave the impression of coming out of "the mouth of nothingness." It was unheard of. Ah, I said to myself, they're really making progress in the movies nowadays.

To make conspirators come so naturally out of the dark, a dense darkness that works on your emotions, full of mystery—this was something no one had ever accomplished until the present.

Now I could only follow the action against a background of thoughts, of interpretations, of particular admiration, and still crowds kept coming out of the dark, from which they seemed to flow into reality. And those moving masses were only part of a larger, deeper, more disturbing mass. A marvel, almost a miracle made perceptible: the infinite (on one side), in touch with the finite on the other, and flowing into it!

I was dumbfounded, as if I had found myself at the exact turning point of an era, changing before me: thanks to a new discovery (which had been kept secret till now), it was displaying the sign of its newness before my very eyes.

Meanwhile at the mouth of the cavern the procession was interminable. It, too, was extraordinary—I had never seen images anything like that. As attentive as I might be to those men passing by in fairly regular ranks, it seemed to me I could only see one leg, the one that came forward, and I could barely make out the half of their bodies that was vaguely hidden in the same indefinable way.

Truly we were dealing with essential, typical conspirators. It would be impossible to dream up better ones: out of prudence and distrust (through an inspired expression of their distrust), even as they marched by they kept themselves partly hidden, literally emerging from emptiness.

A well-justified prudence, no doubt, but a most singular way of walking. Or perhaps not so singular, as after all this was a theatrical action, which tried to suggest that these were partisans, who by definition had to escape our gaze and our certainties.

I was burning to know the name of the amazing director. Not only had he invented this disguise by removal and partial dematerialization (as befits conspirators who intend to conceal themselves as long as possible), but he had another find: it consisted in maintaining, by means of some new technical mechanism, a certain purely mental vibration transmitted by a physical technique. Whatever it was, it communicated the impression of life itself, of life in danger.

Rapid variations of an unknown nature, hardly perceptible commotions, admirably rendered the apprehension of men in danger and those swings between daring and fear that a band of troops must feel as they get ready for a surprise attack—emotions that cannot be denied, that go right to your heart.

I was more than a spectator, I was *there*. Forcibly bound to them, I felt myself in those places, with them. I had never been so transported. All I lacked was the power to touch them, and even so! there were moments when I jumped back, so real did their movements feel to me.

Never had a performance rendered me so present, participating, engaged.

My life as a spectator had just found a spectacular new development. Without planning to, I had entered the next era. I marveled and soliloquized.

Suddenly a shooting pain stopped me, and stopped my emotion, my participation, and soon would give quite a different answer to my previous questions.

Hemianopsia. Yes, it was an attack of hemianopsia that was happening to me; it had slipped in and subtly joined the performance! From it, the oscillations, the trembling vibrations, stronger on the left than the right... and the mysterious darkness, deep and vibrating—that was my hemianopsia, too.

The attack of ophthalmic migraine must have occurred when I walked into the theater, coinciding with the first images, provoked by the overly intense light of the dazzling luminous beam on the screen.

The spasms of the tiny cerebral arterioles had supplied the seemingly emotional vibrations, the partial obliteration of the bodies, the "magic" of the conspirators, their surprising dissimulation, their anxiety so admirably imitated with such physical depth. The elements combined in the drama came from my own trembling, an invasion of the theatrical by the physiological, a confusion of the spectacle with the visual ailment of the spectator.

The material becoming mental, that's what was needed to produce that marvelous accuracy, otherwise unattainable.

As for the new era in film—well, we would just have to wait.

TRIP KEEPING ITS DISTANCE

An endless trip, always keeping itself at a distance. It was on one of the most suffocating days of an oppressive summer... Depressed, I had left Paris to go to the North for a bit of cool air, and I intended to make a stop on the way, to visit an old friend confined to his room by a serious illness.

Long are the hours in a suffocating compartment on a train. Arriving late, with the temperature quite as high as the heat I had left in the morning, I find myself stopped that evening not at the main station, but at a little branch station where I have to change to a local train, bursting with passengers, noisy and almost boiling. Finally, when we reach the city itself, it is unrecognizable, its medieval look lost under a mass of monotonous modern constructions.

Instead of fresh air, a stormy atmosphere with the sickening, stale smell of oil stagnating in it, no doubt coming from the refineries they had built on one of the bends of the river. In this Flemish port, the inhabitants' new behavior toward the French language, which they now pretend they no longer understand, completes the break, for me, with the familiar city of days gone by.

Without going up to my room at the hotel, I go directly to the new address where a nondescript apartment building has replaced the old house in which I had met him.

I expected to find him lying in bed. He steps forward to meet me with an enviably rested look, whereas I am so exhausted I would really like to lie down. The conversation does not take away my fatigue, which it would be unseemly and ridiculous to mention—but it increases so much that I become dizzy, and refusing his insistent offers to spend the evening together, I precipitously take my leave, with a guilty conscience and vague promises to return.

I plan to eat in a calm spot I know where I won't have to talk.

Another failure: restaurant closed. With an empty stomach, worn out, I gain my room—unpleasant, puritanical, on the sixteenth or the eighteenth floor. I go to bed immediately.

It is already quite late when my half-sleep is interrupted at one point as if by an injunction, seeming to condemn me.

A sort of sign communicates this to me... and suggests it is my fault (?), because of something no longer where it should be.

It is three A.M., a bad time on bad nights.

I open one of the windows and push apart the shutters. I can't manage to get my bearings. The air comes in sluggishly, warm and heavy.

Narrow street. I glance down into a deep black pit; I can't look at it without getting dizzy. From the high story I'm on, I look over the low house across the street: with its roof smashed in, shutters ripped off and its windows broken, it seems abandoned. It is black, a black that means not only no light, but a cut-off circuit; it looks like a building that has been looted, ransacked... condemned.

Rooms I imagine bare, like what remains in a house that has been pillaged, bombarded. The city actually was bombarded and besieged, but at least thirty years ago, during the last war.

Can they really leave these houses abandoned, neither completely destroyed nor rebuilt? Under demolition?

An unhealthy sight, wretched, a part of the street, like my day—another wreck, to which it is anchored. And in a certain sense I am condemned, too, as a bad friend perhaps, guilty of indifference once again.

Finally I close the window and go open the other that at least doesn't face this narrow, demoralizing street.

Before me is an extraordinary, luminous spectacle: broad, ample, lit bright as day for no apparent reason.

Madly, wildly ablaze as if to answer the needs of heavy traffic, but nobody's there, not even a dog, a very broad boulevard, ostentatiously lighted, in the taste of the inhabitants of this northern port, one of the biggest in the world—they are quite proud of it.

...just waiting, it would seem, for the eye of the beholder.

The street at the other window is blank, dull, dead, damned, but its precise contrary, the wide artery stretching out before me, is bright enough to hurt the eye, lit up as if for parades or for an official reception... at this time when there's not a passerby to be seen.

Powerful, tightly sealed cars race by from time to time at top speed without ever stopping, without slowing down, like couriers impatiently expected at the other end of the city.

Like a stage, and yet concrete and real as can be, this bewitching stretch of city with an artificial look—a new shock, a new malfunction of my day which is decidedly hard to set right, to restore to reality—flashes out its excessive brilliancies for nothing, like yelps, stridences, and it forms with the narrow street next to it (that can't be seen from this window) an incredible double vision: dreamlike, an unreal whole, impossible to accept.

Fake boulevard, with its pointlessly definitive look, put there, one would think, just for one night. An isolated chunk of city, brilliantly prepared for some review, but without inhabitants (destroyed, absent, all absent?). Or the set for an unknown play, ready to be performed, already being wordlessly, speechlessly rehearsed by actors helped by mechanics and technicians... fake intersection connected to my day on which I have no "hold."

As for the dead side of the street, when I come back to the first window and without any transition find myself once again looking down at the black house in ruins, it seems to come from another age, not far-off, but still out of place, a part impossible to plug back into the other.

Meanwhile, the moon has risen over those dilapidated buildings, an exaggerated, red moon. It, too, is unacceptable, a moon like the huge eye of a cyclops in a trance, and as for its size: like the biggest sun you can see in the country at twilight, a sick, wicked moon weighing down on the city, on this part at least, keeping a close watch over its poverty, its progressive disappearance.

A wicked, unbearable watch.

A bizarrely disturbing situation, with two segments of the city always impossible to unite and in different ways deprived of inhabitants, life and naturalness: the two absolutely cannot manage to make a whole, and remain hooked into my fatigue, my vertigo—colossal, disparate fragments, I don't know what to do with them... and I wouldn't know whom to tell about them in this foreign city.

The hotel, a big, high tower, abnormally silent: its excessive soundproofing makes it feel almost like a tomb, a tomb out of all proportion, another improbability. Here, too, reality has been taken away from me. Will it never return? Will I have no more right to it? It's ridiculous. But the idea won't go away.

...

Slowly time passes. A pile of time still to pass before daybreak.

...Inside the sinister room, the color of a prison, but dizzying as soon as I lean out, now opening one window or the other, now going back to bed, uselessly closing my eyes for some rest that does not come, I remain in a state of non-defense.

Reality depends on so little. A city depends on so little! So does guilt! I see it now: nothing like a little guilt to sap things, to disintegrate them.

. . . .

The next day, first thing in the morning, without trying to get any information whatsoever, I clear out like a thief in the night on the first train to the northern border. There, innumerable canals and such different houses—the dress and general look of the inhabitants are different, too—call one's attention to other exteriors, structure themselves to compose a people, a country... and thus replace the huge, one-eyed city of the day before.

My guilty conscience couldn't follow me either. The other one, the usual one could. Its turn had come again.

For one last time, I had left the land of false premises.

It was also cooler.

LAZINESS

Lazing away: endless dream undisturbed
dreams up life (a fluid parenthesis)

All around, projects, plans, departures,
Buildings fall, rise, rise again,

Laziness dreams
of its well, deepening

TORSO-SITUATION

Torso without a head, farewell to the head,
that extra, always interfering
The torso can do without spying smiles,
words, tying strings
tying again
restraining

Complete without an explanation, the torso
equal to a Pharaoh
Who can strip a torso?

Now wholes...

We watch torsos passing by

ON THE STEM

On the high stem of a ship plowing through the waveless sea
someone standing, leaning forward

Other stems go by obliquely
their occupants leaning in the same way

No port. Unknown ports

A few signs sometimes from stem to stem
Then they move toward each other.

A bit of the prepared product remained when a few days later, I was offered a garden in the country. Someone wanted to make an experiment.

A weak dose, calm spot, clear sky. This person had prepared a few records. At the last moment she showed some apprehension.

As for me, I don't begin well: anguish. Have decidedly become unfit for these experiments.

On her, the effect is good. Happy surprise replaces worry and drawn features.

She is interested, participates, differentiates; in a murmur, she describes the transformations of the visual zone above all—hollows and folds in a painting or the wall.
Distances in the depths of the garden are easier to see, "Seem," she says, "to want to attract our attention."

(. . .)

Meanwhile my heart of flesh and muscle in my chest is making me suffer, producing pains, discomfort, and unpleasant thoughts.

(. . .)

A record. A *lied* was put on, then dismissed. I did not want the European impulse, certainly not from that era.

Another record replaced it—Carnatic music. The first notes, suddenly of unprecedented importance, sounded as if struck inside the ear itself. Never in life had such music been heard so close by. It gathered us up in its passage. The inner force of India, more intensified still; it introduced distinction, urged grandeur, united with fervor, an impersonal fervor.

As water moves forward in the bed of a river, so the music moved forward in the bed of my being, conveying, maintaining spaciousness, and a longing for spaciousness.

My suffering had disappeared, and apprehension.
It was forgotten.
Through *breakings* of all kinds, and especially of a strange kind, the chosen music had covered everything over in its unique way.
.   .   .   .
then was lost inside of me, lost as an independent entity, in a vaster sea.

And the garden was *there,* quite differently there.
From the beginning a subtle depth had reached its limits. Now we had something quite different, and even a quite different garden.

Without ever leaving, the music had united with it, in a union I could not understand, so intimate that I was forgetting it, a union particularly strong with the dominant tree over there which had a very leafy double crown, moving, ceaselessly moving, in uneven, tumultuous movements, embraced by a breeze that had become "passionate"—an unheard-of whole.

Crazy aspirations were speeding, and, it seemed, feeding, in hundreds of branches and leaves—longings made marvelously generous, natural, overflowing, by the sounds of an invisible *vina.*

I had seen it as so unpromising, with no particular character or style when I had walked into it and by it, and now this ordinary garden was suddenly changed, had become a paradisal garden ... and there I was a few steps in front of it, and so naturally that I no longer knew for how long I had been there, in this Garden of Gardens, the one where you think of nothing more, which overwhelms you and no thing in this world can go beyond it, not even time—a real garden of paradise.

So it was possible, and no apple, no serpent, no punishing God, only the unhoped-for paradise. And without having to move, in front of the very tree that formed its center, with its vast crown of yellowing fleshy leaves, gilded, foreshadowing the coming autumn.

A breeze had arisen, waking the sleeping branches and the languid leaves with their sovereign spaciousness, expressing bliss, the highest degree of bliss, and desire, desire for more bliss, blisses of all sorts offered up and a second later ripped away, reconquered, reconquered, reoffered for sharing and adoring, for the passionate gift.

The exalted world of the East was there, one, total, expressing the highest point of ecstasy in the name of everyone, of everyone on Earth.

What branches and leaves can depict, no arm and no body of a man or woman, no human or animal dance could have achieved. There were overflowings, endless overflowings, elastic and in all directions, sometimes slackening lazily and unexpectedly bounding up again, unleashed in an instant, unsurpassable.

Kneelings, supplications, intertwinings, disentwinings, extractions, dives forward, withdrawals, retreats, reembracings and always to the limit, in each leaf, in each branch now a worshiping being, bowing and bowing again deeply, the expression of infinite homage rendered, which for a long time now it seemed each fragment, having become a whole, wanted to render, unrestrained at last and as if inexhaustibly... and high up.

For these passionate excesses were taking place at the top of a tree (and this did not surprise me), on an old walnut tree with a broad crown, so rare in that species, a double crown almost triple, almost unparalleled, a company whose every member, untiringly excessive, was rushing forward, withdrawing, rushing forward again without rest.

Exasperation, but nobody there, but all parts of it, branches, leaves and twigs, were somebody and more than somebody, more deeply moved, upset more, upsetting more.

Individually, not communally, in an accelerated rhythm sweeping away every slackening, in which the real wind did not seem the main thing.

All the leaves bowing low, rapidly, then impetuously shooting up again, then carried back, then going forth tirelessly to surpass themselves again, crumpling, uncrumpling almost savagely, and yet, through a kind of consecration, with unique grandeur.

Beauty of palpitations in the garden of transformations.
Fulfillments and unfulfillments were streaming from the tree of ravishments.

Appeals going out to the thirsty, appeals heard at last, granted. The supplement awaited since the beginning of time was received, was given.
The infinite rumpling–unrumpling had met.

Opening, closing, of infinite desire, an unweakening pulsation.
Between Earth and Heaven—its bliss surpassed—a savagery unknown was referring us to a delight beyond all delight, to the highest as to the innermost transgression, where the ineffable remains secret, sacred.

And now, adding to this, agglutinating to it (from who knows where), there came an imperturbable scansion, a dull, strong beat, but equally inner, like the hammering of a heart, a musical heart, from the trees, a heart we didn't know they had, a heart they had hidden from us, born of a great vegetal heart (it seemed planetary), a heart participating in everything, found at last, perceived at last, audible to those possessed by the sovereign emotion, the one that accompanies every thing, that carries away the Universe.

PASSAGES

These are collected meditations (essays, poems, and unclassifiable prose texts) on art, music, writing, and living—hence the names I have given to the subsections in *Passages*—written over a twenty-six year period and published in various journals; they seemed an appropriate Afterword for this anthology. Ironically enough, for an artist who constantly displays the fragmentation of the self, their unity is striking. So is their eccentric wisdom.

A word about his "Reading" of Zao Wou-ki lithographs and "Adventures of Lines" in Paul Klee's still lifes: traditionally, poems based on works of art move between precise description and general reflection; a classic example would be W. H. Auden's "Musée des Beaux-Arts" ("About suffering they were never wrong, the Old Masters . . . "). As we have seen—particularly in "Ravaged People" (*Paths Looked For, Paths Lost, Transgressions*), but also years earlier in his "Drawings With Commentary" from *The Night Moves*—Michaux takes an entirely different tack.

(*Passages* (1937–1963), Gallimard, 1963)

PAINTING

Those who already have a form

crystallize themselves through painting.

Those who do not yet have a form

are born through painting.

CHOU KING-YUAN

The transfer of creative activities is one of the strangest of all voyages into the self.

Strange decongestion, putting to sleep one part of the mind, the speaking, writing part (part, no: rather a system of connections). You change clearing stations when you start painting.

The word-factory (thought-words, picture-words, emotion-words, motor-words) disappears, is simply, dizzyingly drowned. It no longer exists. The sprouting stops. Night. Localized death. No more desire, no more appetite, for talking. The part of the head that used to be the most concerned with it cools off.[a] It's a surprising experience.

And how restful!

A strange feeling. You locate the world through another window. Like a child, you have to learn how to walk. You don't know a thing. You're buzzing with questions. You constantly try to guess... to plan ahead...

New problems. New temptations.

Every art has its own temptation and its gifts.[b]

[a]The veins that stood out in my left temple and the warmth on this side of my forehead have been reduced, have almost disappeared (1950)

[b]A novelist said to me one day, thinking himself profound "I've noticed there are no descriptions of smells in your books Strange   You don't have much of a sense of smell " What a conclusion! For a man like me, tortured by his nose   There are countries, regions, cities I avoid because of their smell (   )

But to write about them, no To write about smells is too long, too indirect, too inefficient No point trying It's another art

But give me a gadget to emit odors and make them disappear quickly, you'll see if I remain passive, you'll see how I crowd the things into my horizon, how I revenge myself in smelly accents on all the bastards in the world who have made me suffer all my life, you'll see how it stayed inside me, really, all I'm waiting for is the gadget, I'll take care of the inva-

All you have to do is to let them come, let it happen.

For the moment I'm painting on black backgrounds, hermetically black. Black is my crystal ball. I can see life coming out of black alone.

(1938)

---

sion Far more than by any other means, it seems to me I'd give back whatever I can't manage to produce through writing or drawing

Or am I wrong?

will is the death of Art.

Draw without anything particular in mind, scribble mechanically: almost always, faces will appear on the paper.

Since we lead an excessively facial life, we are in a perpetual fever of faces.

As soon as I pick up a pencil or a brush, ten, fifteen, twenty of them surge up to me on the paper one after the other. And most of them wild.

Are all those faces me? Are they other people? From what depths?

Couldn't they simply be the consciousness of my own thinking head? (Grimaces of a second face: just as, out of shame, the suffering adult has stopped crying when he's unhappy, only to suffer still more in the depths of his soul, so he has stopped grimacing, only to grimace still more inwardly.) Behind the face with its motionless features, deserted, now no more than a mask, another superiorly mobile face contracts, seethes, simmers in an unbearable paroxysm. Behind the set features, desperately seeking a way out, expressions like a pack of howling dogs...

There they are, somehow flowing from the brush in black blotches: they are breaking free.

You're surprised, the first few times.

Lost, sometimes criminal faces, unfamiliar yet not absolutely unknown to you (a strange, distant correspondence!)... Faces of sacrificed personalities, "I's" stifled, killed, by life, willpower, ambition, by a propensity for rectitude and consistency. Faces that will keep appearing to the very end (it is so hard to stifle, to drown anything out definitively).

Faces of childhood, of childhood fears whose structure and object have been lost more than their memory, faces that don't think everything has been settled by the transition to adulthood, faces still afraid of some horrible return.

Faces of the will, perhaps, which is always ahead of us and tends to shape everything in advance: faces, too, of seeking and desire.

Or a kind of epiphenomenon of thought (one of the many that the thinking will can't help provoking, even though it is perfectly useless for intellection—but it can't be stopped any more than you can stop yourself from making vain gestures on the telephone)... as if one were constantly shaping a fluid face in oneself, ideally plastic and malleable, forming and unforming from ideas and impressions, automatically sculpted into an instantaneous synthesis, all day long and in a sense cinematographically.[1]

An infinite crowd: our clan.

The mirror is not the place to observe yourself.

Men, look at yourselves in the paper.

(. . .)

(1946)

READING

Books are boring to read. No freedom to wander around. You are asked to follow. The trail is traced, one way.

Paintings, quite different: immediate, total. To the left, also to the right, in depth, as you like.

No path, a thousand paths, with no signs for stopping places. As soon as you wish, the painting again, whole. In an instant, everything's there. Everything, but nothing is known yet. Here's where you have to begin to READ.

An adventure few seek out, although it's there for everybody. Everyone can read a painting, can find matter in it (and months afterward, new matter)—everyone: respectful or generous or insolent people, people faithful to their own minds, people lost in their own blood, lab workers with pipettes, people for whom a line is like a salmon to fish out of the water and every dog they meet a dog to put on the operating table to study his reflexes, people who would rather play with the dog, get to know him and themselves in him, people who with someone else never enjoy anyone but themselves, and those who see above all else the Great Tide, which carries painting, the painter, the country, the climate, the environment, the whole era and all its factors, events still unsuspected and others already beginning to madly ring out their bells.

Yes, all of them have something for themselves in a painting, even good-for-nothings, who simply let the sails of their windmill turn without really feeling the difference—but it does exist, and how instructively!

Don't wait too long, though. This is the right time. There are no rules yet. But they'll be moving in on us soon…

READING[c]

Slowly
from the other side
slowly swim the fish
cruisers of a meditation on hunger

[c]Of two lithographs by Zao Wou-ki (Text *L'Espace du dedans,* revised edition, Gallimard, 1966)

Those in the obstacle of air look
at those in the obstacle of water
foreigners

How many friendships lost because one doesn't have gills!

Dream of a full life
silent
fulfilled in droplets
spheres
pushing away spheres

In space without a bend
looking serious as the rules of precedence observed
modeling and remodeling their form
like a virtue
under the gentle pressure of invisible watery spindles
the placid ones conquer

Sovereigns still exist!

Sovereigns? From their long lateral auditory line
ceaselessly they have to listen ceaselessly
to attenuated signs from the outside

Powdery shadow darkens them
their beautiful watery home is surrounded.

II

Busy trees looking
for their branches breaking
exploding
falling

trees frightened

hunted

trees like nervous systems dripping blood

But no human being in this terrible story.

The modest man does not say "I am unhappy."

The modest man does not say "We are suffering

Our families are dying

Our people have no homes."

He says: "Our trees are suffering."

(1950)

ADVENTURES OF LINES

(Preface to W Grohmann, *Paul Klee*)

. . . .

When I saw the first show of Paul Klee's paintings, I remember I came back bowed in a great silence.

As painting was a closed world to me, I don't know what I saw in it. I was not too eager to know, all too happy to have gone to the other side, in the aquarium, far from the cutting edge.

Above all, perhaps I was looking for the mark of the man who was to write: "What artist would not want to set himself up there, where the organic center of all movement in space and time—call it the brain, call it the heart of Creation—determines all functions?"

I was reaching the musical, the real *Stilleben*.[2]

Thanks to the constantly moving, minute modulations of his colors—which did not seem applied but exhaled in the right spot, or naturally rooted like moss or rare molds—his "still lifes" in the delicate tones of old things seemed to have ripened, to have acquired age and a slow organic life, to have come into the world by gradual emanations.

A few red dots were singing tenor over the general pianissimo. Nonetheless one felt that one was underground, looking at water, at enchantments, with the soul of a chrysalis.

The complex network of lines appeared little by little:

Lines living with the little people of dust and dots, crossing crumbs, going around cells, fields of cells, or turning, turning in spirals to fascinate—or to find what had fascinated— umbelliferous plants and agates.

Lines walking around. ——— The first the West had ever seen walking around in this way.

Travelers, lines that don't so much make objects as trajectories, paths. (He even put arrows in them.) The problem children have and then subsequently forget, the one they put into all their drawings at that age: locating things, leave here, go there, the distance, the directions, the path leading to the house as necessary as the house itself... that was his problem, too.

And penetrators: contrary to the possessors—eager to envelop, to surround, makers of shapes (and then what?)—they're lines for what is underneath, finding their nerve centers not in a feature of the face but in the inside of the head, where an unknown eye watches and keeps its distance.

Lines contrary to the ones obsessed by the container—vase, form, modeled mountain of the body, clothes, the skin of things (he hates that)—are seeking, far from volume, far from centers, a center nonetheless, a center less obvious but more master of the mechanism: the hidden enchanter. (Curious parallelism, he died of scleroderma.)

Allusive ones, presenting a whole metaphysics, gathering transparent objects and symbols denser than those objects, sign-lines, poetry-tracing, making what is heaviest light.

The ones that are mad about enumeration, about endless juxtaposition, repetition, rhymes, notes indefinitely repeated, creating microscopic palaces of proliferating cellular life, countless pinnacles in an ordinary little garden with thousands of different plants, labyrinth of the eternal return.

A line meets a line. A line avoids a line. Adventures of lines.

A line for the pleasure of being a line, of going ahead, as a line. Points. Dust of points. A line is dreaming. Before then, no one had ever let a line dream.

A line is waiting. A line is hoping. A line is rethinking a face.

Lines of growth. Lines the height of an ant, but not an ant to be seen. Few animals in the temples of his nature, and then only once they've been stripped of their animality. Plants are preferred. The meditative fish is welcomed.

Here's a line thinking. Another is fulfilling a thought. Lines at stake. Line of decision.

A line rises up. A line goes to see. Winding, a melodic line crosses through twenty stratified lines.

A line is germinating. A thousand others around it, bearers of thrusts: a lawn. Grasses on the dune.

A line gives up. A line rests. Stop. A stop with three clinging roots: a habitat.

A line closes itself in. Meditation. Threads are still sprouting from it, slowly.

Dividing line there, a ridge line, further on the observatory line.

Time, time...

A line of consciousness has formed again.

You can follow them easily or not so easily, without ever running the risk of being led into eloquence, eloquence is always avoided, the spectacular always avoided, always in the construction, always in the proletariat of the humble constituents of this world.

Sisters of the spots, of his spots that seem to be still blotting, have emerged from the depths, the depths from which he comes and will return, to the place of the secret, in the moist belly of the Earth-Mother.

.   .   .   .

I'll stop. Paul Klee probably wouldn't like us to keep raving away. Too Goethean for that. With his watchmaker's attention to what is measurable, he wouldn't have liked us to walk along with him down such imperfectly parallel paths.

Luckily none of this has the slightest importance in order to walk right into his paintings. It is enough to be among the chosen, to have remained aware that we live in a world of enigmas, and that it is best to respond to it with enigmas, too.

(1954)

Before I took up drawing, I had a desire that no doubt stood in the way; I had to fulfill it first at all costs. I felt it corresponded to my real needs and even to a general need. Instead of one vision, excluding others, I would have liked to draw the moments that little by little make up life, to let people see the phrase within, the phrase without words, a rope indefinitely unrolling, winding, accompanying in its intimacy all that comes in from the outside, and the inside, too.

I wanted to draw the consciousness of existing and the flow of time. As you might take your pulse. Or again, on a more limited scale, what appears when the evening has come and the film of impressions created by the day plays back to you (muted, though, and shorter).

A cinematic drawing.

Certainly mine was important to me. But I would have gotten so much pleasure from lines other people had made, by following them like a magical string full of knots and secrets, reading their life in it, holding its path in the palm of my hand.

My film was hardly more than a line (or two or three) crossing into a few others here and there, here forming a bush, there an interlacing, further on doing battle, rolling itself into a ball or—as feelings and buildings intermingle naturally—drawing itself up to its full height, self-respect, pride, or castle or tower... something that could be seen, that I felt should have been seen, but that to tell the truth almost nobody ever saw.

(1957)

Since I never went in for playing with sand on the beach as a child—a disastrous deficiency from which I was to suffer all my life—when the age for it had passed, the desire to play came to me, and now to play with sounds.

Oh! what a strange thing at first, that current suddenly revealed, that liquid unexpected, that passage bearing something in itself, always, and which *was*.

You no longer recognize your surroundings (the hardness has left them).

You have stopped bumping into obstacles. You become the captain of a RIVER...

You suddenly have a strange (and dangerous) propensity for fine sentiments. Everything is slope. Your means are already paradise.

You can't find the brakes, or not as fast as you find wonders...

The currency you put into circulation is water.

Like a bell ringing out a catastrophe, a note, a note listening only to itself, a note piercing everything, a low note like a kick in the belly, an aging note, a note like a minute that has to cross a century, a note sustained through the discord of voices, a note like a death warning, a note has been warning me this whole hour through.

In my music, there is a great deal of silence.

There is mostly silence.

There is silence above all, silence must settle in.

The silence is my voice, my shadow, my key... a sign that does not drain me, that drains into me.

It expands, it spreads out, it drinks me up, it consumes me.

My great leech lies down within me.

.   .   .

When nothing comes, time always comes,
a bit of time

with no top or bottom,
a bit of time,
on me,
with me,
within me,
through me,
its arches crossing through me as I worry and wait.

Time.
Time.
I auscultate myself with Time.
I feel myself.
I hit myself with Time.
I like myself, I irritate myself...
I like myself, I fight myself...
I plot myself,
I raise myself,
I transport myself,
I *hit* myself with Time...

Pick-bird.
Pick-bird.
Pick-bird.

What am I doing here?
I'm calling.
I'm calling.
I'm calling.
I do not know the one I'm calling.
The one I'm calling does not know.
I'm calling someone weak,
someone broken,
someone proud whom nothing could break.
I'm calling.

I'm calling someone from out there,

someone lost far away,

someone from another world.

(Was it really a total lie, that solidity of mine?)

I'm calling.

At this instrument, so clear,

it's not the way it would be with my muffled voice.

At this singing instrument that does not judge me,

which is not watching me,

abandoning all shame, I call,

I call,

I call from the depths of the grave of my childhood,

which is sulking,

contracting further,

from the depths of my present desert,

I call,

I call.

The call amazes me.

Late as it is, I call.

To smash through my ceiling, above all.

To break the stranglehold, perhaps,

To drown myself, perhaps,

drown myself without suffocating,

drown my pikes,

my distances, drown what is inaccessible in me.

To drown the pain,

pain and the angles of things,

and the imperatives of things,

and the hardness and callousness of things,

and the weight and encumberment of things,

and almost everything of things,

except the passage of things,

except the fluid and color and perfume of things,

the bushiness and sometimes the complicity of things,

and almost everything of man,

and so much of woman,

and so much, so much of everything,

and of me, too,

so much, so much,

much

...so that my torrent of angels may flow through at last.

. . . .

in peace, in fluid, decomposing me.

My stones, my tooth decomposes in it,

my stubborn resisting decomposes in it,

and expands me,

and expands me into the suffering of others.

Forgetting about human dignity,

I calm people, I console, I heal,

I raise the woman from the dead,

I open the doors,

I move forward to bless,

I speak for all.

Rainbow.

No more trials.

I plant the breadfruit tree.

Marked by the breaking of a deep pain, a melody, melody the way an old, one-eyed, rheumatic hound is still hound, it's a melody

Emerging perhaps from the microquake of a sour minute in a difficult afternoon, a failed melody, and falling ceaselessly into failure

Without rising, a melody, but also determined not to give in completely, mangrove knocked around by the waters held back by its dug-in roots

Without strutting like a peacock, a melody, melody for me alone, to confide in myself, a cripple like me, to be recognized in it, sister in uncertainty

Indefinitely repeated, it would tire out the friendliest ear, melody to babble between us, it and me, freeing me from my real, stammering word, never yet pronounced

A poor melody, poor as a beggar would have to be to express his misery wordlessly, and all the misery around him and all that answers misery to his misery without listening to him

Like a call to suicide, like a suicide in progress, like a perpetual return to one recourse: suicide, a melody

A melody to save time, to fascinate the snake, while the tireless forehead goes on seeking its Orient in vain

A melody...[3]

.   .   .

. . . Like a dreamy child, sticking his fingers in his nose, musing on a great problem, pregnant with fifty others, throwing stones in the water for the big circles that are going to spread out, out...

playing, and my fingers playing with my ignorance, the big, good, true companion of my whole lifetime, my ignorance, my support, my interior, or quietly forming a slow road of islands...

tired of pictures, I play to make smoke.

.   .   .

Against noises, my noise. And this noise pushes away all others, noises of the moment, from before, from the whole day, bringing them together through an extraordinary miracle into one perfect nothingness, complete relief.

As the night progresses and my self goes further into the sounds, under the kindly roof of darkness, friends, the feeling of friends being there that one keeps as a protection after they have left, the memory of encounters—of incidents that were important during the day, that for a moment had surfaced again as weak echoes—fade out, become scarce. They have stopped coming in.

I remain alone, abandoned by those close to me, now so far away.

No one, no one left.

Alone, my silence-breaker sails through the night.

.   .   .

. . . I used to think the skin of a drum was necessary. Now I see that's not true. Any old wood will do, as long as your fingers, your hand, can drum on it. Fast, faster, less fast, slowly, very slowly. Your whole life concentrated into this. (. . .)

.   .   .

They were encouraging me to record. For the year I've had the machine, I've tended to give it the cold shoulder. The needle to watch out for, the record to watch out for, the record to change after three minutes, the needle to watch out for again, the groove to watch while you play, to think it's a *piece* when it so happens you don't like pieces, but repetitions, long boring passages, just going my way, but there is no way, to return, to return to the same thing, to be a litany, a litany like life, to take a long time before the ending, not to decide really to make human music and especially not composer's music, and especially not Western music rather make sparrow music, of a rather indecisive sparrow, perched on a branch, a sparrow who could be trying to call out to a man...

.   .   .

Heard Spanish music yesterday. Tells me nothing. Music to be happy or lament together, some people. In sum for entertainment.

What I want (not yet what I produce) is music to question, to auscultate, to approach the problem of being.

.   .   .

Evil: the rhythm of others.

Why I play the tom-tom now?[d]
For my dam
To break through your dams
To cut through the rising wave of the new preventers
To auscultate myself
To take my pulse
To hurry myself along
To slow myself down
To stop blending in with the city with THEM with the country with yesterday
To stay on horseback

Against Versailles
Against Chopin
Against the alexandrine[4]
Against Rome
Against Rome
Against the juridical
Against the theological
Against Rome
Tom-tom on criticism
Tom-tom crushing

[d] I should really say the African drum

Tom-tom top spinning
upright with my back turned to the grave
with no bishopric no dynasty
no paralyzers no trustees
no caresses no bows
Tom-tom of the breast of the earth
Tom-tom of men with hearts like punching fists
Against Bossuet[5]
Against analysis
Against the pulpit of Truth
To smash
To counterpunch
To counter
To pound
To accelerate
To precipitate
To throw down
To leave the workplace
To laugh in the fireplace
To rush down
To rush down
Against the sisters of the harp
Against drapery
To rush down
To rush down

To rush down
To rush down

Against the Golden Number.[6]

(1949)

As soon as I write, it's to begin to invent. Hardly is it out when I start putting up bars of reality all around it and once this new whole has been achieved, putting new, still more real bars around it, and thus, from compromise to compromise I get, well, I get to the point where what I write is invention taken by the throat, without the fine existence it seemed to promise.

It is, however, in this belated honesty—but rigorous and by degrees, and then still more rigorous but always more belated—that I find one of the joys and one of the torments of writing.

.　　.　　.

Quite aware of my own injustice, I write less and less (and very little) about other men. If stones and nature could hear me, I would no longer dare to speak and would soon say nothing. For it is impossible to speak about anything at all according to its merit. Luckily they don't know anything about this and I don't have to take it into account. But the headache it gives me to be truthful even toward them holds me back and paralyzes me more every day.

(1942)

from OBSERVATIONS

I write to go through myself all over. Painting, composing, writing: going through myself. That is the adventure of being alive.

In sum, for over ten years, what I've been doing above all is occupying myself little by little.[e]

(...)

.   .   .

Sincere? I write so that what was true should no longer be true. Prison revealed is a prison no longer.

.   .   .

It seems a writer has no need for more than one major feeling. Love, or envy, or fear, with deep, multiple ligatures and a good basic complex—he can get along pretty well with that. But he does need one feeling. On this wave he modulates the others and his whole universe. It's his *carrying feeling.*

Experience has proven a hundred times over that if an envious man wants to express love, love will only come out "modulated" by envy. And in a loving nature, hatred will acquire strength and life only on a wave of love. Only this wave is "carrying" and able to "carry" hatred and to make it carry. Otherwise it would be a notation of no importance.

A writer is someone who knows how to keep in contact, who remains welded to his disturbance, to his vice-laden region, never appeased. *It* carries him.

.   .   .

[e] But all is not gain for the explorer-scientist The more he finds, the less time he has to realize his new ignorance

My imaginary countries: like buffer-States for me, so as not to suffer from reality.

While traveling, when almost everything jars me, they're the ones that take the shocks, and then *I* can see what's funny about them, and have a good time.

My "Emanglons," "Magi," "Hivinizikis" were all buffer-characters provoked by a trip. (Plume disappeared the very day I got back from Turkey where he had been born.)

In the past, whenever I had a bad experience, I was only in difficulty for the short time I had to face it alone. As soon as I had found a character (when I had "retreated" into him), my difficulty disappeared and so did my suffering (at least the worst of it, the intolerable part). It's up to you now! That's why the foreign country was the occasion, the provocation for characters, to whom I gave the job from then on—both of having pleasure and of suffering from foreign, hostile, people and things. The characters themselves were composed so as not to care and turn everything topsy-turvy. Thus the Magus (from the "Land of Magic") was begun the day after I arrived in Rio de Janeiro, successfully separating me from the Brazilians: I was having such a hard time relating to them (their caffeinated intelligence, all reflex, no reflection) that despite all the time I spent there, I could almost say I never met any.

(1950)

CHILDREN

The child is more man than the man.

If everyone is misunderstood, essentially misunderstood, because it's impossible for a stranger to get inside your skin, to coincide with your whole being even for an instant, the child would seem one of the most misunderstood of all, and this misunderstanding is strange. An anemic becomes congested in the skin of a red-blooded person, but he does not become red-blooded; not even for an instant can he feel what it's like to have limbs bathing in rich blood, quick to repair the body.

In vain does a man wish to imagine himself with breasts on his flat chest. He can't imagine the astonishing, mysterious, forever unknown phenomenon of being a woman, simply woman, not beautiful, not ugly, but woman; and no love will ever make him understand it.

Nor will the hyperthyroid understand the hypothyroid, nor the slim man with a long neck be able to picture inwardly how a man feels with a broad, short neck glued to his shoulders.

He can't do it. He may be excused. He never went through it. But man was a child. He was a child for a long time and, it seems, quite in vain. Something essential, the inner atmosphere, an indefinable something that linked everything together disappeared and the whole world of childhood with it; like a fishing port we've glimpsed somewhere, linked in our memories only by a smell of tar and caulking: it can be resuscitated only by that smell; but the smell of childhood in us is far more buried and irretrievable. The Time of the child, that special Time, a physiological Time created by another combustion, another vaso-respiratory rhythm, another speed of scarring, is completely lost to us (man has an execrable memory for the coenesthetic). He leaves childhood like an illness and has no memory of the illness; he has lost its pulse.

Even if we recaptured his Time, we would remain separated from the child by thousands of lost virginities. Nothing separates, removes, like the loss of virginity. What can be more difficult than to picture the "before," everything that came "before," not yet realized, everything that came *for the first time;* for now everything that used to be surge, appeal, has become satisfaction—that is, nothing at all.

The special way children look at things, rich from not yet knowing, rich in extent, in desert, big from nescience, like a flowing river (the adult has traded space for boundaries), a gaze that isn't bound yet, dense from everything that escapes it, nourished by the undeciphered. The gaze of a foreigner, for he comes to his body as a foreigner. He's the newcomer in the studio, everything has to be explained to him: how the voice carries, where to look, how to pick up his feet.

He also comes as a stranger to our civilization and to this earth. Age of questions. "Why are there so many days? Where do the nights go? Why are there constantly things? Why am I me and not him? Why is it God who is God?" The golden age of questions; man dies of answers.

The child moves forward in a world of masses that everywhere express themselves, moves forward, ventures a frail sign. First head drawn by the child, so light, with such a delicate frame! Four thin threads, a line that elsewhere will be leg or arm or the mast of a ship, oval that is mouth or eye, and this sign is the youngest and oldest human project—that of an ideographic language, the only truly universal language, reinvented everywhere by every child.

At the age of eight, Louis XIII makes a drawing similar to the one made by the son of a New Caledonian cannibal. At eight, he is the age of humanity, he is at least two hundred and fifty thousand years old. A few years later he has lost those years, he is only thirty-one, he has become an individual, he is only a King of France—a dead end, where he remains. What is worse than being a finished product?

Adult — finished — dead: nuances of the same state. You have played out all your trumps.

"All the progress of man is perhaps due to the fact that he remains for a long time in childhood." (John Fiske.)

And yet: "He does not keep his promises." (Goethe.)

The worst criticism one can level against Aristotle is this: that he was definitively Aristotle. Before dying, one becomes all bone.

(1938)

from CROSS-THOUGHTS

The most penetrating, the most disarming, most indigestible emotion of my life was when I heard my heart on the electrocardiographic loudspeaker (I wouldn't swear that is the correct term!).

"*That's* my heart? That pump with no bite, no get-up-and-go!"

Embarrassed, I looked at the simple, kindly technician who seemed to pay no particular attention to it. Heart after heart filing by all afternoon did not dispose her to be full of reflective attentiveness.

For me, everything was becoming clear, and intensely discouraging. That smooth, slow, dutiful, dull thing—that was what was controlling my slumping life, and I uselessly perked it up and nagged at it, at the mercy of fatigue, of insomnia, but stubborn, too.

A heart with no real kick, not made for action, not made for "pointed" work and occasionally a sort of hesitation in its pumping sound, a dull, secret turnaround: a bad sign. Me, bound to that thing forever! If you gave that cursed motor to the most brilliant mind, what would become of it?

Any study of psychology and self-analysis should begin in this way, it seems to me. In a word, I was discovering cardiomancy. Hidden behind the newcomers, I listened to the sounds of the hearts being recorded around me. There were hearts of many kinds. Some of them very striking, as I would have liked mine to be, hearts for an epic, if the time was right. Others were "cavaliers." After a few lively ones, another appeared all muffled, uncertain, which I wouldn't have wanted in my chest or my life for anything in the world; muffled, but without giving the impression of a double bottom, as mine did.

My heart made me think, irresistibly, of a cistern.

P.S. If there is a Karma and a natural expiation in some future life, the legacy of a defective heart would be among "the most avenging, expiating legacies."

(1942)

OBSERVATIONS

Of course I don't want to claim I can dance—I don't even know how to walk[f]—but I did finally become intrigued (none too soon!) by movements, by the influence that movements might exert on me.

That's when I noticed it: There is a left man who wants nothing to do with my right man and who wants none of his competence... no matter how useful it might be.

For a long time I had been watching him, not very happy about it: he couldn't even turn a key in a lock.[g] Lack of strength, I used to think, that's all. Then I decided to give him a chance, to see what he would like to do, for I'd noticed that as far as movements were concerned, he didn't even try to make the movements of the right (arm and hands); he was a complete slacker—and something else, too.

What he had was a totally different style, which he showed when he began to shift for himself a bit and gain confidence, although still only slightly.

As for the right, he seems to have an easy tendency toward brilliancy—a brilliancy that doesn't go very far, no doubt, but brilliancy nonetheless. He wants to show his speed, his turns, his starts, his (quite relative) sprightliness.

The left... well, aside from being really clumsy (he'll be less so in a while), he's dreamy, hesitant. He may have his own grace. Perhaps he will have it. A certain tendency to retreat (like me) and a way of being inner, although like any arm, necessarily outer. Naturally: when I started for real, it was a bit late.

If someone had wanted to repress me completely, my left man is the one he would have changed above all: made him do sports, forced him to come out of his shell, depersonalized him.

---

[f]This is the fault of our Western gymnastics, mechanical gestures pushing away from oneself And our people don't suffer from moving away from themselves? Not at all! It even excites them And their dances go even further "outside"
    Why did I have to wait so long to get to know Hindu dance, a dance that takes care not to decenter the dancer, not to move him away from himself.
    The eye, the neck, the fingers—rather than the outlying legs—make almost all the movements, movements of thought, movements in order not to be multiple, in pieces and helter-skelter, not to be distracted, movements not to be disunited
[g]I had already noticed it at the piano—despondently We are not at all in tune (left hand to right hand), a baby's hand (the left) playing with a giant's hand (insofar as relative strength is concerned)

My reserve would certainly have disappeared, have joined the game (their game), the action, the series—and they would have "got me," I would have become social, a "team player," a "mass man." Thanks to my laziness, I escaped.

I'm a bit surprised people don't give out more information about their left man and their right man. No doubt it's because they haven't tried to maneuver them, to have them live apart from one another, as individuals—something really worth trying.

Even if you only do it to untire yourself (by untiring the right), the movements of the left will surprise you, upon acquaintance.

▪   ▪   ▪

No one has succeeded in teaching dogs to count, to read, or write. But in a few sessions, with simple, well-studied methods, you can succeed in driving them mad.

For want of a better one, this is a new common denominator.

Whatever one may say, it brings us closer. You can't drive a cedar mad.[h]

▪   ▪   ▪

My face is so unknown to me that if I were shown one of the same type I couldn't tell the difference (except perhaps since I've been doing my study of faces).

More than once, at the corner of a street, when I've come upon a mirror in a store window all set to surprise us in this way, I mistake the first comer for myself, provided he has the same raincoat or the same hat; I do feel a certain unease until I appear in the reflection of the mirror in my turn, and I make the correction, slightly embarrassed.

But the face gets lost a bit further on. For the past twenty years, I have stopped keeping myself under my features. I no longer live in these places. That's why I can easily look at another face as if it were mine. I adopt it. I rest in it.

Also, at a Metro stop—for that's where this happens to me most often—when the face I'm contemplating (or should I say, accepting) disappears with the body, I feel more than

---

[h]They have recently succeeded in driving ants mad There's still hope (*London Linnaen Society,* 1950)

sad: *dispossessed* and faceless. It has just been ripped away from me. If it were merely love! It's my face that has been taken. Where am I going to find one now, in the course of the day? She (if it's a woman) went away because of a perfect misunderstanding.

(1950)

As old people are quite aware that young people can't stand them—don't want any old folks around, and on the contrary will flee as far away as possible—they have taken the precaution, among other stratagems, of having children; so they have them, they're there, can't leave and are obliged to be present and even caressed (grinding their teeth), even ordered about... and—a still more delicate pleasure—controlled through the blackmail of affection and sacrifice.

So it seems they've made all their arrangements and are sitting pretty. Not in the slightest! For most of the time their sons are not at all the ones they would like to have around, nor their grandsons (and even their daughters, not their type, unfortunately...). They would rather see them squatting and rotting in the dung heap. The ones they would like to see in their home are other children, glimpsed briefly in the street, in the Metro, and they stab themselves with the impossible adoption, deserted by the young people they would have wanted so much, so much, to have, while the hardening mask of old age gets thicker and thicker on their faces, an unliftable bark.

And the royal gift of a tender, bright-eyed girl's face, with neat skin so admirably woven it's better not to think about it, goes to another family that may not value it and talks bitterly about failed exams, wounded family pride, and laziness.

In short, almost all of them have bungled their job.

(1949)

NOTES INSTEAD OF ACTS

Through streets, dump heaps, empty lots, roam the dogs.

Learned in smells, they rummage through the latest detritus that has just been thrown out. Attentive, with the look of experts. Never do you see them hovering over a rose or a violet (odors for those who have no nose, as sunsets are splendors for people who don't know how to use their eyes. The epitome of the amateur.). An incredible file in their heads, constantly updated. Who knows the map of stenches any better? Perfumes don't distract them, but over the zones of the most intimate, revealing secretions an ideal horizon arises for them. They think it over. Got it! Now they know. Then these innocent beings come back to us, with no transition, affectionate, with the gaze that comes from a clear conscience.

. . .

The wasp relates: "It is often not difficult to enter the dwellings of men. There, the sugary abounds.

When you want to leave, it has happened more than once that you suddenly come up against an extraordinary, absolute prohibition. In vain do your eyes roam over the whole field of the visible. Flowers wave quite near you in the breeze (not perfumed, it is true). No use trying to reach them. All you get are peremptory knocks on the head as soon and as many times as you try to reach them. So what can you do? Giving up all reasoned action, you have to throw yourself into the most violent delirium and, flying around blindly in all directions... suddenly you find yourself outside, safe and sound! This is the Secret. We don't know any other way of getting out of that jam."

(1959–1960)

THE RHINE FAIRIES

It was in the evening, not far from the low-arched bridge that crosses the Rhine where it is still a young river with tumbling, noisy waters. I was standing in the darkest part of one of the banks, far from the lighting and animation of humans and their vehicles. Beyond the lampposts, instant night.

Despite its width and its prestigious name, this part of the Rhine seemed not to be one river at all, judging by the way it was flowing, but a number of bankless streams squeezed into one, rolling side by side, fending for themselves, pushing each other around, thrusting each other away. As the waters hissed by—sometimes caught, sometimes breaking away, but always vigorously—they seemed to be struggling painfully, seemed to have to struggle, against their many neighbors equally rushed and rushing, diverting and pushing away each others' waves. Multiple liquid spindles, fighters, rustling shapes, all gave out murmurs, an abundance, an extraordinary number of murmurs vanishing rapidly, being reborn, re-forming indefinitely, coming from everywhere, out to the middle of the river from where I could hear individual, passionate murmurs rising here and there, as if from people living in those places.

But not just any people. They were unmistakably the murmurs of young girls (between laughter and speech as they often are, among themselves), hurried, unelaborated, unfinished and yet effusive. What I was hearing was their whispered secrets, their confidences thrown like a bottle in the sea, their distress blurted out in all directions for whoever would listen, a call always shy, delicate, but breathless, pffweeet... pffweeet... confidences thrown over their shoulders as if they were about to be swept further along, hurried messages, delivered with their last breath.

Phenomenal, and so unexpected! But once I had heard them, I could no longer not hear them, those momentary dramas, both frantic and unbelievably discreet, dramas I was witnessing in silence, without moving. The water fairies! So this was what the call of the undines was like! After so many, many, many times from my childhood on that I'd walked dreaming along the water's edge, how was it that today was only the first time I was able to hear them—that, through a singular openness, I was ''receiving'' them? Whereas it's strikingly obvious.

Now I could understand the poets of times gone by, simple, sensitive, openhearted, the first to hear them and report back to the incredulous public: the whispers of these murmuring "nearvoices," confidential, exhaled, hurried, moving, and *calling*. That undeniable call drawing us in, making us feel so strange; voices that other men, satisfied by their distractions, do not hear, voices so attractive that those poets, the real ones, who had heard them once, could not stop there. They couldn't be satisfied with simply making a few rhymes about them, they could do nothing else but throw themselves into the water to join them in order to go on hearing their secret (for only an indecipherable fragment of it can be received from the banks) a secret from the depths of the heart, from the secret, mysterious heart of humble, swarming nature, trampled underfoot, powerless, countless. Yes, those presences whispering at your sides and rapidly whisking away the rest of their messages are attractive, *unbelievably* attractive. You have to struggle not to be carried away. Hearing those quick confidences whispered intensely to you, it's as if you couldn't help thinking that only by letting yourself go, by plunging into the water with those fleeing fairies, near them, in the heart of their people, would you hear them at last, completely, marvelously.

Immensely gratified to have found the fairies once again—and they had always seemed to me the product of a contemptibly sentimental invention, not even religion, linked to nothing, a legend put about by a few impotent whiners who don't believe in them much more than in a metaphor—I remained fixed to the spot, motionless, or just about, turning, turning this way and that. Increasingly embarrassed, too, like someone who has heard an appeal and does nothing about it, listening without responding. But how was I to respond?

I took a few steps. I began to walk about. Accused myself, told myself I was exaggerating. I walked to the bridge, then up to the street and the little square where a few noisy cars were still going by. As soon as I'd got back from my little walk and put human vulgarity behind me—once again, unmistakably, unchanged, indisputably, again those sighs, addressed to me as to any chance passerby, a call of a delicacy that cannot come from the daughters of men but only from the daughters of the river, the sirens, an insinuating invitation to come share their existence, or rather to go with them to the very places of their existence, where such marvelous delicacy is expressed... and doubtless exchanged.

It was those tempting, voiceless voices, exquisite sighs, charming, fascinating—it was those voices that drew to their death the men who had the heart for this adventure, men dissatisfied and yet in a sense at peace, indifferent to their own fate. I was troubled, torn between a number of different feelings. And *they* kept going by... and I let them go by. What else could I do? Sometimes a spindle of water rustling over a slight obstacle would naturally become a vague, pearly shape, a phantom that might have been whirling around to send me its little passing nfft, psseet a bit more meaningfully among the many softer, half-resigned calls darting gently out from all over.

Finally, I left the place. I was wondering: if there's some guard watching me from a distance at this late hour, what will he think? Won't he suspect me of wanting to commit suicide, staring at the waters as I must have done? A rather silly apprehension, probably the sign of something else. Sign of a guilty conscience awakening in me for some other reason. Why? Because, in a sense, I had just been a traitor to all human beings. Hadn't I not "dropped" them? That can't happen without a bit of guilt. With human beings one must always keep at least a shred of contact, without cutting it off. Otherwise you set up a supertribunal of men inside yourself that treats you as the accused. Again and again, I would start to go away, troubled by this new train of thought, only to come back to the murmurs that were still calling, that perhaps I would never hear call again.

At last I went away for good. Their world, however, accompanied me. I had found—unhoped for and indeed never sought—the water fairies. As demons were made by noises and rumblings, far more than by sights, murmurs made undines, the sirens. I had just learned this. I was coming back from it.

(1963?)

NOTES

1. Compare this paragraph from "Observations" (1950): "Modeling with clay. how can you get accustomed to that cursed dirty earth that sticks to your hands? No, I'll never get used to it Still, there is this pleasure, when you're sculpting a head: to close the eyes that were looking at you! Definitively, without protest, the eye disappears into the earth. It is an action that is hard not to repeat."

2. "Still life," in German in the text (with the same connotations of "still" as the English word) and title of works by Klee

3. The preceding part of "First Impressions" was selected by Michaux to appear in *Choix de poèmes* (1976), this is the text translated here The rest is taken from *Passages* (1963).

4. The alexandrine is the classic meter of French poetry

5. See "Slices of Knowledge," note 1, in *Facing the Locks*, above.

6. Numerical ratio traditionally used to determine the "right" proportions, in music or the visual arts